Riches of the Earth

Ornamental, Precious, and Semiprecious Stones

by

Frank J. Anderson

special photography by
George C. Roos

Specimens courtesy of The Collector's Cabinet

To the memory of my mother,
Margaret D. Anderson Sheppard,
who taught me to love nature
and the beauty of stone

Page 1: *Two variations of tourmaline showing different forms of crystalization. The example lying down displays the characteristic elongated crystals found in some pieces.*

Page 4, top: *Smithsonite is named for the founder of the Smithsonian Institute, who was the first to distinguish it from a similar mineral called hemimorphite.* Bottom: *Variscite is a light, translucent phosphate, semihard, with a glassy or waxen luster. Generally used for ornamental purposes, it is sometimes substituted for turquoise.*

Page 5, top: *Celestite on barite. Celestite's name refers to its coloration, that of the celestial, or heavenly, regions. The principal ore of strontium, celestite is used in making fireworks and in a variety of industrial applications. Barite is a common but very heavy mineral. Mixed with cement it forms an effective shield against intense radiation. It sometimes forms the natural rosette known as Desert Rose.* Bottom: *Adamite is of wide occurrence and is still found in the ancient silver mines of Laurinum, Greece. Its grapelike masses, generally bright green in color, are favorites with mineral collectors despite their heaviness and fragility.*

Riches of the Earth

Ornamental, Precious, and Semiprecious Stones

by
Frank J. Anderson

special photography by
George C. Roos

WINDWARD
New York

Book design by Allan Mogel
Edited by Jay Hyams

Copyright 1981 in all countries of the
International Copyright Union by W. H. Smith
Publishers, Inc. All rights reserved.

Published by Windward
A Division of W. H. Smith Publishers, Inc.
112 Madison Avenue, New York, New York 10016

First Printing 1981
Printed in Italy by A. Mondadori, Verona

Library of Congress Cataloging in Publication Data

Anderson, Frank J. 1912 –
Riches of the earth.

Bibliography: p.
Includes index.
1. Precious stones. I. Title
QE392.A67   553.81   81-10567
ISBN 0-8317-7739-7   AACR2

Specimen courtesy of The Collector's Cabinet

Specimen courtesy of The Collector's Cabinet

Specimen courtesy of The Collector's Cabinet

Specimen courtesy of The Collector's Cabinet

INTRODUCTION

During the past century we have learned more about the physical properties of the mineral world than in any comparable period of our past. We have progressed from simple imitations to the ability to synthesize precious stones at will; we have measured their age with ever increasing accuracy; and we have harnessed them to industrial uses unimaginable only a few short decades ago. Our scientific advance has been so swift, opening so many new avenues of technological proficiency to us, that it has had a strong tendency to obscure the accomplishments of the distant past. It is to correct that imbalance that this book has been written.

While it is true that we no longer have to scrabble about for workable pieces of flint with which to amplify our somewhat inadequate powers, it is also true that if our ancestors hadn't done just that mankind might not have survived as a species. As we explored the capacity of stone to provide us with more efficient and durable tools to improve our daily life, we gradually created a technology that helped us to form cultures and eventually civilizations. All of those discoveries have a legitimate place in the story of the man and mineral relationship, but we are in imminent danger of forgetting them. We also tend to discard legends, with all their color and drama, as we increase our store of hard facts. But those legends are records of our past modes of thought, representative of carefully constructed responses to questions that once demanded answers, but answers that we were then incapable of supplying. Where exact data is lacking myth always steps in to fill the void and to satisfy our importunate curiosity as best it can. In the process it provides us with a kind of poetry, a pleasant, savory, imaginative experience that need not be abandoned simply because science exists.

Yet other areas of mankind's involvement with stones rest in their use in art, architecture, ornaments of dress or religious ritual, and the abundance of associations that they have had with famous personages. None of that fits properly into mineralogical or geological treatises, but, if ignored, would result in a tremendous loss of noteworthy material for scientists, collectors, and interested laymen alike. Stones, after all, remain stones until they pass through the hands of man, where they become jewels, architecture, and all the stuff of history.

The Chinese, who have considered such wide-ranging properties for a very long time, indeed, have developed far greater sympathy and understanding of stones than has been the usual custom in the West. Chinese writers and poets speak of stones as "the bones of the earth," calling them "rock friends," and one artist habitually referred to a tall stone, standing in his garden, as "my brother." That concept, strange to us in the West, flows out of the Chinese view of nature, in which all things are given a common origin and are regarded as being possessed of an animate spirit of their own. While the concept recognizes that rocks lack the actual power of locomotion, they do not deny them an internal life of their own, one of the reasons that stones play such an important part as an element in Chinese gardens. Nor are the Chinese entirely wrong in attributing an internal spirit—for the mass, density, and form of stones is the result of their contained force of protons, neutrons, and electrons whirling in endless motion, binding molecules together to give each rock a seemingly individual character and being.

If, like the Chinese, we will view stones as something more than mere inanimate objects we may very well see them from a fresh perspective, with hidden or unsuspected qualities that endlessly await our discovery. Should that increased awareness result from the pages that follow, creating deeper perception and keener appreciation of stones in their many relations to mankind, then the purpose of this book will have been served.

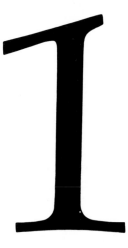

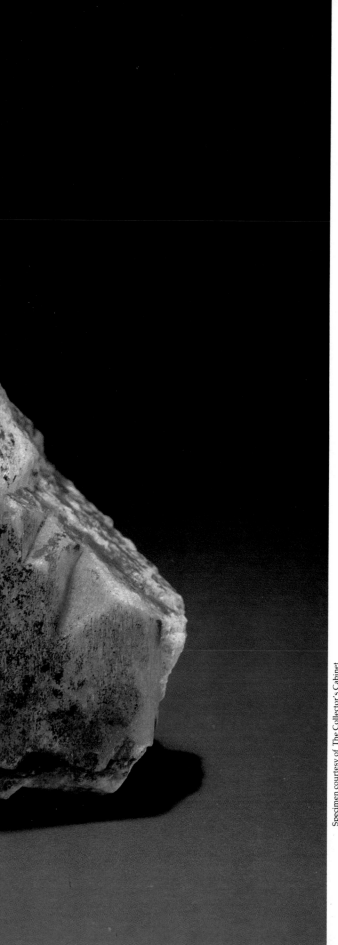

Chapter 1
JEWELS OF THE DAWN

About a million years ago in Tanzania some hairy, apelike man had the notion of chipping a piece of flint, creating mankind's first known tool. From the making of that first tool springs the career of every sculptor, lapidary, and mason working today. When our ancestor, *Homo habilis*, hacked out his first chopper he not only created technology, but with it the possibility of an easier and safer life. From then until the much later rise of agriculture, about 8000 B.C., there was a very slow and gradual development of stone-shaping techniques, one that continued on throughout the Bronze Age. For that matter, stone tools are still used today in some primitive parts of the world, and anthropologists who have both made and employed them testify to their efficiency.

At first only conveniently shaped pebbles were sharpened on one side by flaking off small bits. Next came somewhat heavier hand-axes, which were chipped on both sides. Still later, larger stones were used for the purpose of striking off sizable flakes, those that could be reworked into a variety of tools instead of becoming a single instrument. A further refinement came with the use of a stone punch, or of pressure flaking, utilizing bone or ivory, for shaping and finishing edges and points. These often exhibit a rippled effect. The final stage of refinement combined small pieces of stone with wood, creating spears, arrows, and sickle blades.

The most notable event during man's slow progression through some 975,000 years occurred about 25,000 B.C. He finally became capable of creating art, carving and engraving designs or animal forms on ivory and bone with tools of stone. Bangles, bracelets, and necklaces were made, for man had also developed the concept of personal adornment. Because he was at last capable of perforating certain stones, he wore them openly on his person instead of carrying them about in a pouch, much as a shaman or medicine-man might. By this time some of the chosen stones, especially colorful or translucent ones, must also have acquired commonly recognized qualities and associations. Some, worn as plaques or amulets, conferred the protection and guidance of supernatural beings, while others became the insignia of power and prestige. Jewelry had evolved into both royal and ecclesiastical regalia.

Mankind's desire for ornamentation has been universal and persistent, and is evident in every evolving social group to the present. In such diverse places as Yorkshire, England, where a hunting culture remained active until about 7500 B.C., or among their contemporaries, the agriculturists of ancient Mesopotamia, stone beads and necklaces have been found. In Yorkshire, pebbles of shale and amber provided the necessary materials, while in Mesopotamia a richer repertoire has been found, one that consists of turquoise, serpentine, agate, carnelian, malachite, obsidian, and jadeite. In the West the local materials give no hint of any kind of trade that might have linked settlement to settlement, but in the East, because the stones came from at least four widely separated points, it is plain that trade, as well as agriculture, was established. Once the final ingredient, writing, was developed and added, it is small wonder that civilization blossomed almost overnight in the river valleys of the Fertile Crescent from Mesopotamia to Egypt. All the orally transmitted traditions of medicine, technology, law, and religion could now be given a permanence never before possible, and man could record, combine, and transmit his skills for the greater good of all.

Quite naturally this new-found ability created a local sense of pride in every literate city and kingdom, the just pride of accomplishment. Just as naturally, that pride had to be celebrated with

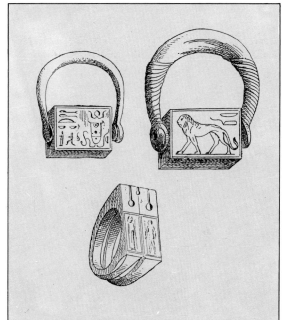

Preceding pages: *Amazonite, sometimes improperly called Amazon jade, is a silicate gemstone and is actually a green variety of microcline feldspar. Its crystals often show the habit of penetrating each other. Left: Statuette of Imhotep. This figure is a good example of Egyptian sculpture from the early Ptolemaic period. Top: The head of Cleopatra as it appeared on a Greek coin. Above: Egyptian stamp seals, evolving into signet rings.*

11

Bracelets courtesy of Navin Kumar Gallery

Specimen courtesy of The Collector's Cabinet

Opposite left: *Pair of bracelets from India inlaid with carnelian.* Opposite right: *Hematite on quartz.* Left: *Serpentine, so-named because its mottled color resembles snakeskin.* Below left: *Stonehenge. The megalithic monuments, made for the most part of bluestone, are one of man's earliest observatories.* Below: *Chinese 18th-century statuette of carved amber. Amber is not native to China and did not reach there until after Alexander the Great's conquests had opened up trade routes from Europe to Asia.*

13

monuments, temples, palaces, and the sumptuous adornment, not only of the heads of state, but of everyone who shared in the glory and luxury that literacy had brought in its wake. The permanence of stone in terms of richness, color, rarity, and worthiness equal to intent was quickly recognized and seized upon to express this new patriotic or civic emotion. The scale of such works was grandiose from the days of the Pharaohs to those of the tsars, although in recent times somewhat less lavishly so. Today, workmanship, availability of material, and the purchasing power of money are no longer what they were, and nobody seems interested in designing a new Golden Age to replace the former ones.

Even in those early days of the dawn of history a great deal of wealth was required to provide suitable settings for the state, its rulers, and its gods. Egypt, beyond any doubt, was the most fortunate of the early civilizations, and was in the best position to create and retain the wealth it needed. Although not geographically invulnerable, it did enjoy a sheltered location difficult to attack, and had the benefit of a highly productive agricultural economy. Rapid and successful development of its physical and technological resources soon gave it a commanding lead over its poorly organized and weaker neighbors. That, of course, provided another form of wealth—an ample supply of slaves. With money, food, and labor at hand it did not take long for the Pharaohs to envision some sizable dreams, and then bring them into being.

As early as 3200 B.C., even before the art of writing was fully developed, Egypt was a power-ful and efficient state capable of raising, supplying, and even directing an army in the field. The carven slate palette of King Narmer fully documents that fact, and also demonstrates the technical skill achieved in his time, for the material is both brittle and hard, therefore very difficult to shape.

Sometime in the late 4th millennium cultural contact was made between Egypt and Sumer. Thereupon two Sumerian influences made an impact on Egypt, although in both cases they were rapidly assimilated and profoundly altered. One was the cylinder seal, of which three examples have been found in Egypt, all of them from Sumer and all antedating the earliest Egyptian specimen. The Egyptians were quick to grasp their usefulness in establishing the ownership and contents of produce placed in sealed jars. They also found them handy in the manufacture of funerary amulets. The designs of such seals were carved down into short, slender, rodlike lengths of semiprecious stones, lapis lazuli being a favorite material of the Sumerians. A much humbler substance, wood, was often used in Egypt for the same purpose. In either case the result was identical, for rolling the cylinder across a bit of soft clay duplicated its design in sharp relief, and could do so an infinite number of times. However, when papyrus documents had to be authenticated by such means it was soon discovered that cylinder seals were not as effective on planar surfaces as they were on pliable clay. The answer to the problem was adaption, so the Egyptians produced the stamp seal, which provided the necessary vertical pressure suitable to the flat surface of papyrus

Chisels, mallets, stone adzes, and sharp-edged plates of bronze with handles, carved out the shallow-draft vessels used on the Nile. Their shape and light weight eased them over or off the river's numerous sandbars.

sheets. At that time all the elements for true printing were present in embryo, but the process had to wait another 4500 years for its actual birth.

The second cultural influence from Sumer was in the art of architecture. No doubt the Egyptians would have succeeded admirably on their own, but the Sumerian example helped them to reach their goal somewhat sooner. Once aware of the huge temple complexes of Sumer, ziggurats heaped high from buttressed brick, the Egyptians began to attempt a little grandeur of their own. They closely copied the Sumerian models at first, making bricks of the same size and shape, and even laying them in the same patterns and courses. Although there is no doubt about who owed what to whom, the Egyptians rapidly outdid their teachers, and created an architecture still capable of astounding the modern world. The prime reason for this, of course, is that monumental architecture depends upon the use of stone, of which Sumer had very little, while Egypt sat upon an oceanic quantity of rock.

Throughout Egypt whatever is not sand or mud is almost invariably stone. It exists there in the greatest abundance and variety, and, what is more, most of it is within easy reach of the Nile. Such a situation is a powerful advantage when transporting heavy blocks of stone over long distances in a non-motorized age. Egypt, of course, would still have had its monuments and architecture, but there would have been differences. Porphyry and granite, save in small blocks, could never have traveled far from their native quarries. Yet, thanks to the presence of the river, stone could be readily moved at the desire of the Pharaoh and his architects to almost anywhere it was wanted, for the Nile offered a 500-mile-long highway.

The major difficulty the Egyptians faced was in building boats that were capable of the task they had to perform. Egypt is not noted for quantities of timber, so almost every large piece of wood had to be imported. It was true enough that they could readily construct light craft from bundles of papyrus, but such boats were scarcely suited to the carriage of obelisks and sarcophagi, many of which weighed several hundred tons. Cedar was very welcome when it could be obtained, but acacia wood was the usual material because it was locally available, and was close-grained, hard, and water-resistant.

The choice of acacia, however, raised other problems. For one, it was only in favorable sites that the tree would grow to heights of from twenty to twenty-five feet and most specimens were considerably smaller. This meant that large lengths of wood could not be cut, so that boats had to be pieced together like a parquet floor. A further difficulty was that the Egyptians knew nothing of nails, and had to fit their boats together by tying plank to plank. Two cubits, or thirty-six inches, was the average length of each piece, and holes had to be drilled all along their edges so that they could be laced. To build such a vessel was no simple matter, while making it water-tight must have been a nightmare. Ancient models and tomb drawings make it clear that there were no ribs in these boats, and that the seams were caulked with papyrus. It is difficult to imagine any high degree of rigidity in such boats, if we are correctly informed about their construction. In the strong river current they must have developed enough sway to occasionally look like water snakes coursing along, unless strengthened by means yet unknown.

Riding and guiding boats downstream from the great granite quarries near Aswan to Sais, in the Nile delta, was normally a twenty-day journey. But we read of a three-year trip that took 2000 boatmen to transport a granite block, 12 feet high by 23 feet wide, and 35 feet long, down the river from Aswan to Sais. Obviously some major difficulties occurred along the way.

Such a block was by no means uncommon, for one has only to look at the obelisks that are now scattered about the world to realize that the Egyptians moved a great deal of heavy stone from place to place. A brief and incomplete census of surviving obelisks will give some notion of the Egyptian accomplishment. There remain twelve in Rome, brought there because the ancient Romans were very partial to them.

The tallest, now standing before St. John Lateran, is just 3 inches less than 106 feet high, and its sides are a few inches less than 10 feet in width. Its weight is a little over 440 tons, yet it has been moved three times without the aid of motorized equipment! The first occasion was when it was

In 1836 J. B. Lebas, engineer to King Louis Philippe, erected this 240-ton obelisk in Paris' Place de la Concorde, using many of the ancient Egyptian techniques. Ramses II first raised it at Luxor some 3300 years before Mohammed Ali, Viceroy of Egypt, presented it to France.

brought down the Nile to the Temple of Ammon at Thebes before 1427 B.C. Its second move came in A.D. 357, when it was brought to the Circus Maximus in Rome by Constantius II. There it was found, lying in three pieces, before being restored and brought to its present site by order of Pope Sixtus V, in 1588. Like many of its kind, its makers should have provided it with a guide book.

Other remaining obelisks are in Istanbul, Paris, London, New York, and Egypt itself, where a few remain on their original sites. For that matter an unfinished one, over seventy feet in length, still rests in its quarry near Aswan. All are monumental in size, as the following table shows:

Istanbul, in the old Hippodrome, 64 feet;
Paris, Place de la Concorde, 75 feet;
London, Thames Embankment, 68 feet, 6 inches;
New York, Central Park, 71 feet;
Egypt: two at Karnak, 97 feet and 109 feet;
    Luxor, 77 feet

The obelisk at Luxor is the oldest to remain standing on its original site, having been erected there in the 19th millennium by Sesostris I. All have slightly convex sides, to overcome the optical illusion of concavity, and their tapering forms are believed to be symbolic of the sun's rays.

While some of the obelisks required stones of great size, so did the tombs and statues of the Pharaohs. A block of granite in the Temple of Chephren weighs 452 tons, while other, smaller ones in the vestibule, range from 38 to 150 tons each. These are dwarfed by the red granite Colossus of Rameses II, now lying in fragments at Thebes, which was 55 feet high and weighed about 1000 tons. It was brought there from Aswan by river, the only practical means of transporting it some 140 miles. Such a mass would be placed on a raft, rather than on a boat, and Queen Hatshepsut is known to have brought obelisk stones from Aswan to Thebes on just such a float, which was about 300 feet long.

That such immense stones could be carried down the river by relatively simple means is understandable; it is how they were moved after being landed that remains a mystery. A thousand tons of stone would crush any wooden rollers available to the Egyptians, and the same would hold true for the wooden runners on the sledges they used for heavy haulage. Moreover such a

mass would have a tendency to plough its leading edge slightly into an earthen roadway, even one that was smoothed and packed. Perhaps the Egyptians placed stone slabs on a prepared causeway, and coated them with fat, oil, or vegetable wax to ease the friction. Until more is known of their technology the matter will remain unresolved.

In the meantime some comparison with a modern example of stone transport might be in order. In 1903 the Cathedral of St. John the Divine in New York City was still in the process of construction. Its choir was to contain eight pillars of polished granite, each 55 feet high, all of which had to be transferred from dockside to the cathedral site, a distance of about 1½ miles. For convenience during polishing, the columns had been divided into two sections, the upper weighing 40 tons, the lower 90. There were sixteen sections in all, with a total weight of 1040 tons, or only 40 tons more than the ancient Colossus of Rameses II at Thebes. Using steam winches and drawing the vehicles over cobblestone roadways, the task took the modern builders sixteen trips and about ten weeks to finish. Nobody knows how long the Egyptians needed to move their monolith from dockside on the Nile to the temple precincts, but the distance was roughly the same as that which the New York workers had to traverse. What is certain is that their route was over rougher ground, that they had no means but muscle power, and were unable to divide the weight. We still do not know how they performed the task, but the use of wooden rollers appears unlikely. When the 90-ton columns in New York passed over thick steel manhole covers they broke every one that they crossed, so it is easy to imagine what a 1000-ton block would have done to any wooden rollers placed beneath it. Twentieth-century technology may have much to boast about, but ancient Egypt knew a thing or two of its own.

One Egyptian quarry in the valley Rehanu, now called Wadi Hammamat, was located about forty miles east of the Nile, and was an exception to the rule of being close to easy transportation. The stone from Wadi Hammamat, which is very hard and heavy, was greatly valued and was called "eternal stone" and "stone of a million years." Its modern name is graywacke, a fine-grained con-

17

stones, that is, sapphire, ruby, and true topaz. Sometimes copper saws were used with emery powder, obtained by trade from the island of Naxos in the Aegean Sea.

Limestone was quarried by drilling holes in a line, pounding wooden pegs into them, and then causing the pegs to swell by applications of water. Modern experiments have proven the method to be both quick and effective. Much the same process was used with granite. While granite has no stratification, such as limestone does, it does have what are called "joints." These result from movements of the earth that are always present to one degree or another, and produce extremely minute cracks and fissures at right angles to each other. That fortunate circumstance permitted blocks with parallel faces to be cleaved from the main mass by the same method used on limestone.

What the Egyptians accomplished with their simple tools still astounds us. Their skill is visible in every major museum in the world, and most particularly in the Great Pyramid of Khufu (Cheops) at Gizeh. There we find some 2,300,000 blocks of stone, each weighing about 5000 pounds, piled to a height of 479 feet on an area of some 13 acres. To envision what those numbers mean, think of a structure whose base is three times the size of that of St. Peter's in Rome and that rises about 50 feet higher. Furthermore, the stones in the interior chambers are so finely dressed that a knife's blade cannot be inserted between them. Most of the original limestone facing, a superior kind from the quarries at Turah just across the Nile, has been stripped away, but the denuded remains are still stupendous.

Even in our own time this enormous mass of masonry was considered the result of cruel oppression by King Khufu for purposes of self-glorification. Now modern scholarship has advanced a view that reverses that theory, for Khufu is seen as providing employment during times of floods, keeping much of the populace busy when unable to work the land. Whether or not the pyramid was willingly shaped by the workmen, it must be admitted that no modern society, with all its technological advantages, could duplicate the effort.

Egypt's supply of building and ornamental stone was not only large and varied, but was also well distributed along the length of the Nile. Be-

glomerate containing quartz and feldspar fragments. Usually a dark gray color, sometimes even blackish, it was highly prized for making sarcophagi. One specific record mentions a block from Mount Bechen (the particular source of the stone) that measured 12 by 6 by 3 feet in size and required three thousand men to move it down to the river. How long that took is not known, but the quarry was ordinarily a two-day journey to riverside for the unburdened traveler.

Blocks of such dimensions were made not only because they took less time to cut than a great number of smaller ones, but also because they resulted in a more stable structure. The earliest masonry was rather small, but by the time of King Zoser, c. 2700 B.C., had become much larger, and during the Pyramid Age, only a century later, blocks weighing from 40 to 150 tons were frequently cut. Hard rock such as granite, diorite, and graywacke, bore inscriptions and forms cut by the use of bronze chisels and saws whose edges and teeth were set with diamonds or corundum

Above: Diorite sculpture of King Sahu-Re' and a figure personifying the nome, or province, of Koptos in Upper Egypt, from c. 2500 B.C. Opposite: Egyptian canopic jar made of limestone and dating to the New Kingdom. This is the baboon-headed Hapy, in which were stored the lungs.

ginning in the south, in the region of the first cataract, there was granite at Elephantine, at Syene (which gave its name to syenite), and at Aswan. Ridges of exposed stone cross the river in that locality, and have been worn smooth through the ages, thus revealing flaws that might ordinarily go undetected before being quarried. This was the frontier of ancient Egypt, and was heavily guarded to ensure uninterrupted work in the important red granite quarries, and to prevent incursions from Nubia.

About forty-two miles north of Elephantine was the town of Silsilis. Hard sandstone was brought from there; it is a material that is found in many Egyptian temples and similar structures. While excellent for building, it was most unsatisfactory for sculpture. Statues made with it usually show the worst and clumsiest kind of workmanship, with the possible exception of works executed in Nubian sandstone from Kertassi, just beyond the cataracts.

Hard sandstone does not exist beyond El Kab, about forty miles north of Silsilis. From there to the delta lies a vast expanse of limestone, within which chert and flint are also found. The best quarries were at Masara, opposite Memphis, as well as those at Turah near Gizeh. Oddly enough the limestone around Memphis itself is coarse, having many deficiencies that taxed the skills of architects and sculptors. Ordinarily limestone was used for building and facing, and was carved in very low relief because it tended to split if it was sculptured in the round. Very often such bas-reliefs in the tombs were painted, and it is possible that many palace and temple exteriors may have been treated similarly. Today the uncolored state of ancient buildings gives us a deceptive view, one quite different from what the Egyptians saw.

About seventy-five miles north of El Kab, and some forty miles east of the Nile, was the Wadi Hammamat where graywacke, dolerite, diorite, and breccia were quarried. Still farther north and east, in the desert, porphyry was found, but it was never greatly exploited until Roman times. The best quality of alabaster came from Hatnub, about ten miles east of El Amarna, while secondary sources were at El Minya, some one hundred twenty miles beyond, and in the region around Alexandria in the Delta. In ancient times quartzite

sandstone was quarried at Gebel Ahmar, and basalt in the Wadi Tumilat, where the Ismailiya Canal now flows. Both places are slightly north and east of Heliopolis.

Gemstones such as garnet, carnelian, and jasper came from various sites in the Egyptian deserts, while turquoise was found in the northern Sinai desert along Wadi Maghara. With such an abundance of ornamental, construction, and gem stones, the Egyptian architects and artisans were able to introduce a wide variety of textures and colors into their sculpture, buildings, and jewelry. The most frequently used stone was limestone; hard sandstone was the next, and granite was the third most-used. Granite was always reserved for the most important sculptures, sarcophagi, and architectural details. Whenever a work demanded unusual permanence it was made of granite. Like graywacke, granite was called "stone of a million years," and "eternal stone"—the Egyptians did not trouble themselves much with fine mineralogical distinctions.

While very hard stones were drilled out into

vases as early as 4000 B.C., the softer, more readily worked alabaster became the great favorite of the artisans. Banded or onyx alabaster was the most highly prized for ornamental objects, such as cosmetic and ointment jars, while the cream-colored translucent kind was utilized for statuettes, small offering tables, and dishes carved into fish or flower forms. Alabaster was also used for the flooring of Chephren's valley temple, as well as his funerary chapel, where thousands of square feet of the stone still remain.

Alabaster was greatly favored for the manufacture of canopic jars, an important part of tomb furnishings. These jars are, on the average, about 18 inches high, including their sculptured lids, and were intended to hold the internal organs of the deceased. They were four in number—to symbolize the four sons of Horus who had been set to guard the body of Osiris—and were capped with the carved heads of those minor deities. Human-headed Imset held the liver, the baboon-headed Hapy contained the lungs, jackal-headed Duamutef guarded the stomach, and hawk-headed Quebehsenuf the intestines. Although the brain was removed, no separate receptacle seems to have been provided for it.

Harder stones were generally used to fashion scarabs and such amulets as the Tet stone. The scarab represented the Sun god Ra, father of all things, as symbolized under the form of a *Scarabeus sacer* beetle, common throughout Egypt. Its habit of pushing a ball made of earth and dung, in which its larvae were hatching, was likened to Ra moving the sun's disk across the sky. Scarabs, which were made of serpentine, jasper, lapis lazuli, hematite, green feldspar (called "mother-of-emerald"), carnelian, vitrified steatite, and faience, served three separate purposes: as amulet, ornament, and seal. Their ornamental use as jewelry is self-explanatory, while the hieroglyphic inscription carved into their flat undersides served as a certificate of authenticity. As amulets scarabs were believed to confer the protective powers of Ra upon the wearer, and, because of the benefit this was thought to bring, they were favorite gifts at the time of the Egyptian New Year. They also became funerary amulets of great importance, the so-called heart-scarabs that were placed in pectorals, resting on the hearts of the deceased. Laid there they were a guarantee of the revival or resurrection of the soul in the ceremony called "the opening of the mouth," and promised a favorable verdict before the tribunal of Osiris. A soul that failed that trial was condemned to eternal death, and had its heart fed to the part-crocodile, part-lion, part-hippopotamus monster Ammit, who crouched nearby in hope of a victim. With all the precautions taken on behalf of the deceased—spells, prayers, and incantations—it is more than likely that Am-mit suffered long stretches of time between meals.

Another amulet was the Tet stone, shaped like a pillar with four transverse bars, or shelves, just below its apex. This was an emblem of Osiris, and was considered to grant stability and power. Its form represented the sacrum of Osiris and thus was credited with a particularly sacred character. Kings and priests annually held the ceremony of raising the Tet pillar, at which time a great festival was held. There is undoubtedly a phallic significance about the Tet, but it is also possible that its shelflike projections, besides representing the joined vertebrae of Osiris's sacrum, may have been meant to receive offerings, or to stand for the branches of plants, for Osiris was a vegetation god as well as god of the dead. A sizable collection of Tet stones is in the British Museum's Department of Egyptian Antiquities.

Besides Tet stones and scarabs there were also rings and necklaces, pectorals, and broad collars made from a variety of gemstones. Even before 4000 B.C., in what is called the Predynastic period, Egyptian lapidaries were able to cut, drill, and polish stones as hard as agate, chalcedony, quartz, diorite, and porphyry. Mace heads mounted like scepters, and probably symbols of authority as well as weapons, are known from very early times. There is even one, carved from limestone, that represents the Predynastic King Scorpion cutting open an irrigation canal, c. 3500 B.C..

There is also ample evidence that mineral cosmetics were used in the earliest eras. Malachite, of which there was a good supply in the Sinai, had been powdered for eye shadow even before 7000 B.C. Just when antimony began to be converted into *kohl* to serve as a black eye-liner is not certain, but small jars and boxes for such cosmetics have been found from before the 1st Dynasty, as have

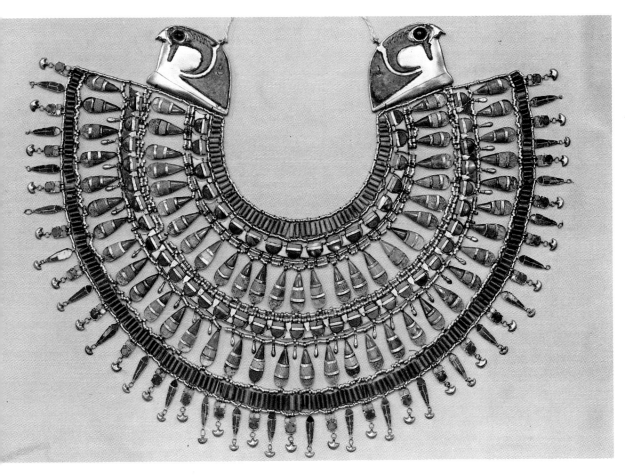

the slate palettes upon which they were ground. Such mineral pigments were not confined to cosmetic purposes alone, but entered into use during prehistoric times in the production of paints and glazes, such as faience. A red ground-color, commonly used in pottery, was derived from powdered hematite. Hematite is fairly hard and heavy, and appears black in the mass, but because it is iron oxide it yields a rusty red when fragmented. It was also faceted and polished for 6th-Dynasty necklaces, made in 2500 B.C. Between 2500 B.C. and 2000 B.C. a hematite paste was made. Beads were shaped from the paste and then heated to solidify. That process finally led, in 2000 B.C., to the production of true vitreous paste, a direct forerunner of glass.

A sophisticated treatment of gemstones began in the 4th Dynasty, about 2700 B.C., the time of the pyramid builders. By then goldsmiths had found ways to place polished stones in beautiful gold or silver settings. Silver, because it was not found in Egypt and was then a rare import, was more highly valued than gold for several centuries.

By the 12th Dynasty, c. 2000–1800 B.C., jewelers' skills reached a peak of style and perfection that has not been surpassed in any subsequent era. The necklace and pectoral of Princess Sit-Hathor-Yunet, now in New York's Metropolitan Museum, is a superb example of the craftsmanship that the anonymous jewelers of Memphis attained. Drop-shaped beads of gold, green feldspar, lapis lazuli, and carnelian form the necklace from which a pectoral of open-work gold was suspended. The design incorporates hundreds of small pieces of turquoise, garnet, carnelian, and lapis lazuli, forming the falcons of Horus; the royal uraeus (a cobra); the sun's disk; the ankh, or sign of life, flanking on either side the kneeling figure of the god of years; and a scarab bearing the name of the Pharaoh Sen-wosret II (Sesostris II),

Egyptian hawk collar made of gold, carnelian, green feldspar, and glass, from the reign of Thutmose III (1501–1447 B.C.).

who was most likely father to the princess. In life or death the piece was a powerful talisman that proclaimed not only the royal status of its wearer, but also functioned as a heart-scarab to safeguard the princess at the tribunal of Osiris in the afterworld.

The hawks who guarded either side of the pectoral were emblematic of Horus, divine son of Isis and Osiris. He was often pictured in that guise because hawks had the habit of soaring aloft in the sky, a region that bore the name Hor in the ancient Egyptian tongue. Further still the sky was envisioned as a divine hawk, whose eyes consisted of the sun and moon. It was thus that the hawk became an important totem from the earliest times onward, and one that became particularly associated with the Pharaoh, in whom Horus was believed to be embodied. Even the hieroglyph for "god" depicted a hawk at rest upon its perch, and so royalty and divinity became inextricably linked in the Egyptian mind.

In fact, anything pertaining to the sacred hawk was considered to carry with it the blessing and protection of Horus. That notion led, quite naturally, to the design of the broad, or "hawk," collar so often pictured as part of ancient Egyptian dress. The divine hawk's plumage was symbolized by the wide bands of colored jewels that formed the collar, hence its popular name. Quite often these many-rowed bands of gems were clasped at their ends by golden hawk's heads with eyes of carnelian or red jasper, traditional colors of the sun's disk. The color red signified Horus as a solar god in addition to his role as protector of royalty and of the dead. These rich complexities of Egyptian iconography provided endless inspiration for the jewelers and lapidaries, freeing them from the necessity of searching out suitable themes, as many of their modern counterparts are continually forced to do. Jewelers and lapidaries could then concentrate, without any further thought, on the practice of their craft.

Building on a foundation of lapidary skills, some established in prehistoric times, the Egyptian jewelers were already adept at polishing gemstones by 3400 B.C. The Cairo Museum possesses a bracelet, from about that date, that is made from beads of turquoise and amethyst, strung on twisted bands of gold wire. It uses the technique of tumbling, so popular with modern amateur lapidaries. At later dates other processes were devised, such as soldering, chiseling, and inlay, so that by 2000 B.C. jewelers had an almost complete repertoire of techniques at their command. The high quality of workmanship is evident from the fact that their methods suffered very little change until the modern era of the Renaissance, and even then some techniques could not be improved.

Much of the jewelry made in those times, probably the greater portion of it, had religious significance, although wealthy Egyptians were never averse to ornamentation as such. Nonetheless many plaques, buckles, pectorals, armbands, and the like, bore images of the gods and carried inscriptions graven into the stones themselves. Selected chapters from the Book of the Dead, a kind of formulary for immortality, were engraved on amulets of carnelian, lapis lazuli, green jasper, and other stones. They were not chosen at random, as far as color was concerned, for each hue had a special reference to the chapter that it cited. The red of carnelian was emblematic of the Sun god, Ra, or else the blood of Isis, depending upon which deity the chapter invoked. Lapis lazuli and turquoise were both appropriate to Horus as god of the sky, because those stones were blue. Green jasper, serpentine, or steatite stood for the green flesh of Osiris in his aspect as vegetation god, and green, accordingly, was the favorite color for the amulet known as the "heart-scarab."

The papyrus scepter, yet another amulet, was usually made from green feldspar, and bore the Egyptian name of *uat*, a word that meant "verdure," "greenness," or the state of flourishing in that language. Its fresh, light green color signified the promise of eternal youth for the soul in the afterworld. Each color had a close association with whatever it was intended to symbolize, and no self-respecting artisan would casually or carelessly substitute one for another. In fact, to do so could easily negate the stone's talismanic value, as well as verge on the edge of sacrilege. For that matter anything linked to Osiris was forbidden to enter the precincts of a temple sacred to Ra. The reasoning behind that taboo was that the presence of Osiris, as god of the dead, might bring disaster and death to the living sun. The ancient Egyptians

were very cautious and conservative about their gods, and they avoided any chance that their gods' divine powers might clash and produce undesirable results.

In the modern world we are so accustomed to creating molded objects of glass or plastic that we can scarcely conceive of having to hollow out pieces of stone to obtain the same result. Yet that is exactly what Egyptian stoneworkers did from about 4000 B.C., in prehistoric times, until about 1000 B.C., in a late era of the New Kingdom. At first it was only the softer stones, such as limestone and alabaster, that were favored. Granular gypsum, which is commonly called alabaster, may easily be scratched with a fingernail, yet is sufficiently solid and impermeable to be useful for storing liquids. Of course most pottery could do the same, but clay does not have quite the richness found in stone, a characteristic that won stone vessels a special place in ceremonial use, and as furnishing for royal tables.

Techniques improved rapidly, and before long basalt, porphyry, breccia, syenite, and iron-hard diorite were being shaped and polished. Blocks of stone were roughly trimmed to the proper size

and form, using nothing more than tools of copper, stone, and powdered abrasives, and the most important ingredient of all—an infinite amount of patience. One theorist has suggested that the Egyptians may have had a method of altering the molecular structure of copper, thus making it as hard as steel for stonecutting purposes. However, flint, emery, and corundum stones in combination with copper saws, chisels, and drills were perfectly capable of meeting every demand placed upon them. For example a syenite vase, two feet in diameter by six inches high, which would easily have weighed over 150 pounds before it was hollowed, could be raised with one finger in its finished state. The sides were abraded until they were eggshell thin, in contrast to later work that skimped on such refinement. In Predynastic times the vases were adapted to domestic purposes, although only the wealthiest patrons could afford them. From about 3200 B.C. they were confined to funerary use only. Once that custom became established there was no longer any need to consider practicality, and eventually only the outer form was retained while the inside was given a shallow token drilling. The superior pieces were

The pyramids of Gizeh, just west of Cairo, are the last of the old seven wonders of the world. The smallest in this view, at the extreme right, is really the largest, known to us as the Great Pyramid of Cheops, but called "the Glorious" by the ancient Egyptians.

23

Top: *Sumerian head of Gudea, in diorite, from c. 2150 B.C.*
Above: *This Egyptian lamp, made of carved, translucent calcite, was among the treasures found in the tomb of Tutankhamen. Each of the lamp's three compartments held oil in which floated a lighted wick, which provided illumination, shining through the carved stone.*

all done in a period of about 500 years, c. 3200–2700 B.C., but high quality was maintained for some two centuries. After that a long decline set in, one that terminated stone-vase manufacture, at about 1000 B.C.

In addition to the remarkable thinness sometimes attained by the Egyptian craftsmen, some unusual shapes were developed by them as well. A bowl, quite dovelike in form, was made from red breccia about 3500 B.C. This called for a high degree of skill, because breccia consists of angular fragments of many kinds of hard rock cemented in a matrix. The pressures that suit one degree of hardness may prove too great for another, so the lapidary must stay exceptionally alert throughout the entire process. In this particular instance, after shaping the bird's body for the exterior of the vessel, it was also necessary to make undercuts within the interior. These cuts extended both foward into the breast portion and backward into the tail, for almost a third of the bowl's diameter in both directions. However, the craftsman achieved perfect symmetry despite having to face these difficulties.

Another example, found in the Sakkara region, is of dark dioritic porphyry that was shaped into a deep rectangular bowl. Its sides slope steeply, and the corners form very sharp and regular angles. What its original purpose was is rather difficult to say, other than it was obviously a food container, and is rather suggestive of a sauce dish. There is no question, though, of the skill and precision required to make it, for every side is as true as if a master cabinetmaker had fashioned it out of wood, rather than from the obdurate rock that was used.

Nowhere is the consummate skill of the ancient Egyptian artisans and sculptors better demonstrated than in the polished hard-stone statues and sarcophagi made from diabase, diorite, granite, and basalt. The nearly intractable hardness of those stones would give pause even to modern craftsmen working with power tools. Nonetheless we find sarcophagi, some with walls six inches thick, which have interiors cut to the dimensions and shapes of the mummy cases they were intended to hold. The smoothness of their exterior finish, bearing the crisply carved hieroglyphics and decoration engraved on the sarcophagi, belies all the difficulties that must have been encountered. The surfaces almost seem to have been modeled in clay and then glazed with ceramic. This is also a characteristic of many of the royal statues. A four-ton sphinx of Queen Hatshepsut, carved from red granite, shows the queen wearing the lion-mane, or *nemes* (headdress), every line of which is sharply delineated, as is every other element of the statue. Despite the size of the sculpture and the hardness of its stone it has been given an almost waxen polish.

Such high finish, fairly common in Egyptian statuary, is the result of a technique called hammer dressing. Balls of dolerite, a kind of granite rock, were pounded against the face of the stone to be polished. This action crushed the molecular structure of the outermost layers, reducing their cohesion. The areas thus altered were then scraped with flint or copper tools to remove the loosened scales. Repeated sessions of hammering and scraping gradually brought the stone to a point where the fine work of abrasion could begin. This was often done with blocks of emery, or perhaps sand, emery powder, or finely pulverized corundum grit that were mixed with water and rubbed on the stone until it achieved a lustrous smoothness. The choice of the abrasive, of course, depended upon the hardness of the stone that had to be polished.

In lapidary work it was often necessary to drill stones as well as to polish them. The early drills consisted of a bent handle lashed to a shaft that held a crescent-shaped piece of flint. To add momentum, two bags of pebbles were tied to the rotating shaft. That simple contrivance was perfectly capable of shaping stone bowls and vases. Shortly afterward a stone bearing united the bent handle and the shaft, permitting greater pressure to be applied, and copper bits were fitted to the end of the drill shaft. When very hard rock was being worked, the drill shafts were sometimes set with fragments of gemstones. A further refinement came with the bow-drill. In the bow-drill a bowstring wrapped around the shaft was sawed back and forth, thus intensifying the drill's speed.

In addition to the flint drill, which was useful for hollowing out concavities, there was also the tubular metal drill. This evolved from the use of stout reeds whose ends were coated with wet sand or emery powder, and then twirled about. Softer stones, such as alabaster, yielded readily to those instruments. The metal tubes eventually bore gemstone edges and were combined with moistened abrasives. The cores that they produced, and many have come to light in ancient midden heaps, are often superior in smoothness to those made by modern tools.

Regarding precision of diameter, the Egyptians were fully capable of very tight control. This is evident in an alabaster water clock made about 1400 B.C. Its form is that of a truncated conic section, with a hollowed interior and an outlet drilled through the bottom. That shape compensated simultaneously for both reduced volume and pressure within its small tank. The diameter of the outlet was also calculated exactly, permitting only a certain amount of water to flow within a limited period of time, much like a sandglass. Quite obviously the Egyptians were no amateurs in the use of stone, and were perfectly able to utilize it in many more functions than we do today.

Mesopotamia

Modern Syria and Iraq lie in much of the territory that the ancients called Mesopotamia, "the land between the rivers." Unlike Egypt, it had a harsh, demanding environment where life, at best, was always threatened and uncertain. Drought, pestilence, or the destruction of war were ever-present possibilities, and the result was that the people of Mesopotamia (the Sumerians, Babylonians, and Assyrians) developed what, for lack of a better term, can be called a regional neurosis. The pessimism and incertitude of the Sumerians graduated to the desperate conquests of the Babylonians, and finally to the nihilistic cruelty of the Assyrians. Although the people of Mesopotamia possessed writing, architecture, and mathematics before the Egyptians, they never achieved the unified stability to carry those disciplines through to their proper ends. Their art was imbued with clumsiness from the first; at the last it glorified scenes of slaughter. However one may wish to define art, there is one thing it can always be relied upon to do, and that is to show us the inward spirit of the society that created it.

Perhaps the major accomplishment of the Mesopotamians was the creation of the cylinder seal. It came into being even before the art of writing was devised, and examples are known from about 4000 B.C. All such seals were drilled through from end to end, and bore designs, generally of geometric or animal forms, cut intaglio fashion as a negative image. They seem to have first arisen as identifying marks of property, but eventually came to have religious significance as well. Until about 2500 B.C. they were chiefly made from either green or black serpentine, as well as from diorite, conglomerate, lapis lazuli, and the core column of large whelk shells. Other stones were added from time to time to the repertoire; marble rather rarely, steatite, quartzite, chalcedony, hematite, agate, and jasper. Here, almost from the very beginning, the craftsmen involved showed confidence in their skill, and were unafraid of any degree of hardness. The materials that they used also indicate a widespread network of trade because many of them had to be imported from great distances.

The favorite stone of the Sumerians, the first notable group of Mesopotamians, was lapis lazuli, prized for its blue color. The death goddess of the Sumerian underworld, Ereshgikal, held court in a palace of lapis lazuli, and the love goddess, Inanna, wore necklaces, bracelets, and other jewelry made of the stone. Over and over again reference is made, in Sumerian literature and myth, to the beauty of lapis lazuli, which remained as an unrivalled criterion all throughout the history of Mesopotamia. Mesopotamians could imagine nothing of greater value, and chose three blocks of the stone to present to Thutmose III as a gift worthy both of him and of Egypt's power and majesty. Undoubtedly the difficulty of obtaining pieces of workable size greatly enhanced its worth in Sumerian eyes, for it came from Media, of which modern Afghanistan was once a part.

So seldom were the Sumerians able to acquire any sizable pieces or quantity of lapis lazuli that they were very thrifty with whatever did come their way. For instance the so-called Standard of Ur, now in the British Museum, consists of silhouettes of shell set into a bed of bitumen, with all the interstices filled with irregular fragments of lapis lazuli. There is no evidence that any of the pieces were smoothed or shaped to provide a better fit. They are simply put next to one another in a crude

jigsaw-puzzle fashion, leaving the bitumen to fill the gaps that remained. No court jeweler of contemporary Egypt would have been so slapdash in his workmanship, but the intrinsic value of lapis lazuli was sufficient to blind Sumerian eyes to the artistic deficiencies of the work.

The motifs of the cylinder seals had long since incorporated the figures of gods, genies, and humans. Within the small confines of those minute cylinders of stone an amazing amount of detail was presented, either engraved, by using copper chisels and emery powder, or cut by a sapphire point. As writing improved and came into more frequent use, more documents had to be validated, and this meant an increase in the manufacture of seals. Quite naturally haste led to poor workmanship, but many of the better seals held to a high standard, particularly in the case of valuable stones. Scenes from the legend of Gilgamesh, the Sumerian equivalent of Samson and Hercules, were very popular, as were depictions of the sun-god, Shamash. There were even seals that showed the bird-god, Zu, being tried for the crime of stealing the tablets of destiny.

Seals continued to be made in the original style, even including cuneiform writing as time went on, but began to evolve in a different direction after 700 B.C. They became cone-shaped, a form better adapted to vertical pressure, and their sides were perforated with holes that gradually enlarged until they could be worn as signet rings. Many of the designs were reduced to mere outlines, and they became even lower and flatter in the period between 300 B.C. and A.D. 300. During that time the tradition that had created the art was dispersed. Fortunately the original style was passed on to later generations of jewelers and lapidaries by the Egyptians, Cretans, and Greeks.

Although the fashioning of these seals suggests that the Sumerians had the ability to make elaborate jewelry, there is little sign that they did. Some of their burial sites, untouched because the kings and cities of Sumer had been forgotten from before the time of Abraham, reveal very discreet personal adornment. Babylon had more taste for display, while Assyria reveled in gold, ivory, and jewels set in precious metals. However, few examples from either remain today.

Sculpture was seriously hampered because of

the general lack of suitable stone. There is scarcely a pebble to be found on the plains of southern Iraq, so most of the statues that have survived are of imported stone. One anomaly, however, does exist, and that is the presence of steatite, gypsum, limestone, marble, and basalt in the middle and upper Euphrates valley. All were available in deposits equal to the needs of the sculptors and architects, but their potential was never fully exploited. What considerations stood in the way of using those resources is a question that only future knowledge can answer.

Much Sumerian sculpture is in the form of statuettes, often eighteen inches or less in height, and carved from alabaster or similar kinds of soft stone. Prominent among these are the "worshiper" statues, perpetually offering prayer to the god of the shrine on behalf of their donors. They are meant to appear devoutly suppliant, but their squat proportions and awkward stance give them the effect of poorly trained servants. Their huge staring eyes always seem fastened in horror upon a guest whose cleavage is about to receive an accidental baptism of gravy.

Diorite and chlorite statuettes of Gudea, ruler of Lagash, and his son Ur-ningursu, were sculptured about 2100 B.C. While they clearly show that the sculptors could equal the lapidaries in the finish they could provide, it is the finish that is more admirable than the sculpture. Sculpture in the round remained something of a rarity among the Mesopotamian cultures, for most carving was devoted to the production of inscribed boundary stones, stelae, and a kind of obelisk, usually only about six feet high. These were made of black marble, and presented about five separate scenes in low relief set one above the other. A most unusual statuette, carved in the round, is that of an Assyrian, King Ashur-nasir-apal, from the 9th century B.C. Only seven and a half inches high, it is made from amber, a rare material in Assyria. In all probability the amber arrived there by trade with the Mycenaeans, far to the west. At the opposite end of the scale is a sculpture of a run-in between a lion and a man carved out of basalt about 1000 B.C. It is eight feet six inches in length, massively and simply modeled in sharply cut planes, and, most unusually, shows a Babylonian getting the worst of the encounter.

Sumerian statuette of a standing male figure in white gypsum with bitumen made c. 3000 B.C. Note the staring eyes and the characteristic supplicant posture.

Above: *Amber with inclusion.* Right: *View of the obelisk
in the old hippodrome, Istanbul, Turkey. At a mere 64
feet, this obelisk is one of the shorter specimens.*
Below: *Variety of pre-Columbian necklaces from Peru.
The stones used include jadeite, carnelian, turquoise,
serpentine, and coral.* Opposite: *The mile-wide rim of
Vesuvius. Many rare minerals have their birth in the volcano.*

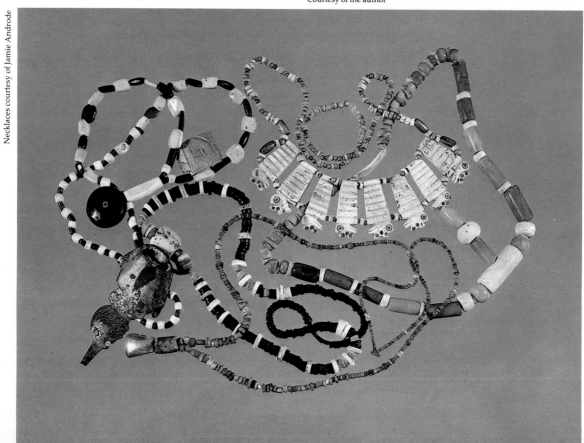

30

In architecture few of the monumental structures that once urged the Egyptians to imitate them have survived. These were built chiefly from brick because captives could be taught how to construct walls more readily from that material than from stone, which required a mason's skills. Such stone did exist, and was utilized by the Assyrian kings, each one eager to outdo his predecessors. Sennacherib had over 2 million blocks of stone quarried, dressed, and set together to build an aqueduct fifty miles long. In some places the artificial channel of stone was sixty-five feet wide. At Babylon and Assur there were processional ways built of gypsum slabs laid over baked brick set in bitumen.

Within the brick palaces there were pavements of alabaster and gypsum, some of them decorated with insets of red breccia. Conical pieces of stone, variously colored, were pressed into the plaster walls to form geometrical mosaic patterns. An early decorative technique was to combine shaped bits of white marble, black schist, and red limestone to form petaled flowers in a border.

But low reliefs cut on slabs of gypsum were far and away the most frequent means of decorating palace interiors. Because gypsum is fairly soft when first quarried, hardening gradually as it dries out, it was an ideal material for the architects and sculptors. On slabs nine and ten feet high they carved the victories of their kings, the legends of their gods, and occasional glimpses of the incidents of day-to-day living. Thanks to those scenes we know how the 9th-century Assyrians breached the walls of cities they were besieging. They simply tunneled under the brick to the timber supports and set them afire.

More peaceful scenes show meals being prepared in cook tents, and genies tending the sacred Tree of Life. True to their heritage, the Assyrians were unable to make even their angelic beings benign. The genies had eagle's wings and beaks, but otherwise had human limbs and bodies. Their duty was to protect the sacred Tree and keep it continually watered. They did that by dipping pinecones, symbols of everlasting life, into little buckets, or *situlae*, of holy water, which they then sprinkled on the branches. The Tree of Life was a date palm, which has, according to an Arabic proverb, as many uses as there are days in the year. It was also beneficial to the Greek architects who derived their very useful palmette motif from it. Further, it became the basis of the fleur-de-lis which is not a lily at all, but a highly conventionalized date palm. Its crest of fronds is at the top; two protective horns, to frighten off demons, are lashed with cords to its trunk, which ends in a splayed foot at ground level. That motif may well endure longer than the tree from which it originated, and has already outlasted several societies.

Opposite: *Top of sarcophagus decorated with inscribed figure of Nut, the Egyptian sky goddess, who is pictured with her hands and feet resting on earth while her body forms the vault of heaven.* Above: *Egyptian statue in black granite showing the* nemes, *or headdress. This statue gives a good sense of the exceptionally smooth quality of Egyptian stonework.*

31

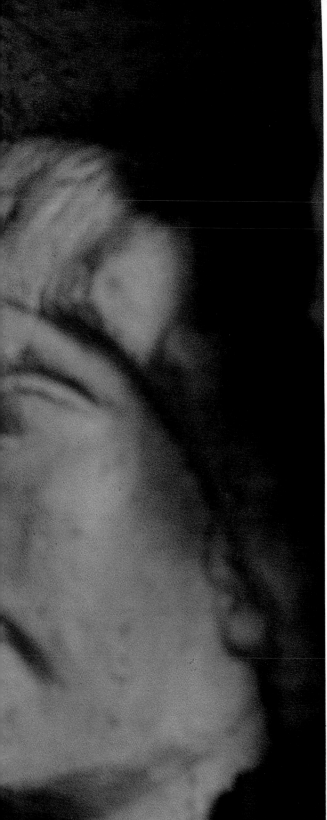

2

Chapter 2
HELLENIC SPLENDOR

Marble is the prime material of Greek sculpture and architecture. Almost from the first the Greeks sensed their affinities with that particular stone, and saw that it would lend purity and dignity to all of their works with it. Its texture and brilliance created a superb effect in the dazzling light of Greece, and its physical properties were perfectly suited to the embodiment of the Greek esthetic ideals.

Before the Greeks absorbed the influences of Egypt and western Asia their work was done with such humble materials as clay and wood; neither of which laid a good enough foundation to build a great tradition of art and architecture. Marble allowed realization of that potential. In fact, it may be justly said that the Greeks were the first to discover the artistic possibilities of marble, and to use it as no other people had done.

Granite, limestone, and diorite gave sculptural voice to Egypt, and Mesopotamia spoke in metal, brick, and compacted gypsum. Even Homeric Greece had not yet learned the language of marble, for the vague term *marmaros* appears only three times in Homer's Iliad and the Odyssey. Each time it means nothing more than "shining stone," and is devoid of all further description. In one particular instance the poem simply refers to the stone as having struck a man. Wherever Homer wants to make his reader aware of rich and regal display he speaks of ivory, bronze, or one of the precious metals; these seem to exhaust his catalogue of sumptuous materials. But who, today, can imagine a palace without a trace of marble in it? That would be like an omelette without eggs.

A further indication that even the Greeks had to be educated to the use of stone in their buildings may be seen in the Heraion, the Temple of Hera, at Olympia. When built in 650 B.C. it possessed some twenty-two wooden columns, probably because the builders did not yet have the skill to make stone ones, or possibly because religious tradition may have insisted on wood. Whatever the case, the wooden columns were replaced one by one, over the centuries, in various styles, and one of the wooden ones was still in place as late as A.D. 160. Just that experience was more than ample to demonstrate that wood and stone were not ideal architectural partners.

Other materials, such as tufa and coarse limestone, were also given fair trial, and proved relatively easy to shape. They did, however, lack one characteristic that is desirable in a building stone—they could not be given either a polish or a smooth finish. Wherever smoothness was desired the builders had to coat those stones with stucco, but in so doing they destroyed the character of the stone itself, transforming it into a featureless piece of plaster.

Because of these circumstances both sculptors and architects extended a warm welcome to marble when it arrived on the scene about 700 B.C. Marble had just the right degree of resistance to the chisel; neither too little, as with some sandstones; nor too much, as with diorite, which slowed sculptural progress to a painful crawl. It also possessed a wide range of color, not only white and black, but every other hue across the spectrum as well. It had sufficient structural strength for architectural purposes, could be textured in every fashion from matte finish to high polish, and, best of all, was widely available. Almost everywhere throughout the Grecian world there were large deposits of marble, generally located near to the great shrines and cities. And should there be any need to transport stone from one place to another, Greek maritime skills and facilities were fully equal to the task.

Among the major varieties of marble that were used were those from Paros, in the Cyclades; Mounts Pentelicus, Hymettus, and Eleusis, near

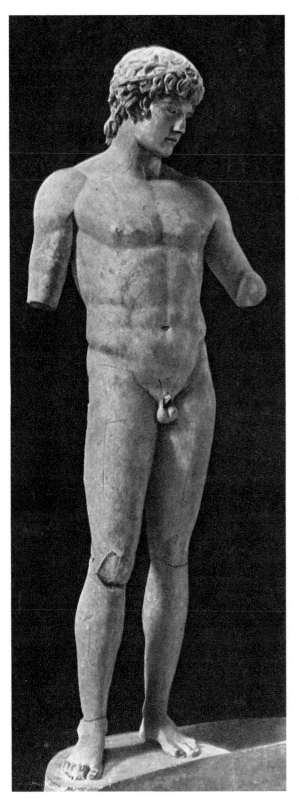

Preceding pages: *The marble faces of a Roman couple, from ruins in Brescia, Italy.* Left: *The statue of Antinous at Delphi, which was rubbed with oil. In its day, the statue probably had a pleasing sheen; today it is permanently stained.* Top: *The porch of the caryatids of the Erechtheion.* Above: *The Temple of Nike, goddess of victory.*

35

Specimen courtesy of The Collector's Cabinet

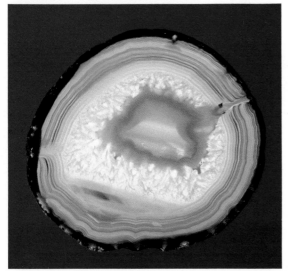

Specimen courtesy of The Collector's Cabinet

Statue courtesy of Rare Art, Inc.

Collection of the photographer

Opposite: *The name of the Parthenon, built under Pericles between 447 B.C. and 432 B.C., means "virgin's place"—an ironic twist in light of the use put to its sister edifice, the Erechtheion. Top left: Geode, also called "eagle stone"* on the ancient belief that eagles placed the stones in their nests to insure the hatching of their eggs. Center left: Agate. Above right: Coral statue on ivory stand. Above: Clinozoisite in quartz. The clinozoisite is the darker portion.

Above: *View of the destruction in and around the Parthenon.* **Right:** *Engraved gems, such as this head of the Egyptian god Serapis, became a specialty of the Greek lapidaries.* **Far right:** *The only remains of the magnificent tomb of Mausolus are some sculpted decorations now in the British Museum.*

Athens; while the islands of Thasos, Chios, and Samos, and others, provided an abundant supply. Parian marble was long considered the best, and was often termed *lychnites*, or "lamplike." The Roman writer Varro tells us that the name came about because the Parian quarries were worked by lamplight, but the glowing, sunny quality of the stone itself seems a better reason for the adjective "lamplike" than any other.

The first building on mainland Greece to be constructed entirely of marble was the treasury of the Siphnians at Delphi, and it was built of Parian stone. Treasury, at that time, signified a place where the people of a city or state deposited and preserved their offerings at a religious shrine. Each, of course, tried to outdo the other, and the people of Siphnos, who had been enriched by discoveries of gold and silver on their island, had the means to put on a great display at one of the most important shrines of all, the place where Apollo delivered his prophecies. No doubt the Siphnians also wanted to make the god mindful that he was not dealing with a batch of ingrates, and perhaps even wished to encourage him to bestow future benefits as well. In any case, their choice of Parian marble was an excellent one, and has conveyed their tribute to Apollo since 525 B.C. Its sculpture may be admired to this day in the museum at Delphi.

Closely rivaling Parian marble was that from Athens' Mount Pentelicus, which provided the stone for the Parthenon and most of the other buildings on the Acropolis. Both marbles have a fine grain, and a warm, creamy color, which ranges from nearly white to a golden ochre. The degree of coloration, as in all similar deposits, depends upon the extent to which iron oxide has infiltrated and stained the stone. Other matter, of course, produces different effects. Hornblende particles cause a blue or green coloration, bitumen or pitch creates black, and most of the rose, or yellow varieties arise from various oxides of iron. One peculiarity of black marble is that its bituminous content often releases an odor when the stone is struck, thus earning it the unglamorous name "stinkstone."

Pentelic marble may also be found at Delphi, where an example of it once graced Apollo's own sanctuary. It consists of a tall column that branches out into acanthus leaves, atop which three maidens seem to be slowly turning in a solemn dance. Because of its seeming movement, Claude Debussy was inspired to write the prelude "Danseuses de Delphes," music that unfailingly evokes the spirit of their motion. Tradition has it that they are the three daughters of Cecrops, founder of Athens, and that their names are Pandrosus, Erse, and Aglaurus.

Pentelic, and other marbles, were often subjected, especially if used in cult statues, to a procedure that sends shudders through the modern soul. It was called *ganosis*, and involved the use of oil to either anoint or polish the statue. An image of Antinous, also at Delphi, clearly shows the result of that practice, still evident today. The upper right shoulder of the statue of the Emperor Hadrian's favorite, Antinous, whose physical perfection caused that ruler to invest him with divinity after his death, is deeply and permanently stained through the oily attentions of his devotees.

Oil was not the only substance that marble had to suffer; it also had to endure the ultimate outrage—paint. Whether this was a holdover from the custom of coloring the stucco finish on limestone, in order to make it look less like plaster, or whether it was simply a matter of preference still remains unknown. What is beyond question is that the ancient Greeks often decked out their sculptured masterpieces with applications of color. Enough traces exist to vouch for the consistency of the practice, but age and chemical change prevent accurate assessment of their original effect. Most art historians are inclined to agree that the practice made the works gaudy, but a stroll through the Acropolis Museum might modify that view somewhat. Pigmentation in ancient times was largely derived from plant and animal sources, and such colors rarely, if ever, approached the high degree of intensity in chroma to which we are accustomed through modern chemicals and dyestuffs. As in most cases, the reality probably lies between the two extremes. The Greeks would likely consider their sculptures, as we proudly exhibit them today, to be little more than bleached corpses of themselves. And we quietly wonder why they ever felt color to be necessary; the form and proportion express it all.

However, the Athenian Acropolis has undergone even worse defacement than mere paint in its 2400 years of history. There was the pious vandalism of the early Christians, who transformed both the Parthenon and the Erechtheion into basilicas with consequent damage to their original forms. Later, in 1458, the Turks converted the Parthenon into a mosque, and about the same time subjected the Erechtheion to the indignity of housing a harem. A worse fate awaited the Propylaea, which was struck by lightning in 1656 while serving as a storage area for gunpowder.

The catalogue of disasters continued in 1687 when the Venetian commander, Francesco Morosini, pursuing his war against the Turks, lobbed a shell straight into the Parthenon. It landed amid a large collection of powder kegs, resulting in damage that has ever since been visible. Morosini was rewarded the following year by being appointed Doge of Venice.

Even the charming little Temple of Nike, just beyond the Propylaea, underwent its share of woe. Before Morosini's attack in 1687 it was totally dismembered to provide stone for Turkish fortifications. Following the Greek War of Independence (1821–1827) it was faithfully restored from the original materials by a team of Austrian and Bavarian architects. A little over a century later, on the eve of World War II, it was discovered that their skill had not been equal to their good intentions, for the structure was on the verge of collapse. But, as so often happens, good luck trailed in the wake of ineptitude (the world would scarcely run otherwise), and the restorers uncovered foundations from the Mycenaean age. That moved the known lifespan of the Acropolis back some six centuries into the past.

Athens and Delphi, of course, were not the only cities to make lavish use of marble. The Ionian city of Ephesus was also notable for its quantity of marble buildings. The nearby islands of Chios and Samos provided most of the material, and in such generous amounts that it was used for paving the streets as well as for construction. Even the seats in the public latrines were constructed with it, and while that may have given those necessary edifices some degree of grandeur it also created a certain inconvenience. Mortal flesh shrinks from the touch of cold marble, and western Turkey, where Ephesus is located, does feel a touch of

winter. It also gets rain from time to time, and wet marble, as anyone who has ever skidded on it well knows, can be as treacherous as the most slippery of skating ponds.

Marble dazzled the eye everywhere in Ephesus. It was fashioned into shrines, theatres (the one at Ephesus held 24,000), multi-storied libraries, fountains, shops, and luxurious dwellings. The most stunning creation of all was the great Temple of Artemis (Diana), one of the seven wonders of the ancient world. It stood on a site that measured some 425 by 220 feet, and was built by two architects from Crete, Kesrifon and Metagenes, in the 6th century B.C.

Its beauty was short lived, though, for it was burned to the ground in 356 B.C. by a native of Ephesus, one Herostratus, who hoped to gain undying fame for the deed. The Ephesians struck his name from their rolls, proscribed any future mention of him, but all to no avail. By coincidence the fire had occurred on the night that Alexander the Great was born, and as his fame rose both events became connected in the popular mind. The result is that Herostratus is permanently enshrined among the villains of history, who always get remembered, while his proscribers' names have blown away with the dust. Today even the temple has vanished. All that remains are some bits of toppled columns clustered about a single reconstructed one in the midst of a shallow marsh. Only the frogs hold nocturnal services there now.

Not far from Ephesus rose another of the seven ancient wonders, the Tomb of Mausolus at Halicarnassus, a building from which the word "mausoleum" is derived. Portions of it survived on the site until they were excavated in 1856–1857, and brought to the British Museum for preservation. It had been overthrown by an earthquake in medieval times, and was later used as a quarry for fortifying a castle of the Knights of Malta.

In its original state the mausoleum stood about 140 feet high, which is the equivalent of a modern 15-story building. It was made largely of marble, elaborately carved by a team of four sculptor-architects whose studios were erected alongside the wall for which each was responsible. Commissioned by Mausolus himself, the work was carried forward after his death, in 353 B.C., by his wife, Queen Artemisia. She died only two years later, leaving the project without a sponsor, but the artists involved continued anyway. They knew that they were collaborating on a masterpiece that would carry their names down through the ages, and all four, Scopas, Bryaxis, Timotheus, and Leochares, hold secure places in art history.

Halicarnassus is also credited with an innovation in marble work, the technique of cutting marble into thin slabs for use as facing material. The Roman historian Pliny tells us that Carian craftsmen, working on the palace of Mausolus, devised the method in order to improve the appearance of its brick walls.

The marble that they chose was from the island of Marmora, near the Dardanelles. Marmora marble was famous in antiquity for its shining white quality. The process used to slice it was very much the same as that employed in modern times. They pressed thin strips of metal into wet abrasives laid along a lightly scored line, and sawed them back and forth rapidly. Today wire strands, or toothed saws of soft iron, working in combination with very fine sand and a constant flow of water, are used for the same purpose. In ancient times marble workers were cautioned against using coarse sand, or even emery, because it was believed that, in addition to wasting much of the stone, a great deal of extra work would be required to polish away the resulting roughness.

One characteristic of marble that has caused damage to many ancient sculptures is its habit of exfoliating, flaking away in thin layers or scales. When subjected to desiccation by heat the structure of the stone changes, allowing the molecules to shift apart. If carried out only partially the marble becomes flexible, bending under slight pressure, or even its own weight. More often the particles separate physically from each other, on a molecular level, and part of the stone will drop away. Projecting portions, such as arms and legs, of statues left standing outdoors in very warm climates, break off for that reason. Very mild heat opens the pores of the stone when marble is being artificially stained, thus permitting the color to penetrate deeply. If too much heat, such as that in a conflagration, develops, then the marble becomes calcined and crumbles into lime, which is how fire destroyed the Temple of Artemis at Ephesus.

Important and colorful as marble is, a much more prosaic stone had initiated commerce and wealth in the Aegean Sea. The island of Cos, later famous for producing Hippocrates, was already a center of trade in the Stone Age, having capitalized on its large deposits of obsidian. That volcanic glass, which flaked down to razor-sharp edges, was highly valued, and many came to Cos to obtain it. In Minoan times the westernmost island of the Cyclades, Melos, became the chief distributor of obsidian, which remained in use for many purposes long after the Stone Age was over. Perhaps the major one was as a mirror, when polished. Obsidian was also engraved as a gem and occasionally shaped into statuary, for there is mention of an obsidian statue of the Emperor Augustus, and four elephants (size unmentioned) of the same material, which he dedicated to the Temple of Concord.

The amount of trade moving through the Mediterranean implies a very early development of shipping, and consequent skill in boat building. By the 3rd century B.C. Ptolemaios IV (222–205) was famous for the enormous ships he constructed, and his barge of state was described as having a length of 300 feet and a height above waterline of about 60 feet. What concerns us here is the ship's elaborate on-board decoration, which consisted of marble statues, some of them the Parian variety, rows of columns made of Indian marble, and panels of agate. Another ship, belonging to Hieron, king of Syracuse, had marble mosaic floors illustrating the story of the Iliad, which ran throughout the officers' quarters. Elsewhere it had floors of agate, and other variegated stones, even a washstand, made from Tauromenian marble, capable of holding fifty gallons. A slight notion of the ship's overall size lies in its capacity to hold 90,000 bushels of grain, 10,000 jars of salted fish, 1200 tons of cargo, a 20,000 gallon tank of water, plus quarters and provisions for its sizable crew.

Gigantic and heavy stone objects such as obelisks were readily transported on similar large vessels available in Ptolemaic Egypt in the 3rd century B.C. They were used ingeniously by one Greek engineer named Phoenix. He dug a canal

41

from the Nile to the site of the obelisk, and then bridged the stream with the monument. Next two huge boats were laden with blocks of the same granite as the obelisk itself, until they held twice its weight. That permitted the boats to come directly under the stone shaft where they were gradually unloaded. As they were emptied the boats rose, and floated the obelisk down the stream, gaining a fifty-talent reward for Phoenix. Since a talent was not an actual coin, but a weight representing about fifty-seven pounds, generally of silver, the obelisk must have been of considerable importance to Egypt's King, Ptolemy Philadelphus, who erected it in the Arsinoeum at Alexandria as a tribute to his queen, Arsinoe.

At the opposite end of the scale in size were the Greek methods of contriving decorative pavements and murals through the use of small stones. Oval-shaped pebbles, worn flat by the action of water in streams or surf, were placed on edge in varicolored patterns, creating a technique of stone setting called "ears-of-wheat," from its resemblance to individual grains lying in the seed-head. Thin marble tiles were also cut into small squares or rectangles, called tesserae, and carefully graded by color and size. Beginning about 400 B.C. these were used to make geometric patterns on floors, but soon advanced to the imitation of paintings, even so far as making attempts at *trompe l'oeil.* Sosus of Pergamum, who created the illusion of bits of debris lying about after a feast (the "Unswept Floor") was perhaps the earliest master of the technique. Dioscorides of Samos, who worked at Pompeii, is another artist whose name has come down to us. But whoever was responsible for "The Battle of Issus," which shows Alexander the Great attacking Darius, remains unknown. The common practice, in fact, was to leave most of these works unsigned, as the bulk of them simply reproduced the design of another artist. They did, however, anticipate Impressionist and Pointillist techniques, achieving the desired effect by the juxtaposition of colors.

An even more important and vastly older art form, used by the Greek craftsmen, was the engraving of gems. Both Egypt and Mesopotamia had shown the way at a very early date with their ability to carve scarabs and cylinder seals, a technique that was already practiced in Crete by 3000

B.C. with the production of prism, or triangular, seals. At first only the relatively soft stone steatite was used, and the designs were confined to hieroglyphs. By 2200 B.C. the skill had improved to the point where they could cut the harder materials such as carnelian and chalcedony, two forms of quartz that rate 7 on the Mohs scale of hardness whereas steatite rates but one.

The difficulties the Greeks encountered in engraving letters rapidly led to technical proficiency in the treatment of plant, animal, and human forms. In a lapidary's shop, discovered at Knossos, lenticular pieces of stone were found. They were convex on both sides, and ranged in hardness from soft steatite, to harder marble, and on to the hardest, jasper and beryl. Examples of inlay work in lapis lazuli and rock crystal were also uncovered, as well as relief cutting that anticipated the carving of cameos. Some of the stones were also adapted to be worn as bangles hanging from the wrist.

Crete, of course, because of its geographical location was open to influences from both the ancient East and West, most particularly through its trading center Miletos, on the Anatolian coast. Nominally Ionian, that city had, in fact, been established by colonists from Crete, and became a focal point not only for the mingling of cultures, but for the development of ideas and techniques that resulted from those interactions. Thus the civilization of Crete, as well as many of its traditions, were not only preserved outside the island kingdom after its decline, but were also eventually transferred to the Mycenaeans.

During the course of excavations at Mycenae, on the Greek mainland, another lapidary shop was discovered. A store of unworked stones, including hematite, sard, chalcedony, and amethyst, as well as a partially worked disc of rock crystal were brought to light. By then both the wheel, a thin metal disc used in combination with emery or sharp sand, and the point, a splintered piece of corundum or diamond set in an iron rod, had become common and important tools in lapidary art. With these tools even the hardest stones could be engraved with inscriptions, designs, representations, or even portraits.

By the 6th century B.C. the Greek lapidaries were engraving scarabaeoids, scarab-shaped stones very like cabochon–cut gems. Names of the designer-engravers also began to appear on the finished gems, among them one of the earliest to be recorded, Mnesarchos of Samos, who was also the father of Pythagoras, famed for his religious philosophy and mathematical discoveries. Another great artist was Theodoros of Samos, who devised a method of supporting the foundations of the great Temple of Artemis in marshy ground, and also introduced new methods for polishing gems. Specialization was *not* the order of the day among the ancient Greeks, who would have found its present popularity difficult to understand.

Laws had already been passed (about 600 B.C.) forbidding engravers to retain impressions of the seals they engraved. This meant, of course, that some of the shadier members of their society had found a lucrative market among the would-be forgers of the day. Alexander the Great permitted only one artist, Pyrgoteles, to engrave his portrait on a gem, which was used thereafter as the official seal. In fact, all of Alexander's rings, which served various purposes in connection with his administrative powers, were also engraved by Pyrgoteles. In transferring his authority, the dying Alexander gave his signet ring, bearing the portrait by Pyrgoteles, to Perdiccas, who had accompanied him throughout his Asiatic campaigns.

Some other noted engravers of gems were Dexamenos of Chios, who carved a flying heron only four-fifths of an inch wide on a piece of chalcedony. It is presently in the Hermitage Museum, Leningrad. Dexamenos is also thought to have engraved the representation of a flying goose, of similar size, on a seal of banded onyx, now in the British Museum. Yet another lapidary of note was Dioscorides, who carved the portrait of Caesar Augustus, which that emperor used as his personal seal. Even during the Roman period the Greek gem engravers continued to be preeminent in their field, for most of so-called Roman art was executed by artists of Greek descent.

While signatures exist on a number of the gems their presence is not always a guarantee of authenticity. Many genuinely old stones *without* signatures acquired them at a later date, at any time from the Renaissance to the present, with a peak of such upgrading in the 18th and early 19th centuries. Only in the case of unimpeachable and continuous provenance, supported by documentation, can anyone be sure that any signature verifies the work as that of a specific artist. Such deception was carried on in ancient times as well as in our own, for great reputations gave as much value to a work of art in those days as in modern times. Phaedros, a writer of fables early in the 1st century A.D., complained of such forgery in one of his stories, and there is no doubt that it was not new even in his time. Closer to the present age is the great German jeweler from Swabia, Lorenz Natter, who died in 1763, after lending his hand to a number of antiquarian impostures at the request of his aristocratic patrons. Heaven alone knows how many of them have eluded detection for years, Natter being expert at his work. He had made a thorough study of the ancient techniques of gem engraving, and even wrote a "Treatise on the Antique Method of Engraving Gemstones."

There are a few guidelines to avoid being deluded by fraud, but perhaps the best of all is not to buy if you lack specialized knowledge and experience. If you do have both there is still a cautionary note: remember that the forger, expert at his trade, stands to make more money if he can impose upon the experts; and many a museum attic will testify to how successfully that has been done in the past.

Most frauds reveal themselves in time, for each generation leaves stylistic traces, invisible to itself, that stand out to those who succeed them. Anachronisms are common, particularly when poorly educated or clumsy forgers are involved. Sometimes even the educated and skillful forger may be ignorant of some small but vital fact, and introduce an inscription in a style that is inaccurate. Both Greek and Latin, the languages of the classical world, had different usages, mannerisms, and letter-shapes that act as hallmark characteristics of both time and place.

Besides serving as seals, engraved gems had other uses, too, and while those would today be considered as nothing more than superstitious nonsense, the ancients felt them to be as real and practical as any activity of their daily lives. From long association with religious ritual many stones had acquired a sacred character, and their colors often linked them symbolically to the planets that were believed to rule human destiny. What was

more natural then than to heighten and focus the occult powers of gems by engraving them with signs or images that would provide the wearer with supernatural aid? The image, in fact, was believed to receive a force impressed upon it by the stars themselves and to emit a particular virtue, provided that both the kind of stone and its ritual consecration were in harmony with its intended use. For instance, one could not expect a stone under the influence of Saturn (always associated with gloom and misfortune) to bring its wearer good luck.

Sapphires or amethysts, both of the oriental corundum variety, were often carved with the head or form of Zeus (Jupiter); Aphrodite (Venus)

appeared on emeralds; and Ares (Mars) on rubies. A lion, engraved on garnet, would protect honor and health, cure the wearer of all disease, and guard him from harm while traveling. A moss (or tree) agate, bound to a ploughman's arm or the horn of his ox, guaranteed a successful crop. Coral was bound to a masthead by sealskin to ward off gales and tempests; but, if it had the name of the moon carved on it with the sign of Hecate, goddess of magic and spells, or the figure of the Medusa, it would preserve the wearer from poison, lightning, and defeat in war.

Medicinal virtues were also ascribed to stones and were administered in wine, or other fluids, if they could be readily pulverized; but if not, they

Opposite: *A piece of the aquamarine variety of beryl.* Top: *Rutilated quartz crystal.* Above left: *Rock-crystal bowl used by Tibetan monks as a ceremonial drinking cup for blood.* Above right: *Marble Ionic capital from Delphi, Greece.*

45

were worn tied to particular spots on the body. These last, called ligatures, were often engraved to lend them greater force. Jasper, an opaque form of quartz, was worn on the thigh to assist an easy childbirth, and two Hellenic physicians, Dioscorides and Galen, recommended such use. Fumes from the burning of jet were used to restore epileptics to their senses, and powdered lapis lazuli was given in cases of snakebite. From the number of remedies for this last condition the snakes of the Mediterranean must have been both numerous and peevish, with fangs continually at the ready.

In earlier, more primitive times, the Greeks used gems rather sparingly in their jewelry, if at all. But with access to wealth and power the notion of display came to the fore, especially after Alexander's conquests made the world conscious of Greek capabilities. Luxury and prodigality became the fashion, and fingers that had touched nothing more precious than wood or wool now dripped gold and jewels. Until the 4th century B.C. gems were set in swivels so that they might be used as seals; then came the habit of mounting them immovably in rings. And their numbers increased for two very good reasons: the glittering ornamentation they offered was irresistible, and they provided a shield for the faithful against the vagaries of fortune and disease.

About the same time a new method of cutting stones came into general use, for cameos began to be produced in ever greater quantities. Accustomed as we are to seeing these made from shells with alternate layers of brown and white, we fail to realize that only such stones as onyx, sardonyx, and banded agate were regarded as cameo material by the ancients. Cameo is a word of uncertain derivation, being neither classical Greek nor Latin, but the suggestion has been made that it comes from the Arabic *khamea*, an amulet. Because onyx was often called the Arabian stone, and amulets made from it generally bore carvings in relief, perhaps that theory has more merit than most.

The art has been in a dying state for the past seventy years, no longer attractive to apprentices who must spend years of demanding practice to master it. One way or another, however, it has survived for 2400 years, and comprises so many aspects of the lapidary's and jeweler's craft that its loss is bound to have serious effects, though it may yet gain a reprieve.

Onyx, which has regular, parallel bands of white and black, or blackish-brown, was one of the favored stones for cameo carving. Exceeding it in popularity was sardonyx, which generally contained red carnelian in addition to its white and black layers. A third material was banded agate. All three of these substances are one and the same in the mineralogical sense, being opaque forms of quartz known as chalcedony.

Because the colors came in layers, each of perceptible depth, and ran straight through the stone from end to end, it was a relatively simple matter to fashion designs from them. Parts of the uppermost layer were cut away to expose a contrasting ground, and then the topmost layer was carved in relief. Because of the slablike nature of most of the stones, few objects in the round were ever cut, although a few exceedingly rare ones exist and have been preserved for us in royal or national collections.

Such a cameo is the Farnese Cup now in the Museo Nazionale, Naples. It is a saucerlike bowl, eight inches wide, carved from a single piece of sardonyx, richly colored with shades of deep brown, the palest of golden ochres, and white that in certain places suggests a faintly bluish tinge. The last color is not physically present, but is an optical illusion resulting from the predominance of warm tones, rather like those of various grades of sherry wine, surrounding areas of translucent white.

The cup is thoroughly Hellenic in style, having been created about 175 B.C. in Alexandria, Egypt. It has a complex iconography on its inner surface showing the Ptolemaic Queen Cleopatra I, her dead husband, and Ptolemy VI Philometor, accompanied by the river god, Nile, the Etesian (northerly) winds, and the seasons of flood and harvest. On the outer surface is a representation of the Medusa, whose reputation for magical powers caused her image to be used for preventing death by poison, suggesting that wine was once served in the cup.

There is also the Cup of the Ptolemies, once known as the Cup of St. Denis, now in the Bibliothèque Nationale in Paris. Like the Farnese Cup it, too, is made of sardonyx, but is in the shape of a *kantharos* or bowl, some four and three-quarter inches high by five and one-eighth inches wide, a vessel intended for drinking wine. Its decoration, carved in relief, underscores that use by presenting the attributes and rites of Dionysus (Bacchus) and Demeter (Ceres), often paired.

The Great Cameo of France, of irregular shape but some twelve by ten and one-half inches in size, is the largest cameo to have survived from antiquity. It is a five-layered sardonyx, and has been masterfully carved to take full advantage of the various color patches that presented themselves. Some twenty-four personages, arranged in three registers, appear on its surface. In spite of their costumes and obvious importance, nobody has been able to determine their identities or rank, except for a few who are plainly captives. Like the Cup of the Ptolemies, this gem is also in the Bibliothèque Nationale, having formerly been in the collection of the Sainte Chapelle. It arrived there in 1244 as a pledge to Louis IX (St. Louis) of France from Baldwin II of Constantinople. The latter was an inept, financially pressed Latin monarch who eventually failed in his bid to remain on the throne of Byzantium, explaining why the cameo remained in Paris.

Probably the most beautiful of all such gems is the *Gemma Augustea*, now in the Art History (*Kunsthistorisches*) Museum of Vienna. It is a two-layered onyx, black and white, of eight and five-eighths inches by seven and a half inches, and shows the coronation of Caesar Augustus by his wife Livia, who personifies the city of Rome. Eighteen other figures accompany them, the Roman eagle, and the astrological symbol of Capricorn, but there is no sense of crowding or confusion. Everything in the design is beautifully balanced, exquisitely carved, and instantly proclaims itself, even to the untrained eye, as a masterpiece of the first order.

The cameo's pedigree goes back to the 15th century when it was known to have been in the possession of the abbey of St. Sernin, Toulouse. Tradition, often more reliable than is generally thought, has it that Charlemagne deposited it at the abbey. Later it attracted the eye of Rudolph II, ruler of the Holy Roman Empire in the 16th century, and he purchased it for 12,000 gold ducats,

approximately $1,000,000 in today's currency. It has been a national treasure of the Hapsburgs and Austria ever since.

The value of such gems has actually safeguarded them through the ages. Relatively few in number, all of the great antique cameos, now in the major museums of the world, arrived there from similar collections, royal or ecclesiastical, and none had ever been excavated. Even some of the smaller ones, despite their pagan subjects, managed to become decorative additions to medieval Christian shrines. Their symbolic significance was generally misunderstood, but their color and intrinsic worth were appreciated.

Many such cameos, which were parted from their original settings and provenance, have created endless problems for art historians ever since. When a Ptolemaic gem, such as the Gonzaga Cameo, now in Leningrad's Hermitage Museum, comes adrift from continuous documentation, or bears portraits no longer identifiable with certainty, centuries may be needed to resolve the problems of its iconography. In the Gonzaga case there remains controversy as to whether the two portraits it bears are of Ptolemy Philadelphus and Arsinoe, his wife, or of Nero and Agrippina. Although there were nearly four centuries between the existence of those two sets of people, the style of the Ptolemies was revived by Greek artisans working at Rome in the 1st century A.D.

Not all relief carvings were done in the contrasting colors of sard and onyx. They were sometimes cut on the face of unicolored gemstones, and the Bibliothèque Nationale owns one of these, carved on an amethyst. No doubts whatever attach to that particular cameo, for it shows a seated Achilles playing the lyre, and is signed by the Greek artist Pamphilos, who worked during the reign of the Emperor Augustus. Thus the identity of the subject, an approximate date, and the name of the artist are all plainly revealed. Other cameos, now lodged in an international variety of museums, display the known figures of mythological personages, which are usually far more recognizable than those of historical ones. Lasting fame is a slippery quality to grasp, and certainly pays no dividends to the illustrious departed.

Ancient cameos, from the classical periods of Greece and Rome, are usually cut on oriental

Left: *View of the Colosseum in Rome showing the underground passages through which animals and gladiators were introduced into the arena.* Top: *Marble statue of Apollo atop a Corinthian capital. Exfoliation has dismembered the god.* Above: *Detail of mosaic at Delos made of chips of marble.*

49

sardonyx, which has a warm, richly tinted quality. They were frequently carved on stones that had previously done duty as bangles, amulets, or necklaces, hence they often have a minute hole, used for threading, drilled through them. Seldom are they carved in high relief, a practice of Renais-

sance lapidaries who carried that characteristic over into their otherwise well-executed forgeries. Very often those portions of cameos that did project to any degree acquired a dulled, somewhat chalklike appearance. That, of course, was an effect of time and wear and usually indicated an authentic gem. But, as with all things, the scoundrels found a means to duplicate it. They enlisted the aid of poultry, cramming the gizzards of large fowl, such as turkeys, with the gems that they wanted to age. The method made use of natural chemistry and the random mechanical abrasion provided by the bird's digestive activities, so it was next to impossible to detect. Antiquity was brought within reach of any lapidary with a poultry yard, and the conclusion of that step in the forgery process always ended with a feast.

When Greek domination of the Mediterranean regions was terminated by the Romans, the lapidary arts did not fade away. The same artists and

Top: *The Emperor Nero, without his famous emerald lens, in a moment of characteristic ill humor.* Above: *Two views of an Etruscan wedding ring. This ring dates to the 6th to 4th centuries B.C. and employs the Etruscan art of gold filigree.*

traditions continued, simply supplying Roman patrons in place of Greek ones. When the Roman general Pompey defeated Mithridates, ruler of Pontus, he captured a cabinet of jeweled rings that had been gathered by that king. When these were displayed at Rome, in the course of Pompey's triumphal parade, they touched off a fad that persisted as long as Rome had any wealth. Furthermore, the Romans quickly outdid whatever Mithridates had been capable of, for some few years later Julius Caesar's collection was considered to be far superior.

About 61 B.C. whatever was left of the old virtues and puritanism of Republican Rome had eroded away. Ostentation became the mark of prestige, and Pompey's triumph in that year opened the floodgates of prodigal display. In it he exhibited a gameboard and pieces made of precious stones, measuring three by four feet in size. There were also gold vessels, cups and trays and bowls and the like, all inlaid with gems, and there were enough of them to fill nine display counters. To crown it all there was a portrait of Pompey, wrought entirely in pearls. The Roman historian Pliny remarked that the disembodied head bore an evil omen, for some years later he was murdered, and his head was carried to Caesar.

Myrrhine cups and bowls had been dedicated by Pompey to the Temple of Jupiter Capitolinus at his triumph, and immediately set a fashion. It is not entirely certain just what myrrhine was, but all the descriptions imply it was agate, especially references to its property of color change by the action of fire, a process still in use. Prices of myrrhine ranged from 30,000 sesterces for a cup, to 300,000 for a dipper, and as much as 1,000,000 (paid by Nero) for a bowl. In terms of present purchasing power those sums translate as $21,000, $90,000, and $300,000, respectively.

Rock crystal, which is pure, colorless quartz, was a substance of some mystery to those Romans who gave any thought to their data about it. The prevailing theory was that it formed only in places of excessive cold, and weight was given to that notion by the derivation of the Latin *crystallum*, our "crystal," from the Greek *krystallos*, which means "ice" equally as much as it means "rock crystal." They insisted that it never formed where there were rivers or lakes, but resulted instead from compacted snow. Nonetheless it was also said to form only in places that faced south, and, besides coming from the Alpine regions, was also brought from India. In fact, a crystal of about eighteen inches in length was reported to have come from the vicinity of the Red Sea, which never approaches anything even faintly arctic in climate. Portugal and Cyprus, two more places that would scarcely qualify as ski resorts, were also cited as localities where it was often found. It was said to be unable to bear any heat, hence its use for holding cool drinks, but experiment has shown it capable of enduring over 1000 degrees Celsius.

Numerous drinking vessels and ornamental objects were carved from it, and for these purposes the Greeks and Romans generally used rutile quartz, which has fine, threadlike inclusions, or pieces with rough or ruddy surfaces. Under the engraver's hands those blemishes were made to disappear, but clear crystals were left untouched. A most unusual use, but one that became more common in later centuries, was to form crystal spheres from it. Roman physicians employed them in cautery, burning or searing the bodily part being treated, and they did so by using them as we would a lens—focusing the sun's rays through them. A substitute was available for these costly crystals, which required much time to shape properly, and it was hollow globes of blown glass filled with water. In short, the Romans were aware of the rudimentary qualities of a lens, and knew how to make them. They even made glass mirrors in the workshops at Sidon (about twenty miles south of modern Beirut), a town credited with their invention.

Then, as now, rock crystal was an expensive commodity, and had the same disadvantage as glass; once broken it was very difficult, or impossible, to mend, forever losing its pristine effect. Nonetheless those Romans who could find any way to acquire it did, and there is a record of a Roman housewife, *not* of the wealthy class, who wanted one piece badly enough to pay 150,000 sesterces for it, roughly equivalent to $45,000. And it is said that Nero, in a paroxysm of rage, after the Praetorian Guards had revolted against him, smashed two rock-crystal cups, bearing scenes from Homer's poems, before his vain flight

Specimen courtesy of The Collector's Cabinet

Bowl courtesy of Navin Kumar Gallery

Courtesy of the author

Left: *A detail of a very peaceable kingdom depicted in polychrome marble at the Villa Castello, Florence, Italy.* Top: *Golden topaz.* Above: *A rock-crystal bowl from India for holding ghee, melted butter, used for ceremonial purposes.*

53

from the palace.

While some engraved emeralds have survived from the Greek and Roman periods there is never any certainty in classical literature that *emerald* is the stone being discussed. In ancient times the word *"smaragdus"* was used to describe the gem that we call "emerald," but it also represented a number of other stones, also green. Among them were malachite, malachite crystals (found in copper mines), green porphyry, green jasper, beryl (another form of emerald, generally of lighter hue), and prase (an opaque green quartz). In a sense we have not improved matters very much for we use the term "mother-of-emerald" to describe a green variety of feldspar, and use the same name, emerald, for the green forms of beryl and corundum, gems which differ completely one from the other.

Until the present a beryl crystal (true emerald) of thirty feet in length and a weight of twenty-five tons has never been discovered, although it is entirely possible that it may happen yet, for beryl formations do attain that size. Beryls of such size that have been found are generally only opaque, grayish-white crystals. If somebody does find such an emerald it probably will not become public knowledge, for the immediate result would be a colossal drop in the prices of emeralds on the jewel markets because of a greatly increased supply.

Perhaps the most famous emerald of antiquity is the fabled lens of Nero, through which he is said to have watched the gladiatorial contests. There is very little doubt that the story is apocryphal, as nobody knew how to grind lenses in the 1st century A.D. If they had tried, however, they would have discovered that both beryl and corundum, the stones usually meant by emerald, require a very long time to grind, as both are rated close to the top of the Mohs scale of hardness. What probably lies at the base of the story is that Nero may have possessed some highly reflective green material that mirrored the action in the arena, or it may have been simply a piece of transparent green glass. In either case the effect of green was considered to be refreshing to the eyes, and such a shield or mirror would have been a welcome accessory at the Circus Maximus, where the vast expanse of bright sand was made positively dazzling by mixing it with particles of mica. Under a strong sun the glitter must have been almost painful, and probably contributed heavily to the already numerous optic ailments of the Roman population. It may be worth noting that when Nero first attended the games as emperor his box was curtained, and he peered out only occasionally through a slit. At a later date he removed the shelter, possibly after acquiring the reflecting or filtering device.

Another nest of confusion surrounded the Latin term *carbunculi*, which became "carbuncle" in English. Rather than being a species of super-boil the carbuncle stood for several kinds of transparent red gemstones, such as ruby, spinel, and pyrope and almandine garnets. Today the name is applied strictly to cabochon-cut garnets, but in former times it meant any stone that glowed like a piece of burning charcoal. No doubt the confusion of these red jewels worked to the advantage of unscrupulous dealers so far as the unwary were concerned, but shrewd buyers were well aware of the various grades and natures of the gems. They would not pay the same prices for garnets as rubies, but detecting fraud was not always simple. The art of staining quartz (which can scratch glass) was known in ancient times, and so was the inclusion of the slight flaws sometimes present in genuine stones. Moreover, glass was often bonded to cores or pieces of the true gems, thus increasing their size. These kinds of deception were also aided by the fact that the stones came from widely scattered locales and had passed through many hands before reaching their ultimate purchasers.

There was also much talk among the ancient lapidaries of the generation of stones in the earth. Workers in the marble quarries at Luna and Carrara swore by every available deity that they had seen the stone fill in holes that had been gouged out of the mountainsides. At Paros the quarriers told of splitting a block and finding a finished statue of Silenus within; and palm branches were said to be found encased in rocks on the site of the battlefield where Caesar defeated Pompey. This last is probably true, and must have referred to fossils found within the stones in that area. Then there were "eagle stones," of both male and female gender, without which those birds were said to be unable to breed. They were, of course, geodes, hollow rocks that contained loose concretions, sand, or crystalline quartz within their interior. It was believed that many other kinds of stones, having sexual differentiation, existed in nature. The male was usually distinguished by a darker color or greater heaviness and hardness. Their original genesis was thought to lie in liquid that held granules of earthy matter in suspension. When fully formed they acquired their sexual differences, and entered upon their career as breeders, a belief that persists in many places to this day. To those who plowed their fields, and kept removing mounds of stones year after year, it must have seemed true. Such activity, being subterranean and inaudible, kept it free from censorial attention in earlier times, and since then the minerals have grown considerably more discreet, giving no modern data on their love lives.

Peridot, another gem valued by the Greeks and Romans, was once known as *topazos*, one more instance of the linguistic traps that lie about in old manuscripts. A center for finding these stones was St. John's Island (now called Zebirget) in the Red Sea, about thirty-five miles east of the Egyptian coast. The gems were said to have been first found by cave-dwellers from the mainland, who had been blown ashore and were seeking roots and other vegetables to dig. They named the island *Topazin*, which, in their language meant "to seek." Another version is that the island was often fog-bound and that Greek sailors, looking for it, called it *topazein*, meaning "to guess." There is a report, from the 3rd century B.C., that a peridot brought from Topazin was carved into a statue, six feet high, of the Ptolemaic queen Arsinoe.

Why peridot, which is really chrysolite, lost the name topaz does not seem to be recorded. Perhaps even words get tired of living in the same old rut. In any case the stones now known as topaz (really varieties of beryl and corundum) are much harder, and range from yellow to sherry-brown in color, instead of being soft and green like peridot.

Another gem that was particularly favored for purposes of engraving was the amethyst. In Greek its name means "not drunken," and wearing it was supposedly a safeguard against intoxication. Consequently a great number of Romans had rings made of it, thus insuring that they would survive the constant round of banquets and orgies. But, in fact, their safety was better guaranteed by the common practice of diluting wine with water in the proportion of eight gallons of water to one gallon of wine. Scarcely the stuff from which heroic hangovers were made.

One variety of amethyst was known as "eyelid of Venus," others as "favorites" (in love, that is), or "love requited." Apparently its gift of sobriety increased one's chances for amour, in direct contradiction to Ogden Nash's lines,

> *Candy is dandy,*
> *But liquor is quicker.*

Yet other unsuspected qualities of amethyst in the classical world were the abilities to assist those presenting petitions to royalty, and to ward off hail and locusts from the crops. When they were inscribed with the names of the sun and moon, and worn as an amulet in combination with feathers and baboon's hairs, they were a certain protection against spells and witchcraft.

The range of Greek and Roman superstition about gems is about equal to their skill in adapting them to use in jewelry, that is to say, phenomenal. Living, as they did, in the early adolescence, perhaps even the childhood of civilization, it is scarcely to be wondered that they fell prey to false logic, inaccurate conclusions, and to the deceits of their fellow men. What is truly remarkable is that they wrought as well as they did, often exceeding our boastful modern selves in skill, and maybe more often in beauty. Without the benefit of tools such as we possess, they were able to shape every stone but the diamond, and they used fragments of that to perform their work. That indicates, of course, that they anticipated, on a practical level, the hardness scale only codified by Friedrich Mohs in the early years of the 19th century. They were also aware that stones, whether precious or ornamental, could bring an added dimension of splendor, dignity, and esthetic satisfaction into the lives of men. Poe's words about

> *The glory that was Greece,*
> *And the grandeur that was Rome*

could very well be lettered in gems and set in marble, to remind us of our debt to the ancient Hellenic world that created them both.

Chapter 3
GEMS FROM ALADDIN'S LAMP

Asia still preserves much of its mystery, even in an age that seeks to pry out all the answers. One glance at a map will show the reasons why, for there are natural barriers on every hand—mountains, deserts, jungles, and great swaths of territory that are uninhabited or thinly populated. Beyond that is the enormous diversity of people, religions, customs, and languages (India has 147), ranging from the most subtly refined forms of civilization to the depths of barbarism.

It is small wonder then that the ancient Western world, lacking accurate maps and adequate communication, held so many inaccurate ideas about the regions to the east. Geography, for instance, was in such a poor state that it was firmly believed that the Nile flowed out of Asia, dividing India from Egypt in its course. As a consequence of that erroneous notion the sources of trade goods, gemstones in particular, became obscured in a cloud of legends and fables. Travelers could, and did, perpetrate the most outrageous lies about the inhabitants of distant lands, telling of people whose ears were huge enough to enfold their entire bodies as blankets might, or else used monstrously large feet, umbrella fashion, to shelter themselves from a torrid sun.

India

Among such fantasies was the tale of how diamonds were gathered in India, for even in ancient times that country had the reputation of producing those stones in great quantity. Supposedly there was a deep pit, somewhere in the mountains, and its floor was covered with diamonds beyond all numbering. The pit was also infested with an infinitude of poisonous snakes slithering about the glittering carpet of gems, so that nobody dared to descend and gather them. Nonetheless the stones were retrieved by an ingenious method. Pieces of meat were flung down into the pit, and

the diamonds stuck to them just as carpet tacks would to taffy. Then hawks, or other birds of prey, were trained to swoop down and bring the gem-studded bits back in their talons.

A further outcome of that story was that diamonds were long considered to be filled with poison, having absorbed it from the venom that the serpents sprayed them with so liberally. Crushed diamond, therefore, became regarded as an infallible means of killing one's enemies. That, however, posed still another difficulty, for *how* did one crush the stone that everyone knew to be uncrushable? It was reputed to split any anvil on which such an attempt might be made. Naturally the solution came in the form of another fable, this time that goat's blood had the power to shatter a diamond and reduce it to dust; the only substance in all nature capable of doing so.

The *Arabian Nights* quality of those stories kept them current and believed from antiquity down to the Renaissance. Benvenuto Cellini, while imprisoned in Rome, chanced to find some hard particles in his food and became terrified that he had been poisoned with diamond dust by an enemy. Recovering some of the suspect material from his dish, he found, to his great relief, that he could crush it against stone. It was nothing more than powdered glass, so he knew he would live to tell the tale. Sometime later he discovered that one Lione Aretino had been hired to prepare the deadly dose, and had been given a diamond for the purpose. The gem happened to be of sufficient size to arouse Aretino's greed, so he substituted glass for it, being certain that it would be just as efficient. Splinters of diamond, of course, will not do anyone's digestive tract any good, but whole or powdered stones have no effect whatsoever. And as for indestructibility—any hammer will fracture any diamond, and a flame of sufficient intensity will cause it to ignite and burn completely. It is,

Preceding pages: *Emerald crystals. A perfect emerald is both one of the rarest and most valuable of gemstones.*
Opposite: *The shah of Persia, Mahommed (1810–48).*

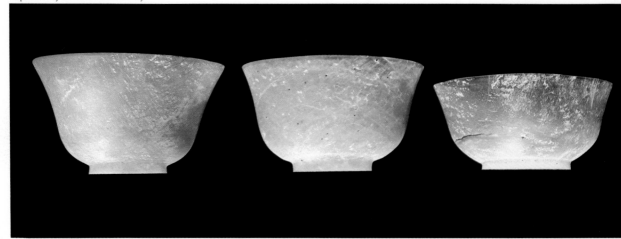

Above: *Cups of carved
jade. These Chinese
vessels are made of
so-called Imperial jade.*
Right: *Ruby.* Opposite:
*Garnet, an inexpensive
gemstone more commonly
used as an abrasive,
especially in garnet
paper.*

Specimen courtesy of The Collector's Cabinet

after all, pure carbon and reacts exactly as coal once the process of combustion has started.

Diamonds and other jewels did come from India, but never in the amounts popularly believed. The country is not, and never has been, rich in precious stones. The profusion of gems that figured in travelers' stories was the result of centuries of accumulation rather than extraordinary natural resources. It is known that Akbar the Great (1542–1605) had an annual revenue of about $400,000 from the diamond mines at Panna in central India, but, even allowing for the effect of our inflation on that sum, it does not represent incalculable wealth. Other districts, such as Madras and the plateau of Chota Nagpur, also produced diamonds, but the major sources of the jewels of India were Sri Lanka (once called Taprobane and later Ceylon), and Burma.

Many of India's "gems" were really only varieties of quartz, and some were nothing more than colored glass. Set into the gilded copper bodies of idols, or mounted into fanciful bracelets, rings, and bangles such stones could be very deceptive to the naked eye. Only jewelers and lapidaries could distinguish what was what, for the standard modern tests had not yet been devised. Most people knew that diamonds would scratch glass, but that was about the extent of their knowledge. Many failed to realize that clear zircons would do the same, and that spinels often stood in place of rubies, and tourmaline substituted for emerald.

The region of Gujarat was noted for its wealth of gems, but they never originated in the soil and rocks of that state. Rather they were the result of raids on coastal shipping when Gujarat pirates boarded merchant craft and dosed both crew and passengers with powerful emetics. In that way the wily merchants who had swallowed their precious stones, or hired sailors to do it for them, were forced to bring their hidden treasure back into view. No doubt the practice occurred elsewhere as well.

Another Indian place famous in the lore of gems was Golconda, a city that has become synonymous with riches and fabled for the quantity and quality of its jewels. Once again the truth was something different, for Golconda was a center for the shaping and polishing of precious stones, and for the making of jewelry from them. The stones themselves poured in and out of Golconda, scattering eventually to all corners of the world, but none were native to the area.

Sri Lanka was a major source of gemstones, as

Opposite top: *Three views of diamonds showing various 17th-century cuts.* Opposite bottom: *Two medieval views of quartz crystal formation.* Left: *Shah Jehan, Mogul emperor of Hindustan and founder of the city of Delhi, first known as Shahjahanabad. He was the builder of the world-famous Taj Mahal, the Pearl Mosque at Agra, and commissioned the jewel-studded Peacock Throne to be made for his palace at Delhi.*

True jade comes in two varieties, nephrite (opposite) and jadeite (right), and a wide range of colors in addition to green. Jade is the toughest of gemstones to work with.

Vase courtesy of Rare Art, Inc.

66

was Burma, Malaya, and parts of Sumatra. Some five hundred gem pits were worked during the dry season in Sri Lanka alone, but even there it was a chancy matter to gain a livelihood from the industry. Much the same was true of all the other places mentioned, for if precious stones existed in great quantity anywhere they would soon cease to be precious.

Also found in the ancient oriental world was lapis lazuli, valuable for making seals and signets and as a pigment. It came from Afghanistan. That country continues as the chief source of supply, with the mines in Badakshan yielding the stone as they have for the past six thousand years. Opal came from Turkey, and was of considerable worth until it gained a reputation in the 19th century for bringing about misfortune. That was undoubtedly the result of having made jewelers monetarily responsible if they damaged the stones while setting them, a frequent enough occurrence in view of the brittle quality of opal, even in expert hands. The finest turquoise came from Iran, and was in great demand, especially in Tibet, where it was combined with coral, and a tasteful assortment of toe and finger bones, in the making of necklaces and other jewelry.

The fame of these stones began to reach the Occident in the 6th century B.C. A Greek explorer and seafarer named Scylax, in the employ of Darius I, was the first to establish a sea route from the Indus valley to Egypt. He sailed from the uppermost navigable reaches of the Indus River, where he built his ship, and then followed the coastlines of India, Iran, and Arabia until he arrived at the head of the Red Sea in Egypt. Darius promptly ordered the ancient channels that had linked those waters to the Mediterranean and the Nile to be reopened, making direct sea communication possible throughout his kingdom. Because of silting, the Ptolemies had to repeat the task some few centuries later, and then the waterway was abandoned again until the 19th century when the Suez Canal was constructed, largely along the same route.

It was not until the 4th century B.C., however, that India became somewhat better known by the West, following the conquests of Alexander the Great. He penetrated to the northwest area of the Punjab before his soldiers—weary, ill, drenched in rain for seventy consecutive days and having been on the march for eight years—demanded to return home.

More and more information continued to flow westward, at first from the writings of Megasthenes, a Greek ambassador to the court of King

Opposite: *Aurangzeb, a treacherous, religious zealot, usurped the throne of his father, Shah Jehan. Some of India's wealthiest cities fell to him, but constant warfare prevented his enjoyment of them.* Above: *Although called "Lion of the Punjab," Maharajah Ranjit Singh was a dissolute, avaricious drunkard who died of paralysis in 1839. The Kohinoor diamond, now a British crown jewel, came from Ranjit's hoard when his empire dissolved after his death.*

Bottles courtesy of Rare Art, Inc.

Above: *Chinese snuff bottles. The example at left is of lapis lazuli;
in the center is one of rock crystal with rutilated quartz inclusions;
at right is one of jadeite.* Opposite: *Indian necklace inlaid with
turquoise with beads of carnelian, jade, and tigereye.*

69

Chandragupta in 302 B.C. In that way some of eastern India and the valley of the Ganges was made known. He was followed by Eudoxos, a Greek merchant in the service of the Ptolemaic king, Euergetes II. Under the guidance of a shipwrecked Indian sailor, who had been taught enough Greek for the purpose, Eudoxos reached the western coast of India. There he obtained a cargo of perfumes and precious stones, which the grateful King Euergetes took in its entirety when it was brought safely into port, about 120 B.C. Such journeys were infrequently made until another Greek merchant, Hippalus by name, popularized the monsoon route between Egypt and India. The winds blew consistently to the northeast from January to June, and then shifted to the southwest from July through December. From 45 B.C. vessels were thus enabled to cross open sea instead of hugging the coastline, and well over a hundred such voyages came to be made annually. In fact, the southwesterly monsoon became known as the *hippalus,* in honor of the man who first made regular use of it.

In addition to the sea-lanes connecting India to the Western powers of Greece and Rome, there were also the overland routes. Although they had been established primarily to convey ivory, silks, and spices, the gem merchants found them equally useful and often safer than travel by sea, which exposed them to the perils of storms and piracy. Few of the ships in use at that time were apt to inspire confidence, and many a merchant, seeing what the harbors offered him, cheerfully took the high road over mountains and desert.

While it was true that the overland routes offered a greater measure of safety for large caravans in time of peace, they also provided ready pathways for invaders in time of war. This was especially true during the eastward spread of Islam in the 11th century. Under the leadership of Sultan Mahmud of Ghazni a horde of Moslems poured out of Afghanistan through the mountain passes into northern India and made their way into the region of Gujarat. There, in the year 1026 A.D., he captured the town of Somnath and its famed Temple of Siva where, over the protests, entreaties, and offers of ransom by the Hindu priests, Mahmud smashed the god's image with his war-club. Once he did so a torrent of gems

spilled forth, the accumulation of centuries of offerings to Siva. The temple had served, much as had many ancient Greek ones, as a treasury for holding gifts to the god, and was destroyed as completely as befitted the divine principle it represented.

Siva, however, also symbolized regeneration, and the jewels that his temple had held were promptly put to new uses in the service of Allah and the Sultan Mahmud, providing wealth for the new regime, and impressive ornamentation for its religious and secular objects and regalia. With every succeeding victory the story was repeated until the Mogul rulers, who eventually succeeded to Mahmud, had become masters of incalculable wealth.

There was, as an example, the Kohinoor (Mountain of Light) diamond with a weight of 162 carats. Now the property of the British Crown it was acquired in 1849, by conquest from the Rajah of Lahore. That stone, however, was merely a remnant of what the Moguls had gathered, for it was one of their number, Shah Jehan (King of the World) who had the famous Peacock Throne built to his command. According to a description from the French traveler and jewel merchant Jean-Baptiste Tavernier who saw the throne in 1665, it was everything that legend has declared it to be. The name came from the presence of two peacocks standing behind it, tails spread, and inlaid with emeralds, rubies, sapphires, pearls, and other precious stones. The throne itself was shaped like a bed, about 4 feet deep by 6 feet wide, and had taken seven years to complete. A canopy rose above it, supported by twelve pillars made of rows of pearls, and the framework of the throne was decorated with diamonds, pearls, and crosses made of 108 rubies and 116 emeralds, all of large size. Tavernier judged that the pearls were the most valuable items in the piece, and that the emeralds were badly flawed.

In any event, the Peacock Throne passed from Mogul hands into Persian ones when Nadir Shah conquered Delhi in 1739. The throne became part of his booty, and journeyed out of India by way of Afghanistan, where it arrived for display at the city of Herat in 1740. What happened to it later seems to be somewhat obscure. Although reputed to be in Teheran as late as the beginning of this century, Lord Curzon, who inspected the royal possessions of Persia in 1903, reported no sign of it. Some portions of it may have been incorporated into the present throne, but it is far more likely that it was broken up and sold piecemeal to satisfy some of Persia's enormous 19th-century debts. Certainly any object as conspicuous as the Peacock Throne would have been highly noticeable to Lord Curzon's vision.

As to the debts incurred by Persian royalty, consider some of the extravagant costumes of Fath Ali Shah who ruled from 1798 until his death in 1848. His portrait shows an abundance of pearls forming the cuffs, armlets, epaulets, and sash of only one of his court costumes, and inset into them were forty rubies, all one to two inches in length, and at least thirty other gems that appear to be emeralds and sapphires.

In another painting, probably done about 1816, Fath Ali is shown seated upon his throne, which even at that date bore no resemblance to the fabled Peacock Throne, and he is flanked by six of his sons, all wearing jeweled crowns only slightly inferior to that of the father. Fiscal responsibility was in very little evidence at Fath Ali's court, and common sense seems to have been conspicuously absent as well. For example, on one occasion, after a disastrous defeat by the Russians, the Shah made a point of appearing before his courtiers in a costume of flaming red, his royal "Robe of Wrath." He fondly hoped that when the Russians heard that he had put it on they would abandon their campaign out of sheer fright. Fath Ali, of course, is not the only king or statesman to act in such a foolish fashion, for it seems to be one of the hazards of the trade.

His immediate successor, Mohammed Shah, also made interesting use of some of the royal gewgaws bequeathed him by his father. He used the point of a jeweled sword to count out tribute piled up for him on some jeweled trays. The tribute was not, however, in the form of gold, gems, or other riches, but of human eyes. When Mohammed Shah found the city of Kerman guilty of harboring his enemy, Aga Khan Malati, Chief of the Assassins, he demanded and received 70,000 pairs of eyes from the city's unfortunate inhabitants. All of these he patiently totaled as the palace slaves bore them in on gem-studded platters.

It is pleasant to add that he died at the age of forty-two after suffering from erysipelas, gout, and a combination of maladies brought on by his excesses.

Despite the depredations of the Persians many jewels remained in the Mogul cities of India. The magnificent Taj Mahal is not simply a beautifully proportioned pile of marble. It is also decorated with a wealth of flower and leaf forms, cut from precious and semi-precious stones, and arranged in scrolls, wreaths, and frets, all of which are set into the marble itself. Because portions of the stone flowers were permitted to project from the background a subtly controlled three-dimensional effect is achieved, and the blossoms seem to be either freshly cut, or growing in the places assigned to them. Agate, jasper, heliotrope or bloodstone, varicolored quartzes and marbles, and the like are still present within the monument, but the costlier stones suffered a heavy toll at the hands of looting soldiery. The jewel-studded golden railing that once surrounded the tombs of Mumtaz Mahal and Shah Jehan was pillaged, and has been replaced by a nearly transparent screen of fine marble, pierced like lacework. Its purity of color would seem to be an improvement on the flashiness of the gems once in place there, and one can always hope that the looters wound up with badly flawed stones, or were cheated by the jewelers to whom they sold them.

The splendor of the Taj was the result of expending unlimited funds over a period of twenty-one years, from 1632 to 1653. The final amount came to about $230,000,000, exclusive of the marble, which was the gift of a neighboring ruler. It was also a splendid example of international cooperation in the arts. The chief architect was one Ustad Isa, from Persia. He was assisted by a specialist in dome building from Istanbul; Shah Jehan's personal French architect, Austin de Bordeaux; and an Italian master of *pietra dura*, Gieronimo Veroneo, who was responsible for insetting the jeweled decorations. Masons, lapidaries, mosaicists, and a host of engineers and craftsmen came from every corner of India and the Orient to complete the task. It was a work for the ages, something as perfect of its kind as the Parthenon once had been; never again to be duplicated. Yet for all its unique beauty it was very

nearly sold for $150,000 to a Hindu entrepreneur who thought he could make better use of its materials. It is somewhat disturbing to think that some descendant of his may be running around out there with the same idea.

In the early years of the 20th century the great wealth of diamonds coming from India had dwindled to a mere trickle, and for all practical purposes has now terminated. Until the discoveries of diamond fields in South America and South Africa in the 18th and 19th centuries, India was the source of all the truly great stones. These were recovered by the most primitive methods from shallow pits dug into the soil at five major locations in central India. Gravel extracted from those pits was transferred to walled areas where it was pounded, crushed, and then subjected to repeated washings and siftings until all precious material, if any, had been removed by hand. That method remained in use into the 19th century, when the only technical improvement was the addition of chains of bowls to remove water from the deeper sink holes. Work was sporadic, and at some locations proceeded over periods of several millennia, while the numbers employed ranged from a few dozen to as many as 60,000.

The formation of diamonds is still a matter of uncertainty , for no typical matrix nor locale has yet been defined, and diamonds are found in meteorites, pegmatite (a coarse-grained igneous rock), clay, and the blue ground of South Africa. Whether they well up from volcanic or other geological disturbances, or are borne by streams or glaciers from distant areas is also debatable. Arguments can be raised defending possible explanations; and to them may be added the possibility that these extremely hard stones may have weathered out of rock formations no longer able to be found, subsequently being transported for untold ages by natural forces. We do know that diamonds can be cleaved readily when struck at the right angle, that internal stress around inclusions can cause them to explode, and that they will ignite at 850 degrees Fahrenheit, and will continue to burn while that temperature is maintained. They are also phosphorescent in the presence of radium, or after exposure to sunlight, and since 1663 have been known to glow in a darkened room after friction has been applied to them.

Among the huge diamonds found in the past was a monstrous 787-carat one that the French jewel merchant Tavernier saw in 1665 in the Treasury of the Mogul Shah Aurangzeb. It had been the property of his father, Shah Jehan, and had remained in its rough state until Aurangzeb ordered it cleaved and cut by one of the Venetian lapidaries of his court. The round rose-cut stone that resulted weighed 280 carats, and was called the Great Mogul. What happened to the other 507 carats is not known, but they were not apt to have been wasted.

There was also the Orloff, a yellowish diamond of nearly 195 carats, which went from a Brahmin temple by means of a French sailor's somewhat sticky fingers, and then into his captain's pocket before Prince Orloff bought it for Catherine the Great for $450,000. Then there was the Pitt diamond, with a weight of 410 carats, purchased by Thomas Pitt, Governor of Madras, for $102,000, and sold by him in 1717 for $400,000 to the Regent of France, the Duc d'Orleans. It, too, shrank considerably in the cutting process, being reduced to about 137 carats. During the French Revolution it was stolen, but was later recovered. Still other notable Indian diamonds were the Nizam, a lightweight of 277 carats, although reported to have weighed 440 carats before being cleaved; the Darya-i-nur, a rectangular stone of about 186 carats; and the Taj-e-mah, a rose-colored, pear-shaped stone of 146 carats. These last two gems formed part of the Persian Shah's collection at the beginning of the 20th century.

One Indian diamond that seems to have had a taste for royal and aristocratic associations was the Sancy, named for its second owner the Seigneur de Sancy, a 16th-century French soldier and diplomat. Its previous owner was Charles the Bold, Duke of Burgundy; and from de Sancy it went on to Elizabeth I, Henrietta Maria (Queen to Charles II of England), Cardinal Mazarin, and Louis XIV of France. After being stolen during the French Revolution it passed to the King of Spain, Prince Demidoff of Russia, and then to an unknown Indian prince, returning to its native land after an illustrious and worldly career.

India has also been the source of some magnificent colored diamonds. First among these was a beautiful blue stone cut down to 67 carats from

Hindu statuette of gilded bronze inset with semiprecious stones.

112 after Tavernier had brought it back to Europe. It, too, was stolen during the French Revolution (which must have given the jewelers a marvelous time of cutting and resetting) and was never recovered. Undoubtedly it was broken and recut, for a stone of that size and color was too recognizable to be put on the market without undergoing a disguise. The nearly 45-carat Hope diamond, now in the Smithsonian Museum at Washington, D.C., is the same color, and is thought to be the remaining section of Tavernier's original stone. There is also a 40-carat apple-green diamond, once part of the Saxon crown jewels, called the Dresden Green, and an Austrian crown jewel, the Florentine, which is very pale yellow and weighs a little more than 133 carats. Despite that list, to which a few more might be added, color appears to be a rather rare quality among diamonds of Indian origin.

Rubies, too, have always been associated with India, although most of the best came from Burma and Sri Lanka (formerly Ceylon). All those areas were once considered part of India when it was under British rule, which accounts for much of the confusion about sources. Even back in the days of Marco Polo (1254–1324) Sri Lanka, which he called Zeilan, was noted for its store of precious stones, among them sapphires, amethysts, topazes, garnets, and, most plentifully, rubies. The king of that island, one Sender-naz by name, according to Marco Polo, owned a ruby some nine inches in length, as thick as a man's arm, and entirely flawless. Because ruby is actually a crystal of corundum (which is aluminum oxide), and huge formations of it weighing up to 374 pounds *have* been found, the story moves into the realm of the possible. Given the usual barrel shape of the corundum crystal, the proportions Marco mentioned would be just about right. In any case, rubies of about two and a half inches in length have been mined in recent times.

These glorious red stones somehow acquired a reputation for being luminescent, and travelers told of the rubies owned by the King of Pegu (southern Burma) that glowed so brightly that they lighted his city at night. Perhaps our modern utility companies should acquire a few now that fuel oil is beginning to approach gemstones in price. Another single ruby belonging to a 13th-

century king of Sri Lanka was reputed to flame as brightly as a torch after dark, and was some five inches in width, which makes it sound very much like the one Marco Polo described.

Star sapphires and star rubies, which are properly termed asterias, and cat's eyes of beryl seem to originate in Sri Lanka more often than other places. All of those stones had a high reputation in the Orient as tokens of good luck, for the moving lines of light that they showed were believed to result from the shining presence of a living, beneficent spirit. The star effect comes about when a stone is cut so that it condenses transmitted light along three lines of crystalline interference. The single line of the cat's eye, called chatoyancy, also results from cutting, and is focused along the line where a crystal has twinned. With an increase in intensity of light the line grows simultaneously brighter and narrower. Still another optical effect may exist in alexandrite, rather rare in Russia where it was named for a tsar, but somewhat more abundant in Sri Lanka. Viewed in normal daylight it is green when seen from one side, but red when seen from another. In artificial light, however, the green disappears entirely.

One stone that remains permanently green, of course, is the emerald, and some from India have been of exceptional size. A rather large example, formerly owned by the Mogul rulers at Delhi, weighed seventy-eight carats. To add to its value an inscription in Persian characters was carved around its edge, stating "He who possesses this charm shall enjoy the special protection of God." Undoubtedly that quote had reference to the belief that an emerald would repel all evil spirits. The Maharajah of Punjab, Ranjit Singh, possessed some prayer beads, a strand made of seventy emeralds, each about the size of a large cherry-pit, and seven rubies of the same dimensions. In addition to their use in counting prayers, the emeralds were considered antidotes to poison, therefore essential to a maharajah's well-being, while the rubies allayed anger and discord, another necessity in a royal household.

Although they are gemstones, garnets are not as highly ranked as rubies, sapphires and emeralds, although they held a very important place in *pietra dura* work, a term applied to setting hard stones into a stone background. The lapidaries of north-

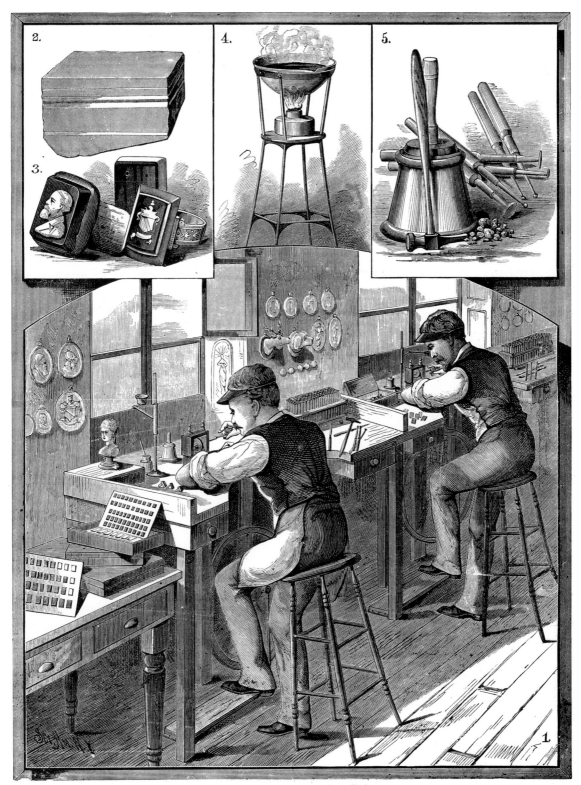

*Lapidaries (1) engraving cameos surrounded by design models; cross
section of sardonyx (2) showing its layers; finished cameo rings (3);
dyeing layers of sardonyx (4) or changing its colors by means of heat;
and (5) the tools of the trade, including hammer and sculpting mallet.*

ern India were well skilled in that art, and frequently set garnets into a tracery of gold let into boxes of white jade. A more unusual use for those stones became popular in 1892 when some tribesmen along the Kashmir border warred on the British. Reasoning that anything red would be more effective in penetrating any red substances such as flesh and blood, they replaced their leaden bullets with those made of garnet.

As it was with the various classes among the Hindus of India, so was it with their jewels, each stone having its own rank, and the wearing of certain gems was appropriate only to a particular caste. The most flawless diamond, for instance, was termed a Brahmin in honor of the priestly class, and conferred riches, power, good luck, and friends upon its wearer. Second in value was the Kshatriya, the warrior caste, and it was worn to prevent the approach of old age, rarely an occupational hazard among fighting men. Of slightly lower worth was the Vaisya diamond, belonging to the farmers and merchants, and which promised them success. The Sudra diamond was fourth in the hierarchy and the least distinguished, as were the Sudras themselves, who were the laborers, menials, the doers. Their stone was to bring them that of which they stood in most need—good fortune.

Even the dwellings of the gods and the realms in which they lived were an endless blaze of precious stones. Krishna's city was ornamented in all four of its quarters and to its topmost heights with cupolas of rubies and diamonds, pillars of emerald, courtyards of ruby, roadways paved with sapphires; all of it shining as brightly as the noonday sun. There was also the Kalpa Tree, which symbolized all of the offerings to the gods. This was a supernatural wonder with pearls dangling from boughs that bore zircon leaves on twigs and shoots of emerald. Its ripe fruits were rubies, and its tender, young leaves were coral, all springing from roots of sapphire and a trunk that was diamond at its base, topaz in its center, and cat's-eye beryl at its tip. The heavenly horticulturists who tended it must have been lapidaries of the first rank.

Even the rather ascetic Buddhists became infected with India's passion for gems; witness the legend of the Diamond Throne. This once stood next to the tree under which Buddha received enlightenment, as it had since the world began. It was one hundred feet around and was shaped from a solitary stone. No matter how earth might be convulsed, the Throne remained steady and immobile, receiving the thousand incarnations of Buddha who rested upon it to experience the "ecstasy of the diamond." There it stood until the world entered its current age, whereupon it was covered with earth and sand and vanished from the sight of men—which says very little for our present non-ecstatic times, no matter how gem-studded they may ever become.

China

From neolithic times the Chinese have been inordinately fond of jade, and have made it an inseparable part of their art and culture. Jade and China, in fact, have become almost synonymous, which seems a natural enough combination until it is realized that not a scrap of jade was native to China when that traditional pairing first took root. For several thousand years every piece of jade was imported from the distant West, from the regions around Kashgar and Khotan, close to the borders of India and Afghanistan. Undoubtedly scarcity and difficulty of access added greatly to the stone's value, but for the Chinese something more than intrinsic worth was involved.

Perhaps a clue to the high regard in which jade was held lies in the qualities that were attributed to it. To the Chinese it was a symbol of life, had protective powers, and stood for the essence of purity. As early as the Shang dynasty (1523–1028 B.C.) it was being formed into two major symbols which have strong religious overtones. The first of these was the *pi*, a pierced ring of jade that symbolized heaven, an abstract region that was also the supreme deity and that sometimes bore concentric circles of bosses representing the stars. In time the *pi* also became associated with imperial power, and the emperor came to be regarded as the son of heaven, an earthly incarnation of the divinity. The other symbol was the *ts'ung*, a rectangular cube bored from end to end by a circular tube. This represented the earth, with its four corners, and also stood for the Earth Mother. Both major symbols were characterized by their open central spaces through which the vital spirit of the universe could flow. To emody those ideas only such a substance as jade, with its given relation to life, protection, and purity could be used.

Another very plausible reason for the popularity of jade in China may be found in the delight taken by Chinese artists and artisans in overcoming difficulties. While true jade is not the hardest of stones, ranking only about 6.5 on the Mohs scale, its structure of parallel or matted fibers gives it an exceptional toughness that resists cutting. Even the hardest metal tools have little effect on it, and the surest means of shaping the stone lies in abrasion by means of garnet or emery powders. Infinite patience is also required for the carving process, if it is to qualify as an artistic production, for it is a slow and deliberate one, exactly the challenge a Chinese craftsman enjoys.

Jade, as a term, is a very imprecise name that has been attached in the gem trade to a variety of stones with similar appearances. Even when one uses the more restrictive designations of "precious jade" or "true jade" the difficulty is not overcome, for both of those terms apply equally to two different stones that are used for ornamental purposes. They are nephrite, a variety of actinolite; and jadeite. Nephrite, more common, is a silicate of calcium and magnesium, while jadeite, also a silicate, is composed of sodium and aluminum, and is found much less frequently, therefore commands a higher price. Both vary considerably in color, and while they differ to some extent in hardness, nephrite being 6.5 and jadeite 7 on the Mohs scale, both are extremely tough, and in fact it takes fifty tons of pressure to break a one-inch cube of nephrite. No simple means or measure seems to exist for determining which of these stones should be called jade, but sooner or later that term will have to be granted to either nephrite or jadeite exclusively, bringing an end to the confusion.

Even the Chinese, the supposed experts on jade, have not helped matters much by calling one variety of jadeite "imperial jade." By that name they are referring to a green, nearly transparent stone, somewhat the color of a kingfisher's plumage. However, some of what passes for "imperial jade" is actually peridot, yet another stone of the silicate group. It is of the same degree of hardness as jadeite, and has long been available to the Chinese from nearby Burma.

The qualities that Westerners ascribe to diamonds and pearls, purity, brilliance and lustre, are outdone by those that the Chinese perceive in jade. They say that its warm lustre and brilliance resemble the nature of kindness, and that its translucency, which reveals its interior being, is like the open attitude of the just and righteous. Its resistant quality—it may be broken but never distorted—they liken to courage, and consider it emblematic of purity because its edges, while sharp, are not meant for the purpose of harm. Last, because it can sound a high and tranquil note when struck, its effect reaches as far and wide as does that of wisdom.

Regarding its musical quality, jade is capable of producing a vibrant, long-lasting note of a pleasant nature. That feature of jade is so well-known to the Chinese that they call it the "sound" stone, and they made instruments from it that roughly resemble the Western xylophone. Each of the tuned pieces was twenty inches long by almost sixteen inches wide, and the tone of each was varied by means of cutting each piece to a different thickness. There were several types, one of which contained sixteen plain stones and was used as a chime in religious or state ceremonies. Another kind, purely for the production of music, consisted of from twelve to twenty-four pieces of smooth, uncarved jade; while yet a third sort, called the "singer's chime," had the same number of pieces, but each was cut into fanciful forms. In every case the instruments were played in the same way—by being struck sharply. So ancient is the use of jade for musical purposes that Confucius is reported to have played the instrument when he sought consolation. As a philosopher who sought to improve and idealize government he probably became an expert and accomplished musician.

The melodious sound of jade was likened to the voice of one's beloved, and the material itself was compared to the very essence of love. It was presented, carved in the form of a butterfly, to betrothed maidens by their future husbands. That custom is founded on the tale of a young man who accidentally pursued a colorful butterfly into a mandarin's garden, a visit that eventually led to his later marriage to the mandarin's daughter.

Jade was also carved in the form of a phoenix, and was given to young girls when they came of age. The intention of making the institution of the family as immortal as the fabulous bird is plain, but somehow the suicidal act of the parent phoenix managed to stay unnoticed.

Besides the toughness that makes jade difficult to carve it is also a dense and heavy stone. This is seldom apparent in the generally small ornaments worn as jewelry, but blocks of it are quite another matter. Once such piece that has a base about 18 inches deep, with a length of some 38 inches, and tapers up to a height of nearly 2 feet, would weigh some 640 pounds. That particular piece, which once belonged to the Emperor Chien-lung, bears the representation of a mountainside dotted with trees, with groups of figures seated in caves and pavilions. It also bears an example of Chien-lung's beautiful calligraphy, which he copied from an outstanding specimen of the 4th century A.D. Considering the nature of the material that had to be carved, Chien-lung's sculptor must have felt that

he, too, had been working for ages, and literally had moved a mountain by the time he had finally finished.

Fortunately for the pack animals and merchants, who had to transport jade over long distances, most pieces were of lesser size and weight than the one mentioned above. Usually they were in lumps that ranged in size from pebbles to small melons, and were recovered from the mountain streams of Chinese Turkestan in the vicinity of Khotan and Kashgar. Young women did the actual finding since, according to Chinese belief, their natures epitomized *ying*, the female principle, while jade was considered to be *yang*, or male. The notion was that male jade would be irresistibly drawn to the female gatherers, and to strengthen their attraction they were required to wade about completely naked. While Shakespeare pointed out the existence of "sermons in stones," certainly the Chinese had to be the first to ascribe sex appeal to the mineral kingdom.

Not all jade came from the rivers, of course, and

Shade is always welcome when the sun beats down in quarries, making rock too hot to touch, so this ingenious Chinese mason carries a light bamboo screen to shield both himself and the stone he is trimming from its rough state.

in fact, most of it was mined. Again this raised the problem of how to extract such an obdurate material, as metal tools were not equal to the task, and it was hopeless to attempt sawing pieces out of the rock matrix. Nonetheless an ingenious and practical method was devised that broke fragments out of the vein through a rapid alternation of temperature. Fires would be lit all along the course taken by the jade, and, when they had heated the stone enough, cold water or ice would be brought into contact with it, shattering loose a supply of pieces.

Bringing the jade back down to the centers of civilization, where it could be processed, required a long and arduous journey, not of days but of months. Weather, terrain, banditry, and natural hazards, such as landslides or sandstorms, made every caravan an adventure in survival. Not least among the trials was altitude sickness, although it was not realized then that lack of oxygen was the cause of the travelers' problems. The difficulties, however, left their mark on geography, for the mountains over which the jade and silk routes ran were the Himalayas, and the effect they had upon those who had to climb them earned them the name of the Headache Mountains. They also provided an ample number of nosebleeds, and bouts of nausea, vertigo, and exhaustion.

Much of the jade ended in the Imperial Workshops in Peking and were made into objects for the emperor's use, or were distributed by him as gifts. However, even more jade passed into the hands of the wealthy and all others who could manage to acquire it one way or another. In China's culture the talismanic power of jade, added to its great esthetic appeal, ensured a nearly universal dispersion of the stone. And to add to its popularity there was the legend of Ho Hsien-ku, one of the eight immortals, who gained eternal life through taking a powder of pulverized jade and mother-of-pearl. That story naturally suggested medicinal uses, such as reducing jade particles to the size of rice grains, and then taking them to strengthen the lungs, heart, voice, and even prolong life itself. An elixir of jade was also made by boiling equal parts of powdered jade, rice, and dew in a copper pot, carefully straining and filtering the result. Taken regularly the concoction was said to strengthen the muscles, make them more pliable, to reinforce the bones, purify the blood, improve the flesh, and bring peace to the mind. When taken over a long period of years it was said to free the body from hunger and thirst, and from the effects of heat and cold. Because jade's fibrous content is somewhat allied to that of asbestos there can be no doubt that it would succeed in doing all those things, though perhaps not quite in the way envisioned.

What must have been an additional attraction of jade for the Chinese is its variability of color. It ranges from white to translucent grayish-white, which is the highly prized mutton-fat jade, to yellowish hues, into the rarer brown and violet, although most often found in various shades of green. It can be almost completely transparent, translucent, or completely opaque, totally pure in color or mottled, and, while never black, its darkest shades of green have that effect. The colors are largely due to the degree of iron silicate and chromium present. However, specimens that have been entombed often exhibit other hues, usually orange-brown, derived from the products of bodily decomposition, or a flaked, white opacity induced by the chemical action of the soil.

While jade was the most important semi-precious stone to the Chinese they were not unaware nor neglectful of the other stones. Marble, usually a flawless white, was used occasionally for sculpture, as in the case of a T'ang dynasty (A.D. 645–907) lion, which combines the epitome of the feline with a soupçon of the reptilian, to achieve a thoroughly Chinese effect. Marble was far more frequently used in architecture, and formed an important part of imperial China's most solemn and sacred place, the Temple of Heaven. There a series of three marble terraces mounted to beneath the building's roof. The topmost, which was ninety feet wide, had a round stone exactly at its center. This was surrounded by nine concentric rings of stones in which the marble was precisely fitted, and the pieces were arranged in multiples of nine, that is the innermost circle had nine stones, and the ninth and outermost had nine times as many, or eighty-one. On the morning of the winter solstice the emperor stationed himself in the middle of that central stone, and was then regarded as being placed in the very midst of the universe, from which he prayed to heaven for its goodwill in the coming year.

Under the Manchu emperors, the last of China's royal rulers, the throne was a masterpiece of carved lacquer, although earlier ones had been composed of more precious materials. The Ming emperor Yung-lo (reigned A.D. 1402–1424) had a magnificent throne that bore six jade dragons on its back and armrests. From the mouths of those divine beasts depended strings of gems arranged in groups of six above and below two jewel-studded enameled plaques. Even on the armrests six more precious stones are to be found, and they could not have provided Yung-lo with much comfort—but then thrones are never built for purposes of relaxation. All of the stones, which are rubies, sapphires, and green jades (possibly the "imperial jade" variety) are completely round, and range in size from that of large peas to glass marbles. Others are set into the framework surrounding the seat and on the legs and base of the throne as well, with a total close to five hundred gems in all. And, as if all of that display was not enough, Yung-lo's belt bore seven large rubies surrounded by groupings of cabochon-cut sapphires, cat's-eye beryl, emerald, jade, and pearls. There is little doubt that most of those stones passed into the hands of the Manchu soldiery.

The skill that allowed such lavish decoration of Yung-lo's throne and person blossomed to its greatest extent under the succeeding Ch'ing dynasty, the rulers of which were Manchurians, and which endured from 1644 to 1912. The Ch'ing emperors, after conquering China, were not at all anxious to hide their glory. Instead they reveled in color, lacquer, silks, jewels, vermilion, gold, porcelain, and everything else that advertised luxury. To indulge their longing for orchards that would remain either in perpetual bloom, or were continually laden with ripe fruits, they commissioned jeweled trees. These examples of the lapidary's craft seem to be visions out of the *Arabian Nights*, brought into being by the genies of Aladdin's lamp. They were set in deep bowls of gilt and cloisonné enamel, with soil of crushed coral surrounding roots and trunks of gold or silver. From the metal boughs sprang leaves of green jade, while the petals of the flowers might be mother-of-pearl, agate, carnelian, or white jade. Fruits might be topaz, jasper, amethyst, or any of dozens

of other semiprecious stones. Whichever were chosen, every effort was made to shape them in as natural a manner as possible; well-detailed even down to the stamens in the center of the blossoms, and to set the leaves so as to appear as if they were actually emerging from the boughs and twigs. Because of the turmoil experienced in China throughout most of the 19th and 20th centuries, it is difficult to say how many of those botanical and horticultural extravaganzas have survived, although any one of them would give a special glow to the collection of which it is a part.

Another area in which Chinese craftsmen outdid themselves was in the creation of snuff bottles. At the height of the snuff craze in the 18th and 19th centuries powdered tobacco, mixed with scent and flavorings, was carried about in small boxes from which it was tapped out and sniffed. Many of the European snuffboxes were works of art, but the best of them never approached the imaginative and graceful little Chinese bottles. Generally about three inches high, they were usually shaped out of a single piece of hard stone, anything from agate to malachite to jasper or quartz or jade. Some were made of lacquer, patiently built up layer by layer and then carved, while others consisted of successive envelopes of glass, blown one over the other, so that a design of several colors could be created by selective cutting. Another feat of ingenuity was to blow a clear glass bottle and paint the design on its inside by means of minute brushes. But far and away the bulk of such bottles consisted of various semiprecious stones. The first task involved cutting out a blank of the proper size and shape and then drilling out its interior. With that tedious bit of preparation out of the way the artisan went on to carve the decoration on the outside of the bottle. In the cases of lapis lazuli or aventurine he usually relied on the inherent beauty of the stone's color and surface, for both of those materials were apt to succumb under the pressure of carving tools. Jade and agate were highly favored, for both often had either inclusions or possessed several different colored layers. Whatever accident of nature presented itself was promptly seized upon by the craftsman, and either incorporated into the design or made the major subject. For example the scattered mottlings on a piece of jade could be envisioned as berries or fruits on a vine, and then be carved accordingly. Again parallel bands of color might be turned into several zones in a landscape, or tones and textures on the stone's surface might suggest that the bottle be given the form of a frog, a fish, or a cicada. The only limit.to the possibilities was that of the carver's imagination. The stoppers for these bottles also required exactitude in their execution, since they had to fit tightly enough to seal off the contents from air, but not require a major struggle to remove.

Very often the caps of the stoppers were made of rounded and polished gemstones, or balls of coral, and were shaped like the button atop a mandarin's hat. That last article of dress, incidentally, came in nine grades, five of which called for either precious or semi-precious stones. All were spheres, one inch in diameter, and were ranked as follows; ruby, first grade; coral for second; sapphire third; lapis lazuli fourth; and rock crystal fifth. The remaining four, in order, were shell, plain gold, figured gold, and engraved silver.

That progression tells something about the basic Chinese character and philosophy. Only two precious stones are listed, ruby and sapphire, and coral is rated above one of them. It is also noticeable that both rock crystal and shell rank higher than gold and silver, and that decoration indicates a lower status. The Chinese, who could and did make jewelry of butterfly wings set in hair-fine gold wire, did not need precious materials to create a dazzling effect. They preferred the understatement of jade to the brilliant blaze of diamonds, and were the first to realize how the lowly silkworm's unpromising cocoon could be exalted. And what other people took earth itself, and fashioned it into the beauty of porcelain? Their praise is reserved for excellence, not the accident of rarity, and the humble paper that carries the words and brushwork of a sage deserves the highest praise of all.

Japan

What jade was to China, rock crystal was to Japan—the "perfect jewel." As had been the case with the Greeks and the Romans, the origin of rock crystal was thought to be from ice frozen under pressure for so long that it could never again revert to the liquid state. There is also more than a hint of the Greek idea that stones resulted from exhalations of the earth, for small quartz crystals were said to have been formed from the breath of the White Dragon, and larger ones from that of the Purple Dragon. Dragons, in the Japanese view, were the supreme creative powers of the universe, so the high regard in which they held rock crystal is evident.

Although agate and topaz are found in Japan, as well as quartz, the country is not notable for any wealth of gemstones. As a consequence their arts rely more on exquisite craftsmanship than on intrinsic value of the materials used. Studied simplicity and the most subtle refinements of proportion, harmony, and line more than compensate for any lack of jewels or precious metals. This, in turn, led to a characteristically Japanese treatment of rock crystal. To them it symbolized both purity and infinity, hence they generally gave it the form of a sphere, the shape of perfection.

Infinite patience and persistence, very like the standard demanded of the jade carver, was asked also of the crystal polishers. Beginning with the raw quartz crystal, which was hexagonal, terminated in a point, and had a hardness of 7 on the Mohs scale, the artisan had to shape a flawless, perfectly round ball. The initial steps involved the use of a chipping hammer with which a sphere was painstakingly cut from the crystal itself. According to the nature of the precise area upon which they were working, either hammering or chipping techniques would be used in alternation, ending in the production of a globe that needed no further work other than polishing to bring out all of its beauty. Polishing took place in half-cylinders of perforated iron, and the balls were kept constantly turning in a mixture of powdered garnet, emery, and water until they achieved the desired diameter and smoothness. They were then passed on for final polishing with finely powdered hematite, which we call jeweler's rouge. From start to finish the entire process was conducted entirely by hand, and all measurements were gauged by sight and touch alone. In Japan those transparent spheres were admired for the clarity and perfection of their depths, a lesson that the charlatans and crystal-gazers of the West should have taken to heart instead of seeking knowledge only from superficial reflections.

4

Chapter 4
MEDIEVAL MAGNIFICENCE

The Middle Ages were truly the time of the lapidary, for we see his handiwork everywhere from royal regalia to the ornamentation of church furnishings. The effect is that of a great enameled golden casket, tipped to pour forth a flood of jewels. Half barbaric in its splendor, and half a transcendent vision of paradise, the medieval period took its character from the aims of its two great patrons: the Crown and the Church.

On one hand the kings, possessed as their ancestors had been with a thirst for gold and gems, sought to set their thrones upon firm foundations of wealth, whereas the clergy was duty bound to spread its creed and lead men toward storing up treasures in heaven. Seemingly opposed to each other, these very different goals were not, however, irreconcilable, but met and blended on the grounds of their mutual need for security. The kings provided the strength of the state against the enemies of the Church, while the Church sanctioned the acts of the kings with divinely appointed authority.

All that remained of the power of Rome was its tattered technology, and it was there that the conquering invaders, skilled metalworkers that they were, felt best equipped to benefit from the world they had overthrown. The old crafts, and the men who knew and practiced them, lingered on long after the fall of Rome, only now their efforts were no longer bent upon satisfying the demands of luxury. Instead they were turned toward taking care of themselves, and shoring up their newly found independence. If the so-called Dark Ages were without light it was because they had not yet had time to build a dynamo on their own plan.

If the fires of civilization and learning were banked in Western Europe they still blazed brilliantly in Byzantium, spreading their glow abroad wherever men were willing to look for the light.

Ravenna was just such an outpost, and it is there that we can see the spirit of the medieval emerging from its matrix of Goth and Roman. The tomb of Theodoric the Great, while showing how skills had barely suffered in the aftermath of Rome's fall, also demonstrates the aptitude of his Ostrogoths for absorbing and putting to use the lessons in engineering and construction that they had learned. Only a few generations earlier these warriors from Eastern Europe were forest folk who knew nothing of building in stone; but before A.D. 526 they had become proficient enough in masonry to equal the ancients. Atop the two-storied structure that they erected to hold Theodoric's remains they placed a low-arched dome. By itself that would not have been remarkable, but when the fact is proffered in conjunction with the dimensions—36 feet in diameter—and the knowledge that the dome was a monolith weighing 230 tons, then the fact of the structure's existence becomes quite remarkable indeed. The skills required to quarry, transport, and shape that stone were of the highest degree, as were those needed to raise and set it into place. Add to that the realization that the elements of construction were so well ordered that the building has preserved its integrity for nearly 1500 years. It is highly unlikely that any recent examples of architecture will endure as well.

Yet another example of Ostrogothic talent can be seen in an engraved portrait of Theodoric, last known to have been in a collection in Bern, Switzerland. Cut into an amethyst (apparently a piece of amethystine quartz) the barbaric heritage of the lapidary who made it is plain to see. It has none of the finish typically created by the Greco-Roman gem engravers; instead its statements are bold and direct. The strong Germanic features of Theodoric's face are presented beneath a thick shock of hair, and convey a certainty that this *is*

Preceding pages: *The magnificence of the Middle Ages is evident in this* flabellum (fan) *made of silver, jewels, gilt, and filigree, c. 1200.* Left: *the top of the Farnese Table, designed by the Italian sculptor Jacopo Barozzi da Vignola (1507–1573) near the end of his life.*

how he looked, differing widely from the stiff and highly conventionalized Byzantine images of him on the coinage of his reign. The portrait on the gem, despite its minor crudities of execution, pulses with life and vitality, while that on Theodoric's coins is as remote, lifeless, and artificial as a two-dimensional cutout.

In a very real sense the Goths, the Franks, the Vandals, and all the other northern tribes that had prowled the edges of the Roman Empire, revivified its arts with their own vigor. The sheer delight their craftsmen took in pure color, in masses of jewels set in glittering gold, is apparent in every-

thing they made. Their very naiveté swept aside the effete mannerisms of the declining Greco-Roman world, replacing them with that most difficult of all conditions to attain—and one impossible to maintain—simplicity. It is that characteristic that redeems any awkwardness present in medieval works, and clothes them with a springtime charm. While other schools might struggle with the rules of perspective, composition, and draftsmanship, the medieval artists and craftsmen took the shortest route to whatever statement they had to make. They were completely free of the need to depict this world as it is, for they were intent upon revealing the one beyond.

Furthermore, they placed the precious things of God's creation at the disposal of the Church, decorating ecclesiastical furnishings with the jewels He had made. What better way to glorify the words of the Lord than to cover the gospels with gems? It was with that logic that St. Martial of France, who was daily called upon to handle sacred objects in his celebration of the Mass, had gloves made of the finest white leather set with precious stones. Not only did they prevent his touch from profaning the sacred books and vessels, but the beauty of the stones honored and glorified whatever he held. The notion had much religious intent to commend it, but even saints cannot always foresee unfortunate consequences. One day while wearing his magnificent gloves he chanced to witness an act so sacrilegious that it shocked him to the ends of his fingertips. Thereupon the gems, so long accustomed to the quiet habits of holiness, leapt out of their settings, providing St. Martial with great amazement, and the not-altogether-innocent bystanders with some degree of largesse.

The Ostrogothic craftsmen preferred far more substantial settings for their jewels, and commonly placed them in cells of molded goldwork, massing 200 or more garnets, almandines, and pieces of lapis lazuli in one design. The finished product, called a *fibula,* was a large brooch that served to clasp the heavy folds of a cloak when it was draped as a garment over the shoulder. While animal and abstract forms were quite frequent, the most popular design of all was that of an eagle, thus establishing the national emblem of Germany as early as 500 B.C. In a sense the technique

of cloisonné enamel, later perfected at Byzantium, was anticipated by the Goths, although they performed the more difficult task of cutting the stones into the shapes of the cells instead of filling them with powdered glass. All in all they were not unworthy successors to the lapidaries of classical times.

With the rise of Christianity, following the conversion of many of the Germanic tribes, the development of the crucifix as an ornamental object soon took place. At first the crosses were small and made simply of gold, being used primarily to identify the orthodox Christians from the Arians, who were still a numerous sect in the 6th century. Quite naturally the more important members of the Christian community felt the need for crosses more fitting their station, and commissioned ones that bore a modest complement of jewels. The result was so handsome that the clergy seized upon this innovation of the laity and created processional crosses to lend more dignity and color to the rituals of the Church.

The gems chosen for decorating the crucifixes were placed in settings raised above the surface of the crosses, and were held in place by prongs, or by either crimping or bending back the edges of the mounts over the stones. The jewels themselves were cut in flat, tabular fashion, or as rounded cabochons, and both the gem and the shape of its setting had religious significance. Lapis lazuli, which is blue, symbolized truth and the hope of heaven, but inconveniently required chastity of its wearer. There was also green jasper or chrysoprase, which stood for faith that is forever fresh; red garnet denoted the blood of martyrs. A circle signified eternity and perfection, a square indicated the world and those yet living in it, while a triangle figured the Trinity. Such shapes and stones can be seen time and again in early mosaics and illuminated gospel books, for the Church had already had several centuries to formulate its symbolism and iconography.

Sarcophagi of various rare or costly stones, such as porphyry and pure white or colored marble, were placed in niches along the walls, or in separate chapels. Pavement slabs of colored or veined marble were laid, and quite often floors were made of marble mosaic. These last presented elaborate geometrical designs rather than those of

Biblical events or personages, since it was not considered proper to trample anything sacred. The patterns, which seldom if ever repeated themselves, spread throughout naves and aisles, giving the look of oriental carpets. Finally, to cast a warm, soft glow of light over these spendid interiors, small windows of alabaster, ground thin as glass, were set into the walls. In small chapel tombs, such as that of Galla Placidia at Ravenna, the effect is superb; but once larger expanses had to be considered other means of glazing had to be devised.

One magnificent specimen of the jeweler's art that survives intact from A.D. 603 is the gospel cover of Queen Theodolinda. This was a rather sumptuous thank-you gift to her from Pope Gregory the Great on the occasion of the baptism of her son Aldobald. Gregory was grateful to her for having aided the conversion of many of her fellow Lombards, an act that not only enlarged his flock, but gave it protection as well.

The cover itself, which was made in Rome, illustrates perfectly the prodigality of art patronage at the beginning of the Middle Ages, and also shows that the level of craftsmanship at the time stood in no need of apology. Both sides of the cover, which is gold, bear 110 gems set into two crosses that are surrounded by cloisonné enamel. The crosses also bear eight antique cameos of classical workmanship. The gems, which consist of pearls, sapphires, amethysts, peridots (or emeralds), garnets, rubies, and topazes, are all expertly cut, polished, and mounted, particularly in the case of the pillow-cut cabochons. These last take either a square or rectangular shape, arch upward from a flat base to rounded tops, and are slightly and slantingly trimmed at either end so that they finish by resembling a pillow. They are very characteristic of medieval lapidary work, which seldom attempted any great alteration in the natural form of a stone, preferring instead to cut simple geometrical shapes.

Such works as Theodolinda's gospel cover were usually commissioned from expert jewelers skilled in the crafts of designing and making precious objects. Some, of course, were produced by monks who spent their lives perfecting their art in the service of the Church, and there was even one jeweler who began as a metalworker, but ended as

the patron saint of goldsmiths. He was St. Eloi, who learned his trade in 6th-century Paris, and came to the attention of King Clotaire II, who wished to have a throne made. Eloi was given the requisite amount of gold and gems for the task, and a detailed and specific record was made of the items entrusted to him, so that he would not be tempted to pilfer or divert any of the material for his own uses. It was then that Eloi's talent for saintliness became evident, for he produced not only one throne from his allotted supply, but two. How the king made use of them, being capable of sitting in only one place at a time, the legend does not tell us, and perhaps it may be wiser not to inquire.

Despite any artistic license in the legends about him, Eloi was real, and so was the throne of Clotaire II. Eloi also served the next Merovingian king, Dagobert I, as Master of the Mint (some thirteen coins bear his name) before he became Bishop of Noyon. In that post he continued with his craft, but confined his efforts to the production of sacred objects such as jeweled reliquaries, chalices, shrines, and Church ornaments. Materials for these were supplied by gifts from royalty, other noble patrons, and from Church revenues. Wealth poured into the ecclesiastical coffers from every quarter, but because not all of the kings and nobles gave piety a high priority, every now and then the wealth would be redistributed by a process of looting.

Although many such desecrations took place in medieval times, the French Revolution was the event that despoiled most of posterity's heritage of St. Eloi's work. St. Eloi's patron and monarch, Dagobert, had commissioned many items from him for the churches of France, such as the Abbeys of Chelles, St. Loup of Noyon, St. Martin of Limoges, and St. Denis of Paris, but all was swept away in 1789 and its aftermath. If nothing else, revolutions have clearly demonstrated that revolutionaries have an appetite for gems at least equal to their desire for reform, and which may even occasionally exceed it.

For example, all that remains of St. Eloi's cross, done for the Abbey of St. Denis, is the end of one arm, and that is bereft of the nine gems it once held. Luckily the 15th-century Master of St. Gilles depicted it in place on the altar at St. Denis, so we have, at least, a record of what it looked like. Another pictorial survivor of St. Eloi's superb craftsmanship is an engraving, done in 1653, of the chalice he made for the Abbey of Chelles. It was gold, about eleven inches high, thickly set with red, blue, green, and white stones—probably a combination of pearls, sapphires, chrysoprase (often taken to be emerald), and almandine garnets. The stones were set in panels around the body of the chalice, forming a checkered design with central chevrons of cloissoné enamel, and edged with vertical rows of garnets. At top and bottom were wide bands of cloisonné that held cabochon-cut gems, all in all a work that would have conferred sainthood on Eloi even if he had created nothing else.

Other kinds of church furnishings also began to gain in popularity, besides such articles of divine service as chalices and crosses. These were the reliquaries containing physical remains of sacred persons, or artifacts connected with sacred events. Almost anything imaginable might be found in them, from a piece of the true cross to the blood of a martyr. Wonderworking properties were ascribed to most of these relics, and many of them became the goals of pilgrimage. Not in an altogether disinterested fashion the various shrines housed their artifacts and anatomical remnants in the most elaborate casings they could afford, and the goldsmiths and lapidaries rejoiced. Here could be found the skull of a saint covered with a sculptured portrait in gold or silver, and bearing jewels in appropriate places such as a collaret about the neck, or sapphires set in enameled eyes.

A considerable number of these reliquaries were fashioned during the period of the Crusades when knights passed through Constantinople and the Holy Land, encountering enterprising merchants along the way. It was a time when the mendacious prospered, selling the Crusaders such items as a vial containing a tear that Christ supposedly shed over Lazarus; paintings made by angels; the head of St. Anne, mother of the Virgin Mary; and two heads of St. John the Baptist, only one of which had the remotest chance of being genuine. There was also the chalice used at the Last Supper, which was reportedly carved from a single emerald, but turned out, on examination, to be nothing more precious than glass. On one oc-

casion that same chalice was pledged to a pawnbroker for the sum of 100,000 crowns. However, when the time for redeeming the note arrived, seven claimants, each in possession of a chalice and a signed pledge, stepped forward for payment. The pawnbroker in the meantime had had six copies made and, by selling them as well as the original, gained far more money than the interest on a single pledge would have brought him. The broker, of course, vanished with his ill-gotten gains, leaving behind the problem of which chalice was genuine.

By and large, however, most relics were genuine and had unimpeachable provenance since they had become essential to the consecration of a church. Encased in suitably decorated small caskets, they were sealed inside the altar at the ritual dedication of a church, a practice that led in time to the acquisition and application of other relics for special purposes. Quite common were those visibly displayed in vessels of rock crystal, generally used to intensify an act of blessing the faithful. Others were kept in elaborate purse-shaped receptacles of jewel-studded gold, in place of the customary cloth or leather, or in containers that reproduced an anatomical form when they held a fragment of a martyr's or saint's body.

One notable example of the latter type is the reliquary of Ste. Foy, a virgin martyr whose skull and girdle are housed in a statuette of the saint. Only a little over thirty-three inches high, she is shown seated on a decorated throne. Since acquisition of her likeness by the Abbey of Conquès in the 9th century, many gifts have been bestowed upon the statue's little figure by devotees visiting her shrine during a pilgrimage to Santiago de Compostela. In addition to cabochon-cut gems on her robe and a heavy Byzantine crown, many more jewels are set into the sides and border of her throne, which also has finials made of rock-crystal spheres, each about two inches in diameter. Although richly ornamented and bedizened, the reliquary creates a bizarre effect, and few, if any, such pieces have been shaped as an entire figure.

When the relics consisted of several small parts, or did not lend themselves to a specific representational container, they were often deposited in jeweled golden pouches. Such a purselike form

Top: *A 16th-century Spanish reliquary cross, which contains eight separate relics, made of gold and enamel on a body of rock crystal.* Above: *Charles V, ruler of an empire "on which the sun never set," wearing, instead of the famous Iron Crown, just an ordinary crown set with a few precious stones.*

instantly symbolized that the contents were treasure of inestimable value, having greater worth than the gems with which the reliquary was ornamented. One particularly beautiful reliquary of this sort can be found in the cathedral treasury of Monza, a small town outside Milan, that has long been famous for its collection of historical and religious relics. This reliquary purse is said to hold the teeth of St. John the Baptist, and is decorated with the great splendor befitting such a very rare possession. Upon its golden surface, covered with filigree work, are 186 gemstones, 20 large pearls, and a border of 130 smaller ones, all arranged in the masterful style of the 9th-century Carolingian workshops. Although the reliquary underwent some restoration about A.D. 1680, and accordingly can no longer be vouched for as an unaltered design, it does preserve the rich character and materials of 9th-century work.

Yet another kind of relic is also found at Monza, one that combines sanctity with the power of the state. It is the Iron Crown of the Lombard kings, bearing six enameled and jeweled plates bound, on their inner sides, by a circlet of iron reputedly made from a nail of the true cross. It was used to crown kings and emperors throughout the Middle Ages, among them the famous Frederick Barbarossa. In 1530 Charles V crowned himself with it at Bologna, and in 1805 the Emperor Napoleon I did likewise, saying "God has given this to me; Let who interferes beware."

Those who tried discouraging the accumulation of relics, even such level-headed and unbiased critics as Guibert de Nogent (1053–1124), a Benedictine monk and a historian of the Crusades, met with dismal failure. About two hundred years after Guibert's pointed criticisms, Edward III of England had an inventory made of the relics he owned. A partial extract from the list includes a rock-crystal vessel partly cased in gold, and containing an unspecified number of unlabeled relics, apparently a neglected hoard whose nature prevented Edward from disposing of it decently. Another was in the form of a chest that contained four silver-mounted containers of rock crystal holding parts of the chasuble and alb of St. Edmund the Confessor, an arm bone of St. Amphibalis, and some of the blood of St. George.

Nothing was said about what the fourth vessel held, for medieval inventories were often casually and maddeningly incomplete. Still other items held in rock crystal were a large bone of St. Jerome, relics of the martyr St. Stephen and a tooth of St. Adrian. There was also a purse that held part of the column to which Christ was bound during the Flagellation. Obviously Guibert had had no effect on the passionate yearning for tangible links with the past, and neither had his successors, for John Calvin was still thundering against the practice in the 16th century.

Because pilgrimages to relic-rich shrines were often physically difficult, or too expensive, some cathedrals and churches devised labyrinthine paths as substitutes for penitential journeys. Some of these, marked out with polychrome marble, may still be seen set into walls or pavements. Perhaps the most famous example is that in the nave of Chartres cathedral, made of blue and white stone, though the blue now borders on black, having absorbed much discoloration through traffic. It has an entirely symbolical nature: blue signifying heaven, and white purity, meaning that only the pure can attain the goal of salvation. The number of marble slabs that make up the path to the center of the labyrinth is 521, the components of which total eight—the number assigned as the symbol of the Resurrection that occurred eight days after Christ's entry into Jerusalem. It is interesting to note that these pavement patterns were often called the Road to Jerusalem, goal of the Crusaders, and the object of many penitential pilgrimages. The entire design is placed within a circle, symbol of eternity, and holds at its core twelve pieces of white marble which form six groups that surround, in their turn, a disc of the same stone. Obviously that grouping of thirteen represents Christ and his twelve apostles. The length of the pathway to the central goal is about 450 feet, every inch of which had to be traversed on one's knees while reciting prayers.

The wall labyrinths were considerably more merciful, for they simply required tracing the course with a fingertip, again reciting a prayer as each part of the design was touched. It was very similar to telling a string of rosary beads. One such in the cathedral at Lucca is only about twenty inches wide, and formerly enclosed a scene of Theseus conquering the Minotaur. Still another, in San Savino at Piacenza, is accompanied by a verse that warns that while the world is wide at its entrance, the way out is difficult and narrow for those who carry a burden of sin. A variation of the pattern is sometimes found with a series of circles representing the nine heavenly spheres of the upward path to heaven. An example, which has been improperly restored, can be found in Santa Maria in Trastevere at Rome.

An octagonal labyrinth, eight being symbolic of the bodily resurrection, was once to be found in the nave of Amiens Cathedral. Laid down in 1288, it was forty-two feet in diameter. It was destroyed in 1825, and only a record of its design was kept. At Reims another labyrinth was removed even earlier, in 1779, by order of a canon of the cathedral, who objected to the noise and disturbance made during divine services while children and their elders pursued the route. It is very possible that a number of others disappeared for the same reason, though some, or portions of them, have survived in cathedral museums.

In addition to labyrinths picked out in marble, the stone also provided elaborate pavement designs for much church architecture. At Ely Cathedral in England, there are reddish, brown, white, and grayish marble flagstones that are set out in geometric patterns of rectangles, chevrons, and diamonds, giving a warm glow of color and something of the effect created by the shields and banners of the medieval knights. And at St. Mark's cathedral in Venice the floors are crowded with a tesselated paving of polychrome marble, thoroughly Byzantine in style, bearing more than a hint of Arabic influence. At Siena, however, an old intarsialike Roman method was used.

Intarsia work, which involves the insetting of pieces of variously colored and figured woods so as to create geometric designs, landscapes, or even portraits, was an extremely difficult art to practice. Even more so is *opus sectile*, in which sawed and polished sections of marble are used in place of wood or wood veneers. The technique, which was introduced at Rome in the time of the Emperor Claudius (A.D. 41–54), was never entirely forgotten in Italy. Examples of it done at Rome in the 3rd century remained visible even after the art had been largely superseded by the more flexible technique of mosaic. It is, in fact, practiced to this day on a very small scale in Florence, with one workshop recently in operation very near to the church of Santa Croce.

In late medieval times the art was revived for the flooring of Siena's cathedral, which, with the exception of one mosaic, was done in *opus sectile*. The polychrome marbles used in executing this work are black, from Valerano and some from Pistoia; white from Carrara; yellow, and purplish tones with a red or bluish cast from Siena itself; reds from Verona; and a cinnamon-brown of such wide occurrence that almost any region could be named, although it resembles the pigment burnt sienna so closely that it is probably a local product. Blocks of these marbles were cut into sheets of sufficient thickness to withstand the weight of the expected traffic, and then trimmed to their final shapes by sawing with abrasives. The craftsmen, who followed the drawings of the designers, had to be aware of the peculiarities of their material, and keep within the limits they imposed. Rather like the artists who work in stained glass, they had to avoid strips and curves that would not accommodate to certain pressures, and also to keep pieces from spanning too large an area, so that the shapes would not snap. Careful judgment was always required, for an error brought disaster and a new start.

In all there are sixty designs to be found on the cathedral floor, and while it must be admitted that they make a masterly display, it is also obvious that they are highly impractical. Entire sections of the nave have to be roped off, or placed under hinged wooden covers (removed on special occasions), in order to minimize wear on their surfaces. Small marble tiles that can be replaced as they are consumed through use, or even plain slabs, make a more sensible solution, but the builders of Siena's cathedral were more concerned with glorifying their faith than with the plodding practices of everyday practicality. In any case, as the originals approach their end of usefulness they are preserved in the cathedral's museum, and are replaced by exact copies, so none of the original beauty is lost.

These pictures in marble have one feature that the ancient Roman workers in *opus sectile* never considered, for they include lines that both outline and model their subjects. To accomplish that effect the lines were marked out on the marble sections, then channeled out, and finally filled with a cement paste of powdered black marble, thus making them resemble large drawings.

The subjects of the pavement are quite varied, presenting scenes from both the Old and New Testaments, portraits of the six Sibyls who foretold Christ's coming, a wheel of fortune showing the rise and fall of kings, personifications of the virtues, and more. Despite the jumble of topics, the frequent interruptions suffered, and the number of artists involved—each with a different style—the work displays a surprising harmony. That, of course, results from a uniformly high level of skill, the homogeneity of the material used, and a shared vision and purpose that was the product of their time. Essentially these art works are graffiti, from the Italian word meaning "to scratch a mark," but they are certainly light years away from the defacements that that word has come to mean today.

While most stones in the medieval period became part of the fabric of various structures, or were used directly by the lapidary in creating jewelry or ornamenting precious vessels, some semiprecious stones ended up on artists' palettes. One such was azurite, hydrous copper carbonate, often found cut and mounted as a cabochon gem since it is either transparent or translucent, and has a blue-to-bluish-purple color. As research into the nature of medieval pigments continues, azurite is gradually being recognized as a major source of the blues used by painters in the Middle Ages. Earlier it had been thought that lapis lazuli provided artists with their chief source of supply, but Afghanistan is the principal supplier, and the distance involved meant an almost prohibitive expense in obtaining the material. Nonetheless, medieval paintings exhibit a great deal of blue, so a problem arose until two things were realized: that azurite was fairly common in Europe; and, that it frequently altered into malachite, a closely related hydrous copper carbonate. There are sizable deposits around Lyons, France, and it has been mined from the silver mines of Saxony since the 12th century. Two other clues appeared as well, for sometimes certain blue areas would unaccountably turn black or develop a bright green

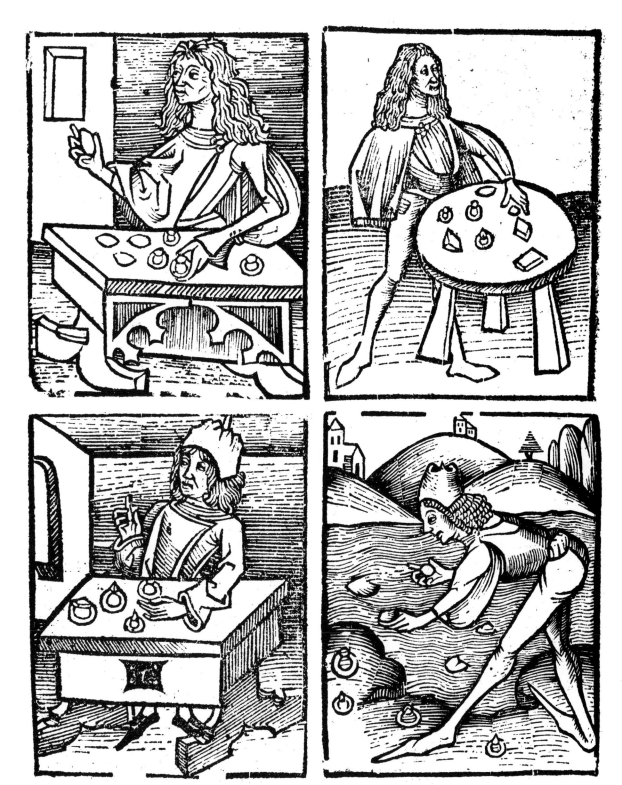

Four medieval (1497) views of stones. Top left: *Stones in their settings.* Top right: *Selling stones and crystals.* Above left: *A dealer in a gemshop showing off his amethysts.* Above right: *Gathering stones from a river. These woodcuts demonstrate the importance of stones during the Middle Ages, both for ornamental and medicinal purposes.*

93

color. Those two phenomena relate directly to the fact that azurite turns black when it loses its water content, and becomes green when it deteriorates into malachite, a change that is very noticeable in the upper church of St. Francis of Assisi.

Depending on the degree of fineness to which azurite was ground, and its basic content of copper carbonate, it gave a wide range of blues, and was called either "mountain blue" or "Armenian stone." Unfortunately for art historians, who have to rely on documentation in their studies, much azurite was labeled lapis lazuli, for that term was loosely applied to many blue pigments. So many traps lie in wait for medieval researchers that the only safe statement they can make about the period is that they still do not completely understand it.

Malachite itself was widely used for the production of bright greens, which still delight the eye on many a panel painting or page of manuscript. Since the Middle Ages have passed so has the abundance of malachite, and nobody would think of grinding it today. Now it is far more likely to be used in small, expensive objects such as boxes, desk sets, or pieces of jewelry. Magnificent large specimens of the stone are to be found in Leningrad, where huge facing slabs of it decorate some of the halls in the Winter Palace, and also form the columns of St. Isaac's cathedral. Massive pieces are still found in the Ural mountains, Arizona, Zambia, Chile, and Australia, and needle-shaped crystals are fairly common.

Before the development of colors from coal tars, and modern methods of synthesizing pigments, the medieval painter had very few reds with which to work. This was hardly a problem in fresco work since large, glaring areas of intense red were not desirable in wall paintings. But brightness was necessary in the illumination of manuscripts, and on the relatively small wooden panels then used by painters. The most brilliant red of all was vermilion obtained from cinnabar, a heavy opaque stone that is just below the level of hardness to qualify it for use in decorative objects. That, however, was actually a blessing because cinnabar is the principal source of mercury, a mineral that can have devastating effects on people. The dull lumps of cinnabar, once they were crushed, were absolutely irreplaceable on the me-

dieval painter's palette, and have become almost characteristic of the art of the Middle Ages.

The other red pigment available came from hematite, an iron oxide that the ancients called "bloodstone" because of its resemblance, when fractured, to the rich, deep red of venous blood. It was extremely useful for the entire range of maroon reds, and also slightly purplish pinks when mixed with white. Luckily it is quite abundant, for it was an important color in frescoes and also for manuscript painters.

Yet a third kind of red, commonly used in dyes, inks, and watercolor washes, was derived from chips of brazil wood. Incidentally, that is a case where a country derived its name from a product well known before the country was ever discovered. The word "brazil" came from the word "brazier," because the color extracted from it sometimes glowed like burning charcoal, and since the South American country had many kinds of trees capable of producing the dye it acquired the name of the wood. While the nature of the solution used to extract the dye could alter its color considerably, it was found that marble dust and eggshells added to the liquid resulted in a beautiful rose color without the least brownish tinge. Thus the refuse from quarries and sculptors' studios unexpectedly proved useful in the dyers' vats.

Far from being refuse, lapis lazuli was one of the most expensive of medieval pigments, which sometimes added to its virtues in the eyes of the purchaser. There has never been a time when prestige has not been an important element in human affairs, and also a purchasable one. The luxury trades could not exist if people did not enjoy exciting a little envy or awe in their fellow beings. Patrons, whether secular or ecclesiastic, often insisted on specifying the most costly materials—in part to do honor to the object created, and in part to glorify themselves as having a purse ample enough to pay for it.

Lapis lazuli, because of the distance that the raw material traveled from its point of origin in central Asia, came to be called ultramarine, that is, "from far across the sea." Evidence points to it being imported in a prepared state from Arab lands because Europe did not have the secret of preparing it as a pigment until the 14th century.

Although it eventually yielded a beautiful blue, its original form offered a most unpromising beginning. Lumps of purplish-blue rock, often with a greenish tint and bearing spots of gray and white calcite, added to brassy yellow pyrites, made up the stone as it came from the mine. When ground and properly prepared it became the richest and most permanent blue on the medieval artist's palette.

To reach that state, however, required a great deal of monotonous labor. First of all the pieces had to be reduced to a fine powder, not altogether easy to accomplish since the stone has a hardness of 5 on the Mohs scale, roughly equal to that of turquoise. The finer it was pounded the better, for that aided the extraction process that followed; but the first view of the result was something like a mass of gray dust. The gray powder was mixed with a paste of wax, oil, and resin all worked together like dough, and then squeezed in a bowl of warm lye until the solution refused to absorb any more blue. More warm lye was then placed in another bowl and the process repeated until no more blue could be coaxed from the lump. The solution was allowed to stand and evaporate into a powder that might then be washed and skimmed repeatedly until all impurities were removed. The entire process might take as many as sixteen to twenty washings and strainings.

To provide a good, hard base upon which pigments could be pounded and ground, the artists followed the lead of the apothecaries, and made use of bronze mortars and slabs of porphyry or marble. In those times only the raw materials were sold, and it was up to the artist to prepare them for his own use. While in his own studio this was no problem, but if he was required to work outside of it then difficulties began to multiply. The porphyry slab upon which pigments were ground and mulled was hard enough to resist considerable wear, and was readily obtainable in Italy from ruined palaces where it had been used as an ornamental stone. Outside of Italy marble became the favorite substitute as a grinding base, and had the additional advantage of being white so that the colors could be judged somewhat better. All well and good; but what artist wanted to haul heavy slabs of stone about with him so as to go about his work? The result was that many of them, engaged

on church frescoes and the like, made use of the marble altars that were right at hand, happily grinding and mixing. The practice grew to be so common that the churchmen, aware of the sacred relics concealed beneath the altar slabs, finally had to impose penalties to put an end to the sacrilegious act.

Regardless of the surface upon which they ground their colors, artists had to observe particular caution when preparing minerals. While lapis lazuli permitted grinding to a fine powder, such was not the case with malachite nor azurite. If the grinding process was overdone the crystals began to lose rather than gain color intensity. A nice balance, obtainable only through years of experience with the vagaries of certain materials, was the only guide. As a general rule crystalline pigments had to maintain a size somewhere between the coarse, which produced the most intense pigmentation possible but was too gritty for brushwork, and the very fine, which flowed smoothly from the brush, but was too pallid from crushing to carry enough color. The most deeply colored ruby or sapphire could be placed on an anvil and reduced to powder by hammering, if anyone was stupid enough to do so, but the result would not be a deep, glowing red or blue, for the complete fracturing would cause the particles to look white.

In one of the legends of St. John the Divine just such a pounding of precious stones does occur. Returning to Ephesus from his exile on the island of Patmos, St. John discovered a Greek philosopher preaching an ascetic doctrine of renunciation. Two wealthy young men, heeding the philosopher's words, placed some gems they were wearing on an anvil and hammered them into dust. The more practical St. John reproved them, saying that the renunciation was simply inverted pride and would have had more meaning if the jewels had been sold to benefit the poor. He was then challenged by the philosopher to prove Christianity's superiority by restoring the stones to their original, unshattered condition, which he did at a word. The result was that he, St. John, gained three converts, aided the lot of the poor, and abetted the welfare of the jewelry trade in Ephesus. The success of such an action, however, as readers must be cautioned, depends entirely upon their eligibility for canonization.

Naturally when saintliness has been proven beyond all doubt there is occasion for building sumptuous monuments, shrines, and other memorials. Such was the case at St. Mark's in Venice, where the Pala D'Oro (Golden Altarpiece) was installed in A.D. 976 by order of the Doge Pietro Orsolo, who commissioned it from the workshops in Constantinople. After undergoing restoration and renovation in 1105 and 1209, it finally took the form in 1345 that we see today. At that time an artisan named Giampaolo Boninsegna cleaned, retouched, and recomposed the altarpiece, giving it the Venetian Gothic style it now has. He also invested it with its full complement of precious stones. Late in the 18th century, in 1796, an inventory was made of those gems, which totaled 2521 exclusive of the cloisonné enamels on gold. It is difficult to imagine any richer an altar than this one, and it gives some slight echo of the wealth that once poured through the hands of the Queen of the Adriatic. There are 1300 pearls, 400 garnets, 300 sapphires, an equal number of emeralds, 90 amethysts, 75 pink and rose spinels, 50 rubies, 4 topazes, and 2 cameos—enough to require several hours, and separate attempts, to count accurately.

In 1797 the French, under Napoleon I, took Venice, removed the famous four horses from St. Mark's to Paris, but left the Pala D'Oro untouched. There is a story, probably apocryphal, that when the French soldiers entered the cathedral and saw the glittering altar they asked the sacristan what it was worth, and if all of the gems were real. With great presence of mind (and visions of bayonets popping jewels out of their settings) he calmly shrugged his shoulders, waved his hand contemptuously at the altar and said "Glass, all glass! And has been for a long time." Remembering that an inventory had been taken only the year before, and that the Venetians might have decided to lessen the lure the altar offered, the sacristan *may* have been telling the truth. If so, only a jeweler, complete with magnifying lens, will be able to settle the question.

What is certain, beyond all doubt, is that St. Mark's cathedral could readily be regarded as one of the world's greatest repositories of marble specimens. Scarcely a variety of the stone, and certainly not a single color of it, has been neglected. That scope and plenitude results from a Venetian practice whereby every shipmaster who sailed from Venice returned with some beautiful or notable item for the ornamentation of St. Mark's. The credit for establishing the custom is given to Doge Dominico Selvo (1071–1084) who first ordered an exhaustive search to be made for marbles and fine stones.

The aggregate value of the marbles, for they formed a very large percentage of the basilica's donations, is beyond calculation. For instance, when that eminent Victorian John Ruskin was writing his three-volume commentary on Venetian architecture, the *Stones of Venice* (1851–1853), he made every effort to determine the worth of the pillars he found in the nave and transepts of St. Mark's. These were white, compacted alabaster streaked with gray and amber; were fifteen feet high from base to top; and were shaped from solid blocks about twenty-two inches in diameter. The only answer he received, however, from every sculptor of his wide acquaintance in the art world was the same. All told him that such blocks were nowhere to be found in the market, and had to be considered priceless. When one realizes that the basilica contains 2500 columns of ornamental stone, it becomes clear that Ruskin was attempting an impossible evaluation, and he had not even taken the facing slabs, bases, panels, or moldings into account.

Because of the extent and long duration of Venetian rule, immense booty and tribute flowed into its coffers. Much of this went into the Treasury of St. Mark's, and piled up there until 1797 when Venice came under French rule. Fifty-five bars of gold and silver resulted from the melting down of treasures, and nobody knows how many gems disappeared. There was a dispersal by sale in 1806 of some 15,250 carats of precious stones, and in 1814 the Austrian successors to Napoleon auctioned off an additional 26,431 carats. The bulk of that latter sale went to jewelers in Istanbul, returning them, in many cases, to their point of origin. In all, a little over thirteen pounds of gems filtered out of Venice, an accumulation of about 900 years, and the amount and time forms a useful gauge by which to estimate other great hoards of the past.

Because both Occidental royalty and religion

Incense burner of carved malachite. No one would think of smashing this beautiful object and grinding it down to make green color—but malachite did make an attractive pigment during the Renaissance.

The cutting and setting of marble mosaic floors is an art practiced throughout Italy from Roman times onward. This example, from the Cathedral of Milan, has rivals in Siena's cathedral and Venice's St. Mark's.

have suffered a great decline in the present century, such treasures flow in ever greater amounts into the great national and civic museums, and are likely to increase still further in the years to come. Immense as the Venetian pile of jewels may seem to an individual, all thirteen pounds of it could be placed in an overnight case, and much the same can be said for the total volume (not value) of the world's holdings of precious stones. If all of them were gathered in one place they could probably be fitted into a building the size of an average modern bank. Comparison then, with the size of the globe, shows clearly why they are called precious and rare, and command the prices that they do. They *are* relatively few in number, and deserve to be well housed and kept.

Many have already found their way into such repositories as museums, where they are both available for public viewing and receive a maximum of security. What was once the occasional privilege of kings and bishops is now open to everyone who has the desire to see; all the great treasures of the Middle Ages are now on display for the looking by rich and poor alike.

At the Tower of London the great, uncut ruby of the Black Prince may be seen ornamenting the Royal Crown of England. This became an English possession in 1367 when Don Pedro of Castile, who was rarely generous at all (and never so much as he might seem), gave the stone to the Black Prince in recognition of his aid in battle. Henry V later wore it on his helmet at Agincourt, but, despite all the glamor of its past association, the ruby is not a ruby at all, but a spinel of much lower value. Don Pedro, it seems, lived up to his reputation.

In the Louvre, at Paris, there is the Eagle Vase of Abbot Suger, an antique vessel of porphyry (probably Roman in origin) converted in 1140 into the shape of a perched eagle. The transformation, made to the abbot's own design, was effected by adding gilded silver wings, head, and talons to the body of the vase, which had been hollowed out from a solid block of stone. Also in Paris, in the Cabinet of Medals of the National Library, is a cameo from the 1st century that was reused to ornament the Casket of Charlemagne. In its center is a portrait of Julia, daughter of the Roman Emperor Titus (A.D. 79–81), cut into aquamarine and surrounded by nine sapphires and six pearls all mounted in the style of the 9th century. This remnant is all that is left of a work that was destroyed during the French Revolution. It is impossible at this date to list the masterpieces that have been sacrificed over the ages to the vandalism of religious and political fanatics, who always seem compelled to improve the world by smashing everything beautiful in it.

Closer to home there is the chalice of Abbot Suger, now in the National Gallery in Washington, D.C. Singlehandedly, Suger probably did more to beautify the world than all the reformers, revolutionaries, and assorted zealots one could list in a week, for he was the moving spirit behind the magnificent architecture of the French Gothic. The chalice that he prized is made of a single large piece of carved sardonyx, with a rim and base of jewel-studded gold. It, too, threatened to join the list of lost masterpieces when it vanished by reason of theft in 1804, but fate relented and restored it to posterity in 1922 when it reappeared on the art market.

Still another splendid souvenir of the Middle Ages is the Lothair Crystal, now one of the proudest possessions of the British Museum. It is silent testimony to the superlative skill of the 9th-century lapidaries who shaped it, and has a most interesting history on its own account. Created at the command of Lothair II (855–869), it bears the inscribed notice *Lotharius Rex Francorum Fieri Iussit* (Made by Order of Lothair, King of the French). Barely over four inches in diameter, it carries eight scenes from the tale of Susanna and the Elders, with ten inscriptions, all engraved on a circular piece of rock crystal. Forty figures, each fully modeled, are presented within the confines of the design in addition to the ten lettered descriptions and statements. However, the work is so well executed and balanced that there is no sense of crowding.

The provenance of this piece guarantees its authenticity as a true example of Carolingian art, for it was in the continuous keeping of the Benedictine Abbey of Waulsort, a small Belgian town near Dinant, from the 10th century until the time of the French Revolution. Looted from the abbey it was subsequently sold for ten francs to an antique dealer, probably being regarded as worth-

Opposite: *Madonna and child reliquary of silver gilt with precious and semiprecious stones from the shrine of St. Remacle, Belgium.* **Above:** *Malachite.* **Right:** *Azurite was used as a blue pigment in many medieval frescoes. It frequently reverts, over time, to a greenish hue.*

LOTHAIRE 3.du nom
Roy de france né a Laon eng 41
et mourut l'an 9 86. agé de 45.ans et l'an 32
de son regne et inhumé à S.Remis de Reims

Par un traité mal concerté,
Ce prince fut blamé de toute la Noblesse,
Et d'un fatal poison, au sort de sa jeunesse,
Mourut sans estre regreté.

Above: *Lothair, King of France, commissioned the rock-crystal plaque that still bears his name. His royal Carolingian line came to an abrupt end a year after his death when Louis V, his son and successor, was poisoned by his own mother.* Opposite: *The Eagle Vase of Abbot Suger.*

less by the thief, since it was split through from top to bottom. Luckily, damage to the design was slight, affecting only minor portions of the lettering and figures. The fortunate dealer realized £267 when the crystal was auctioned in 1855 to the British Museum, and everybody was happy.

On a much earlier occasion, back in the 10th century, the piece was given as a pledge to a Canon of Reims cathedral, so that a Carolingian count could provide himself with a horse. However, when he sought to redeem the crystal the Canon denied any knowledge of the transaction, seriously misjudging the count's capacity for taking care of his own. The count promptly set fire to the cathedral, smoking the Canon out into the street where he was then searched, and the crystal found on his person. The count returned to Waulsort, about one hundred miles away, and performed penance for his sacrilege to the cathedral by founding an abbey where he deposited the little piece of rock crystal that had caused him so much trouble. What penalty was paid by the Canon of Reims for his act of thievery is not recorded, but it is certain that he learned when and where to avoid the wickedness of this world, especially when perpetrated by outraged nobility.

Although, as has just been seen, the art of engraving gems was not entirely lost in the Europe of the Middle Ages, two wildly incorrect popular beliefs about engraved gem formation deterred that art. Because the misconceptions illustrate some of the parochial characteristics of medieval thought, an affliction by no means confined to that particular age, they are worth mentioning here. The first, and most logical of the two, all things considered, was that unaided nature produced engraved gems. That reasoning went as follows: because the original stones were too hard for man to cut (and for many craftsmen they were), it was obvious that only nature could have shaped them. If anyone objected to that idea they were asked why the forces that created mountains should turn incompetent when it came to the much smaller matter of forming cameos? Where nature acquired a knowledge of Latin, Greek, Egyptian, or Hebrew no one inquired, and the accuracy of portraits went unchallenged because almost nobody knew what the persons portrayed had looked like. In any case they, too, would have been asked why nature would have trouble duplicating a model that it had made in the first place.

The second theory, which took into account the evidences of human handiwork, had a very simple and direct explanation, which was that the cameos had been made by the Israelites while wandering in the desert. Obviously such skilled work could only have come from the wiser and more accomplished people of antiquity, for medieval folk consistently gave greater credit to the authorities of the past than to those of their own age. Besides, it seemed reasonable that some occupation was needed to while away the idle hours during a forty-year march. So they conjured up visions of the Biblical fathers gathering up choice stones from the plenty that they found in the desert, and then sitting about their fires at night, chipping away for the benefit and delight of posterity. Luckily for those Israelites, they did not encounter many diamonds, for they would have found nothing hard enough to permit them to cut the designs they wished to shape.

Neither they, nor anyone else for that matter, were able to attempt such until after 1476, when Louis von Berquem of Bruges perfected the process of faceting diamonds. Until then they had to be taken just as they came out of the ground, and occasionally what were called *à pointes naives* (natural octohedral crystals) were found. They look like two pyramids placed base to base, and were sometimes mounted in rings in that fashion. A clasp, or brooch, once preserved at the Abbey of St. Denis, contained four of them, and was said to have originally belonged to Charlemagne. Because of the religious disturbances in France during the 16th and 17th centuries, and the various political ones of the 18th and 19th, the relics of Charlemagne, and a good many others, are gone forever.

It is too bad that the people of those times did not have more faith in one medieval belief, one that regarded the diamond as "the stone of reconciliation." And while they were at it they might have considered some of its other virtues as well, for it was said to be an antidote for poison and also for insanity. Considering that jewelers continue to thrive, there may be something to the old superstitions after all.

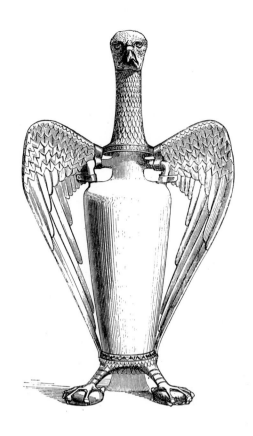

5

Collection of the photographer

Chapter 5
MAGIC, MEDICINE, AND MINERALS

The well-furnished dining table no longer displays an article such as the *arbre d'épreuve*, or a proving tree. That item of tableware was also known as a *langier*, or serpent's tongue, and was a metal standard, often attached to the salt dish, that bore from five to fifteen different stones pendant from its branching arms. The stones had a practical rather than a decorative purpose, and were intended to detect or to neutralize poison in any of the meats or wines served at meals. All the royal tables of Europe had at least one, and a great deal of reliance was placed upon them in preserving the health and safety of kings and nobles. The method of using them was quite simple. The chamberlain dipped the stones, one by one, into the viands and drinks as they were brought from the kitchen. Supposedly the stones would sweat, change color, or exhibit other phenomena, if poison was lurking under the parsley or in the cup, but, as added insurance, a taster also sampled the food. If he survived, the dish was served. If not, the kitchen help were shortly introduced to the executioner, who was then permitted to earn his keep.

Although the stones used on the proving tree were often precious, such as sapphires, rubies, and emeralds, they also consisted of flints, agates, sharks' teeth, or such strange things as toadstones or bezoars. Yet despite the proving trees and the tasters, poisoners still managed to practice their craft, for they generally relied on a course of slow, cumulative dosing, preferably with arsenic, to achieve their ends. Care had to be taken with arsenic to prevent from building up an immunity to it in the intended victim, and in Eastern Europe some of the peasants were addicted to the substance, even eating it daily. In places such as Transylvania its presence in the soil was a contributing factor to the growth of the vampire legend, for bodies buried in arsenical ground re-

mained remarkably well preserved. This, in turn, was a possible link to the custom of taking pinches of arsenic for cosmetic purposes, since it conferred an opalescent gleam to the skin, and may have been imagined to preserve beauty from decay in the living equally as well as it prevented the mouldering of the dead.

Two of the proving tree's stones are as unfamiliar today as is the proving tree itself, but both were real, even if all of their ascribed powers were not. The first of these is the toadstone, which can be either a fossilized tooth, or, more generally, a piece of igneous rock honeycombed with cavities that have filled with deposits of carbonate of lime. It gets its common name in English because it usually has the rough, warty appearance of a toad skin, and very often the broad oval shape of a toad's body. The French call it *crapaudine* because the cavities it contains rupture with a loud noise when the stone is heated, becoming noisy as the booming croak of a toad, *un crapaud* in French.

In medieval times such stones were believed to be hidden within the heads of toads, and were regarded as an infallible remedy for mothers and newborn children against the malignancies of fays, sprites, and pixies. With that sort of reputation they were much in demand, and would have caused much discomfort for toads if it had not been for the provision that only stones gained from living specimens would be effective. To obtain them one had to entice some old and very large toads onto a piece of red cloth draped over a box, it being well-known that red caused the creatures to act with gay abandon, producing results similar to those of cats rolling in catnip. Sooner or later in their delirium of joy one would forget to maintain his hold on the stone and it would tumble out onto the cloth, fall through a hole cut for the purpose, and land inside the box. The poor batrachian would then be unable to

Preceding pages: *According to medieval apothecaries, amethyst was a sure-fire preventive of drunkenness.* Above: *Taking possession of a borax, or toadstone. Once in hand, the stone more than made up for the difficulties suffered to obtain it, for it was thought to be an antidote to every poison.*

107

reach and reclaim his lost property, and it could then be set into a ring or shaped into an amulet.

For centuries the bezoar was regarded as the principal antidote against all poisons, and had an assured place on the proving tree. Although a mineral composed of lime and magnesium, it was formed not in the earth but as a concretion in the intestinal tracts of oriental deer and goats. Such formations might be small in size, in which case they were mounted in the bottom of a cup or dish, or were carried about for touching suspected foods and drink to neutralize poison. Sometimes they were scraped gently, and the powder added to a prescription; or if they were large enough in size they were shaped into cups or small bowls. A very high value was placed on these stones, and they frequently formed royal gifts. Elizabeth I of England received such a gift from an oriental potentate, had it mounted in gold, and passed it along as a crown jewel to James I. At the height of its popularity a bezoar sold for fifty times the equal weight of an emerald. In addition to their supposed ability to counteract poison, bezoars were also credited with the ability to ward off plague, cure dysentery, fever, epilepsy, and end fatigue. So brisk was the demand for them that apothecaries finally took to renting the stones by the day, a great convenience in case an unexpected invitation to dine with the Borgias happened to arrive.

Proving trees had their greatest vogue during the Renaissance, although they first came into use in the Middle Ages and continued to the time of the French Revolution. Through all that time not only did the heads that wore crowns lie uneasily, but so did their stomachs, and heaven alone knows how many digestive disorders and anxiety-induced ulcers resulted from fear of poisoning. In all probability more damage came about through worry than from the toxic substances themselves. Apprehension affected both the aristocracy and the clergy as this brief list of proving tree owners clearly shows: Edward I of England, the Duc de Berry, the Duc d'Anjou, Charles V of France, and Pope John XXII, who had two of them as gifts from Philip of France.

Sometimes the proving tree itself was made from branched red coral instead of gold or silver, since it was believed that coral turned pale in the presence of poison. It was thought to be particularly sensitive to any venomous emanation, and thus offered the added insurance of an early warning system. Many members of royalty, however, increased their arsenal of protection by wearing prophylactic rings, amulets, bracelets, jeweled collars, or by carrying pouches containing such stones as were thought to prevent poisoning. Anne of Brittany carried a purse of red cloth, which held a fossil "serpent's tooth" and a toadstone, doubtlessly made from the same red cloth that had first beguiled the toad into forfeiting his jewel. Charlotte of Savoy, who seems to have been unusually anxious, wore a bracelet of proving stones, and had a pouch filled with still more of them. Very likely she had good reason for such prudence and caution, since some of the physicians of the day were not above lending their knowledge of poisons to the highest interested bidder. Such was the Bohemian Jean de Grandville, who served first the King of Hungary, next the Emperor of the Holy Roman Empire, and finally Louis II of Bourbon. Then there was Francesco Casini who, in addition to writing a number of treatises on poison, also happened to be personal physician to six 14th-century popes; but whether he was hired for purposes of protection or elimination remains unstated.

Many of the stones used to detect poison were also administered in cases of serious illness, as witness the recipe for compounding the Most Noble Electuary of Jacinth. This consisted of powdered jacinths (now known as zircons), emeralds, sapphires, topazes, pearls, and red coral, with twenty-two other animal and vegetable ingredients. At times this prescription was varied by adding white coral, amber, garnets, and rubies to those already mentioned, and was given in doses of from ten grains to half a drachm. It was usually prescribed in cases where there was either much vomiting or diarrhea, which gives a slight clue to the ailments that carried off Charles VI of France and Lorenzo de Medici, both of whom received that medicine on their deathbeds. The physician who gave it to Lorenzo, one Pier Perleone of Spoleto, committed suicide at the Villa Martelli a few days after his medicine failed. He did so by plunging into a well, though there are some who intimate that his leap and bath were not entirely

voluntary. Malpractice in the Renaissance was not always remedied in the courts.

The confection of jacinth was also given to Philip II of Spain only two days before his death, for it was a standard item in the pharmacopeias of the time. It did, in fact, persist in medical use until *after* 1720 when it made its appearance in Quincy's *Pharmacopoeia Officinalis*, or the *Compleat English Dispensatory*. Quincy, however, felt that the crushed gems were the worst part of the mixture, and suspected, quite rightly, that the stone fragments operated like glass splinters in the patient's intestinal tract. He mentions that apothecaries, in grinding the mixture, wore away as much marble or porphyry as the weight of the powder they obtained. How then, he asked, could body tissues absorb and assimilate substances that reduced the hardness of stone to dust? Even an intelligent person such as Francis Bacon was prevailed upon to accept a treatment of pearls made into a paste with lemon juice; harmless but expensive and ineffectual. However, for sheer expense Pope Clement VII seems to hold the record for all time. In 1534 he was given some 40,000 ducats of pow-

Opposite top: *Stags were believed to be the enemies of serpents, cutting them in half with their hooves. When bitten by a serpent, the stag would submerge itself to the eyes in water, and the venom would flow out of its eyes, as shown here.* Opposite bottom: *Charles VI of France went mad at 24. In the hands of his* physicians for the next 30 years, he survived all their prescriptions *save the Most Noble Electuary of Jacinth, a crushed-jewel remedy given him in his final illness.* Above: *Philip II of Spain was given a dose of jacinth. He died two days later.*

Curing a nosebleed with heliotrope. The pressure and the coldness of the stone may have done the trick.

however, the gems were said to give off a subtle fragrance, as was reported by one Olaus Borrichius, writing in the fourth volume of the *Collection Académique*, Paris, 1757. There he states that the powder should be so fine that it will not grate upon the teeth, and to obtain that degree of perfection he gave a medical student a month's lodging to perform the task. An ounce of each stone—emerald, zircon, pearl, sapphire, and ruby—was provided. That is approximately 7500 carats in all, so Olaus must have been either rather wealthy or related to the noted liar Baron Munchausen. Using mortars and pestles of iron, and later of glass, the student took many hours each day for three weeks to accomplish his task, at which time the entire, sizable room became redolent of March violets. Since neither those flowers, nor anything else aromatic, were in the room, it followed that the odor, which persisted for three days, had to come from the stones. It is doubtful that modern perfume makers will try Olaus's method for economic reasons alone, if no others.

There was, however, quite a trade in providing the sick and wealthy with as many powdered gems as their bodies could handle, since the efficiency of remedies was often rated according to their rarity and price. More often the stones were kept intact, and used for purposes of touching the afflicted parts of the body. Sometimes they were steeped in fluids to transfer their power so that it might be imbibed, or were simply bound to, or suspended over, diseased organs. They were highly regarded as therapeutic agents, and a medical work of the 15th century, the *Hortus Sanitatis*, lists 144 stones and the means of using them medicinally. The practice, however, had begun long before that, for the Ebers Papyrus (c. 1500 B.C. but copied from a manuscript of c. 3000 B.C.) listed lapis lazuli and hematite among its curative substances. Theophrastus, a disciple of Aristotle, wrote a book on gems and some of their medical uses in the 3rd century B.C., as did the Greek pharmacist Dioscorides, and the Roman encyclopedist Pliny, in the 1st century A.D. Later Hildegarde of Bingen, writing in the 12th century, continued the tradition, which lasted to the 18th century when many of the stones were still listed in the pharmacopeias of the day.

Some few of the remedies, such as those made

dered gemstones in a period of 14 days, the most expensive of which was a diamond administered to him at Marseilles. In terms of the present U.S. dollar that sum comes to over $3,000,000, outrageous enough, but rapidly being approached by hospital costs in current non-Renaissance times. Had Clement refused to take his medicine he would, in all probability, have lived somewhat longer, perhaps a *great deal* longer. Any constitution that could resist a daily input of so many minerals had to have been far more reliable than the medicines pumped into it.

The immense labor of grinding such hard stones to a powdery dust that would dissolve in water was a contributing factor to the high cost of such prescriptions, although it is doubtful that they were ever given that amount of effort. For perhaps the first century that confection of jacinth was given, the apothecaries pounded and ground with all their might, but after noting the effects on the patients they probably did not trouble themselves too much. When thoroughly pulverized, of powdered stones with absorbent or styptic properties, had slight usefulness, but the vast majority were simply expensive ways to accomplish nothing, or, what was worse, do the patient irreparable harm. Most were the outgrowth of sympathetic magic, as like curing like by applying red stones to inflamed or hemorrhaging areas; others were plainly superstitious in nature. Opal, for instance, was something in the nature of a panacea because it possessed all the colors of all the stones, and therefore seemingly had all of their curative powers as well. Amethyst was a well-known preventive of drunkenness, permitting its wearer to drink the house dry without suffering any ill effects. The Greeks originated that legend. *Methyo* in their language meant to be drunken, but the letter "a" prefixed to the word reversed the meaning, thus signifying *not* to be drunken. Because the Greeks mixed their wine with twenty parts of water, the stone probably got the credit for any of the resulting sobriety.

The yellow color of topaz singled it out as a healing stone in cases of jaundice, which gives the skin a yellowish tinge; and bloodstone, also called heliotrope, was considered ideal for stopping nosebleeds because it bore tiny red spots like drops of blood. Jade was prescribed for kidney troubles and for all ailments of the urinary tract, and got its English name from the French *l'éjade* which came, in turn, from the Spanish *hijada*. It was thought that jade had the ability to break up kidney stones, and one Italian poet even wrote some lines on that very unpromising theme:

White stones should serve to build palaces or temples fair,
Yet mine do but mark days filled with pain and gloom,
Well do I know that Death doth whet his scythe
Upon these my stones, and that the marble white
That grows in me is there to form my tomb.

Very often the placement of a therapeutic stone was every bit as important as what kind of gem it was. Jacinth or zircon was to be worn either on the neck or the index finger if it was to keep its owner free from plague, welcomed with dignity and honors at the dining tables of his peers, and certain to receive justice in any court of law. Diamonds, however, had to be worn on the left arm where they would make the wearer invincible, capable of reconciling quarrels and strife, free from

melancholy and madness, and untroubled by nightmares and demons. The authority quoted for these last two statements was the one-time bishop, Marbode of Rennes (1035–1123), whose book *De Lapidibus* set forth the lore and uses of some sixty stones. One of the most popular works of the Middle Ages, it gathered all the pertinent matter about the powers inherent in stones that had been written from antiquity until Marbode's own time. Over 140 manuscripts of the treatise exist in the major libraries of Europe, and eighteen printed editions have been published between 1511 and 1977. Although its medical value today is nil, Marbode's book can still tell us much about symbolism, medieval names for a variety of stones, and the psychological processes of the people of his era.

A sample is to be had from the writings of Qusta ibn Luqa who lived in 10th-century Syria. His statement about the value of the placebo, which most of the gem remedies were, is this: "The state of the mind affects the state of the body. Sometimes belief in the curative value of a prophylactic is enough." Ten centuries later there is no way to improve his observation.

Many of those mineral placebos were worn as ligatures bound onto arms, legs, or around the body. Still others were contained in belts, often of lion's skin, or were worn on cords of varying lengths as suspensions that touched particular areas of the body. Jasper, which is an opaque or cryptocrystalline variety of quartz, was judged to assist childbirth if worn on the thigh. It was also said to prevent hemorrhage during the birth process, and Hildegarde of Bingen, who wrote a medical book in the 12th century, advised expectant mothers to keep the stone on their person at all times as a defense against evil spirits. Others commended jasper for maintaining purity of heart and a preference for chastity, in which case its other virtues would have been superfluous.

The emerald, when worn suspended from the neck, was said to ward off malarial chill; it was also credited with the capacity to improve eyesight—as green was considered soothing to the eyes—and even to prevent epileptic seizures. It was also credited with curing moods of fury, and those of lust and license, as well as calming tempests in the sky. Emerald was also prescribed in

which also harmed the brain. And only a fool would wear onyx, since it carried nightmare, fear, and misfortune for its owner. What was more, flawed or imperfect stones, which might be considered to be useful as medicine since they had failed as gems, were ruled entirely out of the apothecary's mortar. Only perfect stones would do because otherwise no cure would result, and very likely damage would be caused instead, ranging from simple lameness to pleurisy, jaundice, or leprosy. Sales promotion methods it seems have always been with us, and so have the skeptics who resisted them. There is the famous answer of Charles V's jester to a question about the most valuable property of the turquoise. Expecting the usual reply that the stone would sustain all the damage of any great fall the questioner heard these words instead: "Why, if you fell from a tower while wearing a turquoise on your finger, the *turquoise* would remain unbroken."

No such disbelief was held by Ivan the Terrible, in whom it would have been quite reasonable to expect considerable doubt about the real nature of things. Shortly before his death in 1584 Ivan gave a brief tour of his treasury to some of his Boyars and to an English ambassador to his court. Placing pieces of coral and turquoise on his arm and hand Ivan invited all to see how they changed color "into paleness declaring my death." He called the diamond the richest of stones, but confessed that he had no fondness for it. As he went on to say the diamond restrained fury, an appetite for luxury, abstinence, and chastity, making it clear that such a stone was less than sympathetic to his character. The emerald he called an enemy to uncleanness, which probably abounded in the capital of his day, and he had nothing but praise for the sapphire, his favorite gem. He declared that it both preserved and increased courage, gave joy to the heart, pleased all the senses, cleared the sight, and strengthened all the muscles and sinews. All present listened attentively, voicing no disagreement, and finally the tired Ivan asked to be carried out to rest, not feeling any benefit from his treasures.

Agates, while having very pleasing colors and banded patterns, would appear to have been too common and well-known, thus avoiding any strange notions about being blessed with special

cases of demoniacal possession, as an antidote to poison and poisoned wounds; it even being said that if the victim was already on the point of death a dose of eighty barleycorns in weight would bring about recovery. As if all that was not enough to move out any lapidary's stock of the stone it was also believed to cure ophthalmia and to end hemorrhaging. The green color of emerald was, of course, responsible for most of those notions, acting on the principle of sympathetic magic, but as to another of its properties, that of increasing wealth, the purchase price alone would seem to work in the opposite direction.

In 1628 Robert Burton, writing his ever-delightful but completely misnamed *Anatomy of Melancholy,* said that sapphire not only cured melancholy (then a morbid psychological condition leading to insanity), but released the mind from care, and mended manners. Had it been true, the 20th century would have had a perfect remedy for its troubles. The stone was also believed to cure sore eyes, dysentery, heart disease, skin ailments, bruises, and inflammations, and, being emblematic of chastity, was often set in rings to be worn by the clergy.

Not all stones were helpful, however. Selenite, or moonstone, drove away sleep, as did the ruby, properties—but not so. With a number of other stones, agates are grouped in the category of cryptocrystalline quartz, and are formed by deposits out of solutions that are rich in minerals. Nonetheless agates have had a number of powers ascribed to them, among which was the ability to attract whatever woman one might desire. While that feature might have opened possibilities of future troubles, agate was also endowed with the faculty of shielding its owner from all danger. Additionally it made its wearer agreeable company to everyone, persuasive to all, and favored by God, an essential gem for every practicing politician. Still further it cured insomnia, brought pleasant dreams, conferred a bold heart, and overcame any and all obstacles, even acting as a protection against the most evil of Evil Eyes. Eye-agates, which had a white ring in the center, were especially useful for that purpose, and were an important item of trade in the Sudan during the 19th century. The German centers of stone-cutting and polishing at Idar and Oberstein, which are still in operation, were kept busy around the clock trying to meet the demand, bringing in an annual revenue of about $30,000 per factory, or well over $100,000 at current rates. Where the poverty-stricken natives of the area got all the necessary money is another question, but for a time they were capturing military and civilian supplies from many British settlements.

The same type of eye-agate was also employed in providing eyes for some of the Asiatic and African idols, and was used throughout the Near and Middle East to cure what was called the "Aleppo Boil." This was a hard, raised area with a ring of inflammation about it, and rudely resembled the eye-agate that provided relief for the parasitically induced sore. Farther to the east, in India, the agate was given a more esthetic task, for it formed a portion of the ramparts about the mythical royal city of Kusavati, with other walls of gold, silver, coral, beryl, and crystal. Within those walls grew palm trees made of the same materials, save that those of agate bore leaves and fruit of coral, and the coral trees carried fruits and leaves of agate. When stirred by the wind the trees gave forth a melodious, musical sound that charmed and intoxicated the listener with its beauty.

But of all the notable things concerning agate its

Opposite: *Even the distraction of taking his dog for a walk can't relieve this unfortunate medieval gentleman of a painful eye-ache. The application of an opal, however, may have helped clear his view of Rover's path.* Above: *A medieval salesperson vending garnets or rubies.*

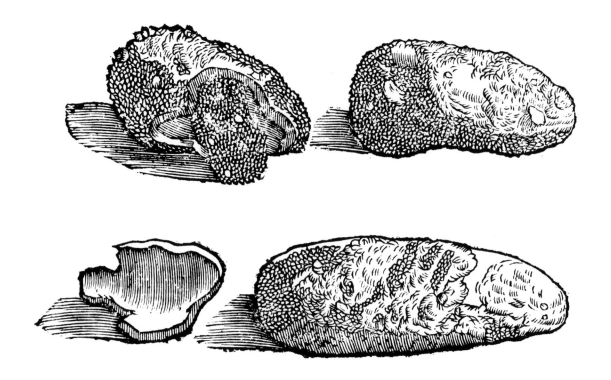

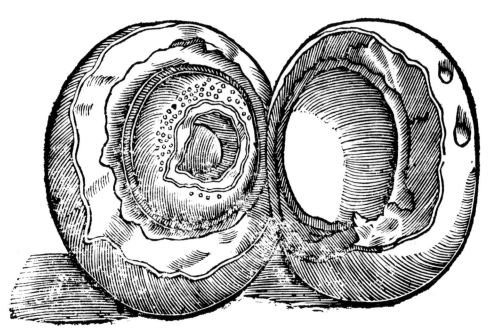

A 16th-century woodcut illustrating the "birthing" of a geode, or "eagle stone."

place in the history of aeronautics is probably the strangest. In 1670 a Jesuit professor of natural philosophy at Brescia, one Francesco Lana, conceived the concept of an airship to be borne aloft by four thin copper spheres from which all air had been removed. Neither the Montgolfiers, the Wright brothers, nor Count Zeppelin had anything to fear, however, for the design had overlooked a few necessities, to say the least. Some thirty-nine years later his scheme was refined and resurrected, and on the 5th of June, 1709, a courier from Lisbon rode into the streets of Vienna proclaiming the first flight made by man. To prove it he carried a stock of broadsheets (poster-sized printed announcements) that related the full story, and a woodcut of the vessel that had achieved the feat. Conveniently the event had taken place sometime earlier in Brazil, at the request and expense of the King of Portugal. Naturally that made it a bit difficult to check the story, but everyone was so overjoyed that such an idea never entered anyone's head; it was enough that the marvel had come to pass.

The print that illustrated the wondrous ship also bore an explanation of how it was done, though a few details remained unclear. The most important thing was the addition of an iron framework, set with coral-agates, to supplement the vacuumized copper globes of Lana's original design. Coral-agate is very much what its name implies, that is, agate that has replaced coral by a chalcedony formation. The theory was that when the agate gems warmed in the sunlight (another reason for the choice of Brazil for the initial flight) they became magnetized, and would then act on magnetic spheres, hopefully placed fore and aft at the corners of a canopy. The intrepid pilot sat midships between two globes, one astral, the other terrestial, which he used as navigational aids, peering through a telescope from time to time as he plotted his course. The hollow globes of Lana's ship had been replaced by hollow tubes, with valves through which the air could be pumped out. Oddly enough the ship's rudder, above which flew the flag of Portugal, was also constructed of the same tubes, on the principle of never having too much of a good thing. Best of all was the landing gear, which consisted of rows of feathers apparently attached to flexible leather hinges. These doubled as a kind of paddle in case the wind died down, or could be swung outward to form a sort of parachute during descent, and, of course, also cushioned the shock of the landing itself.

As extensive as the medicinal and physical properties of stones were, whether real or fancied, their magical uses equaled them. For instance there was the alectorius, found in the gizzard of a capon that was past four years of age, or else in the gizzards of very old roosters, who took longer to form it. Sufficient reference is made to this stone in medieval documents to assure us that it was not an imaginary substance, but a real one. It turns up in quite a few inventories of the time, always with the same description, and generally set in rings, so there is little doubt that it was a recognizable stone and a real one, even if its supposed powers were imaginary.

The stone itself was probably a bit of quartz picked up by the bird to aid its digestion. That process occurs in its posterior stomach, an organ with thick, horny walls in which the bird grinds its food by means of stones it has picked up, a necessary step since it lacks teeth and the strong digestive juices of a serpent. These bright, diamondlike stones, when held in the human mouth were supposed to relieve all sensation of thirst, although it would still be advisable to carry a canteen while crossing the Sahara. It also made its bearer invincible, and legend has it that many a gladiator emerged victorious from the arena because he had carried it in his mouth while fighting. Even Milo of Crotona, who built up his strength by lifting a calf every day until it was a full-grown bull, used the stone every time he wrestled in a contest. He was as real as the alectorius, having been a recorded winner on six occasions at the Olympics, and the same number of times at the rival Pythian games, which amounts to a period of twenty-four years. He was said to have carried a four-year-old heifer around the stadium at Olympia—a longish walk—and afterwards ate all of it in a single day, thankfully something our modern cafeterias no longer demand of us. He also commanded an army that defeated the Sybarites in 511 B.C., no doubt because the alectorius guaranteed victory in battle, but also because the Sybarites were a soft, pleasure-loving people who were ill-suited to warfare.

Above and beyond the gifts it bestowed upon Milo, alectorius also restored exiles to favor, even bringing them new honor in the eyes of the public. And, as if that was not enough, it also improved an orator's powers, made personalities more pleasing, and increased an individual's perseverance. It was also recommended to wives, who were thus enabled to overcome their husbands with desire, and rouse them to a rare pitch of excitement. In any case, every housewife was advised to seek it out when preparing a capon for the table.

Another wonder-working stone derived from birds was the chelidonio, or swallow stone, listed so frequently in medieval inventories that it could not have been altogether imaginary. Described as existing in two variations—one having black markings on a purple ground, the other as whitish gray on one side with purple on the opposite face—it was always said to be found in the swallow's intestinal tract. Its scarcity today may simply be the result of not looking in the right place, a habit encouraged by our hordes of packagers who put everything into tidy little bundles that effectively conceal the sources and origins of whatever we buy.

Not a particularly handsome stone, the chelidonio was eagerly sought because it brought many benefits to its fortunate possessor. It was to be obtained only from the largest young birds; and was to be carefully kept from touching water, earth, or other stones, until it was wrapped in linen. Thereafter it was to be worn under the left armpit, whence it would dispense the following gifts and cures: it ended lunacy, headache, pain in the eyes, tertian fevers (those which recurred every three days); restrained temptation, especially from an incubus; hindered goblins, witches, and sorcerers; and even strengthened bodies that were chronically weak. It also stemmed the flow of harmful humors in the body, such as melancholy (which brought about madness); gave its owner a pleasing, gracious personality, capable of great eloquence and, very importantly, set aside the wrath of kings. All things considered it is remarkable that any swallows survived into our times.

Earlier, the amethyst was cited as preventing drunkenness, but, like the chelidonio, it had other potentials as well. It offered protection against treason, though whether from its effects or its commission is not made clear. It also guarded one from deceit and imprisonment, insured that its owner would never be afflicted with blindness nor be troubled by strangulation or choking. Further, it provided a shield against all enchantments, improved the complexion, and prevented hair from falling out. Luckily for a number of our modern remedial, legal, and cosmetic services, amethysts and swallow stones are seldom employed today.

Sardonyx, so often used in making cameos, had some unsuspected virtues as well. Being a stone generated in the earth by the power and heat of the sun, it was said to strengthen the intellect of its owner and to grant a superior degree of understanding. When worn often and consistently it eliminated stupidity, and calmed obstinate and unruly passions. Sapphires, oddly enough, were also credited with the same powers. It seems, however, that the effects lasted only as long as the stone was worn, and left the genetic patterns of the chromosomes untouched, else we would be a race of charming, intellectual giants today.

Fire prevention and cooling were the province of still other stones such as the agate, which, when dropped into boiling water, would cause it to cool on the instant. Much the same property is granted to a gem called galacia, also known as chalazia because of the waywardness of medieval spelling. The latter word means hailstone in Greek, indicating that it was possibly a diamond or transparent corundum. Whatever it may have been, no furnace flame on earth could infuse it with the slightest degree of warmth. Even topaz is to be found on the list of coolants, though there is some doubt that what is meant is modern topaz. Originally that name was attached to peridot and to chrysolite, both greenish-colored stones. In later times topaz somehow acquired a reputation that exactly matched that of haephestites, or pyrites, in its ability to cool water. The latter stone, however, had some additional advantages, for it calmed civil uprisings, hurricanes and hailstorms, kept locusts and blight from ripening crops, and preserved its bearer from all danger. A brilliant stone, named for the Greek god of fire, Haephaestos (Vulcan), it darted forth fiery, golden rays, and had to be worn either on the left arm, or over the heart, to work at its best. Under its original name of pyrite, however, the same stone is described as being fully capable of burning the hand that clutches it, much nearer the truth of its character than that of cooling. Pyrite, on weathering, produces sulphuric acid, and that, in turn, if grasped by a hand that is moist from perspiration, is very apt to react chemically by burning one's palm.

There was even one stone, the zignites, mentioned in the late medieval *Hortus Sanitatis*, that was said to extinguish flames when applied to a fire. However, the compiler who put that into the text had evidently misread his source, and mistook the word gagates for zignites, a very simple matter, but one that was pretty well astray of the mark. He had in mind the strange properties of a stone that caught fire when water was thrown upon it, but which could be extinguished by oil. The stone he was referring to was jet, which, being a hydrocarbon related to coal, can ignite by spontaneous combustion after having been dampened. It was believed that its flames were to be doused only by oil, working quite logically along the principle of opposite effects, though anyone who trusted that line of reasoning was sure to be surprised.

It was generally set on fire for purposes of suffumigation, to bring on the menses, as well as for another common medieval ailment, epilepsy. Burning jet also drove away snakes and demons, dissolving the wicked spells of magicians and all deceitful illusions and prophecies of evil omen. Dropsy was cured by this means, as was the severest kind of indigestion, and in solution it offered a sure way to fasten teeth that had loosened in their gums. The same water, when taken internally, aided a difficult birth and could also be used in verifying virginity, whenever the need arose. If the suspect retained the fluid, though the recipe carelessly neglected to say for how long, then her purity was beyond all doubt, but, if the case was otherwise, then the waters poured forth at once. Whether or not jet was used for that purpose in strait-laced Victorian times would be difficult to say, but it flowed out of the deposits at Whitby in Yorkshire to every jewelry shop in England, Europe, and America through most of the 19th century.

Bloodstone, which is a dark green chalcedony dotted with bright red spots (hence its name), is also called heliotrope, and was thought able to make water boil. Its other abilities were to stop nosebleeds (its major use), to produce rain, a good reputation, expel poison, preserve health and vigor throughout life, to help foretell the future, and to prevent one from being cheated. It had, however, one further use that should have made it the most desirable item in the jeweler's store: it made its wearer invisible. To accomplish that operation required using it in conjunction with the plant called heliotrope, while reciting the proper incantation and performing the correct ritual. Nothing is said about regaining visibility, which could have been an inconvenience if one was permanently trapped in the invisible state. That, however, was hardly likely to have caused a problem since the scribes neglected to set down the ritual and the charm to be recited, or perhaps they were censored by the tax collectors of their day.

Selenites, or moonstone, is yet another magical stone that managed to get its spelling mixed up with a similar word, resulting in confusion about the powers and origin of both. The other stone was chelonites, a name that implies that it came from a tortoise. It was thought to be useful for foretelling the future. Selenites was also said to originate in a tortoise, and was likewise used for predictions, although its powers waxed and waned with the moon, which it resembled in form and color.

And for those who were ambitious to make the world ring with the sound of a voice of brass there was calcophonos, or sound stone. That could link it with jade, which does emit a vibrant, long-lasting note, but the mineral, as described, is black and gives out a metallic ring when struck. Far from being mythical, it has been supposed to be phonolite, an igneous rock that matches the description, and has chemical and physical characteristics not unlike jade itself. It was recommended to all those who croaked out rough, husky sounds. They were advised to wear it around their necks and were assured that their voices would become fully melodious to the same degree that they remained chaste. It also induced sweet sleep, free of bad dreams.

One stone of considerable usefulness in the

good old days, when interrogations took place in torture chambers, was memphites. As its name suggests, it was found in Egypt in the vicinity of Memphis, and probably was extremely difficult to procure anywhere else. No samples of it seem to have survived, but that is not surprising since the method of using it required it to be ground into a powder, which was mixed into vinegar and then applied to those areas where cuts, burns, and other unpleasantries would have occurred. The memphites stone was said to make the victim's body insensitive to whatever pain was inflicted, and two medieval authorities can be quoted to that effect. One was Isidore of Seville, bishop and saint of a city that later gained some small fame for an institution known as the Inquisition. The other was that pillar of medieval learning, Albert the Great, who credits Aaron, brother of Moses, and Hermes Trismegistos with making the pain-killing remedy known to man. For the sake of those who may have tried it, let us hope that, for once, expert opinion was correct.

The person called Hermes Trismegistos was really Thoth, the Egyptian god of learning, under the name assigned to him by the Greeks. Hermes was their equivalent to Thoth, and Trismegistos stood for thrice learned or thrice great. The connection with Aaron stems from a legend that became popular in medieval Europe about the same time as the rise of alchemy, and involves a stone tablet upon which was engraved the secret knowledge of the universe.

Hermes, wishing to benefit mankind with the hidden wisdom of the gods, caused a tablet of emerald to be engraved with everything necessary for a proper understanding of the alchemical process. Emerald was chosen for two reasons: the first was that green was the color of the alchemist's primordial matter, an essential substance for the operation of the work. The second reason was to authenticate the message and its source, it being well known that only the ancients had the knowledge that enabled them to cut letters or designs into gemstones.

All myths, of course, serve a purpose, and this one marked the transfer of secret power and lore from the Egyptians, by way of the Jews of the Old Testament, to the alchemists of medieval Europe. The legend of Hermes' emerald tablet was further shored up by additional circumstantial evidence, such as being discovered in the Sinai desert during the Israelites forty years of wandering. Further credence was lent to it by the involvement of persons of high reputation and credibility, which is why it was Aaron, brother of Moses, and his sister, the prophetess Maria, also called Miriam, who were declared to have found the tablet. Several versions exist, but most state that light emanating from the emerald first revealed it to the pair. Here we have an echo of Isidore of Seville's statement that said that true emeralds suffused the air about them with their vivid green color. Maria is also credited with the invention of the alchemist's *Balnae Marie,* a glass apparatus, much like a modern chemist's flask, in which substances were liquefied by the application of mild heat. Very often the *Balnae Marie* (Mary's Bath) after being sealed at its top, was buried in the sand exposed to the sun's warmth, or within the gentle heat generated in the dung heaps of the barnyard. The paths of lapidaries, alchemists, and mythmakers met here and joined once again, as they did so often in attempts to shape the workings of nature nearer to the desires of man.

The astrologers were equally concerned in determining how best to use the powers that nature had infused in all the parts of creation, and stones, because of their beauty or strangeness or clarity, were thought to contain or concentrate many of the stars' most potent forces. The theory ran that rays from the heavenly bodies, carrying the particular virtues of certain stars, planets, and constellations, became strongly focused on certain stones at certain times. When that moment had been calculated carefully, then the engraving of an appropriate sign commenced on the chosen gem, or the graven jewel was applied at that time in order to effect a cure. In a left-handed, roundabout way such procedures, because of their very complexity, brought about advances in both mathematics and astronomy, and dispelled some of the inanities and lunacies that so many were attempting to preserve and increase.

The preferred gems for the practice of medical astrology always came from India or elsewhere in the tropical regions. It was in such places that the sun's rays struck the earth fully and directly, not with the glancing sort of stroke that occurred in

Francisco Lana aloft over the jungles of Brazil.

the more northerly areas of temperate Europe and America. Obviously the rays from other heavenly bodies followed the same path, hence gems from the tropics always received more of whatever force or power was needed for the task at hand.

To aid physicians in their treatment of disease, all ailments and their remedies were classified according to a system of four qualities, such as hot, cold, moist, or dry. A disease that had been determined to come from a cause that was cold in its nature was cured by bringing it under the effect of warmth, or by applying an opposite in order to bring the fluids or humors flowing within the body back into balance. An ailment with a nature that was warm and dry, as was the case with many fevers, was relieved by treatment with something cold and moist. Astrologically, certain signs of the zodiac were assigned particular qualities that they imparted to the stones generated under their influence. Should a doctor want to treat a patient for quotidian fever (one that repeated in four-day cycles), or perhaps dropsy, both of which stemmed from cold and moist causes, he simply prescribed the use of a stone or stones formed under Aries, Leo, or Sagittarius, since they were regarded as hot and dry in their nature. The tables listed Taurus, Virgo, and Capricorn for stones with cold and dry qualities; Gemini, Libra, and Aquarius ones that were hot and moist; while Cancer, Scorpio, and Pisces influenced stones that were moist and cold. The Arabic compilers of such charts took great care to specify the exact nature and strength of the stones to be used in degrees. Coral was said to be cold in the first degree (a little cool) and dry in the second, that is, noticeably dry, but not too much so. Hematite was warm in the first degree, dry in the second, but, if washed before use it became cold. Marcasite was cold in the second degree, dry in the third, while diamond was strongly cold and dry in the fourth degree, and therefore most useful in curing ailments of a moist and hot nature. Therapeutically the system was not altogether reliable, but it did hit on quite a few things that had beneficial effects. It is noticeable, though, that the great Arabic physician, Avicenna, seldom used gems in effecting his cures.

The vast majority of the stones and gems mentioned in the medieval lapidary books were iden-tifiable, but a few with very interesting properties defy classification. Foremost among these is a white stone that could be made to give off sparks of flame. That, of course, sounds suspiciously like flint, until one reads further and discovers that this strange stone could neutralize "flying venom," of which nine kinds were recognized in Anglo-Saxon medicine. In all probability they were communicable diseases, and the very fact of their recognition would be of value to the history of medicine, even if the supposed cure was ineffectual. Whatever the stone may have been, it was scraped with red earth (probably iron oxide) and put into wine or water, and was given as a curative draught. It also aided the benighted traveler who had lost his way, for, by striking sparks from it before him, it would guide him onto the right path. Even more important, fire struck from the stone acted as a protection against the dangers of lightning, and any fantastic delusions. That advice had best be ignored in mountainous terrain, where the heated air rising from fire or a chimney makes a perfect path for the grounding of electrical current.

Another unidentifiable stone mentioned in one of the lapidaries of Spanish origin, possibly the Lapidario of King Alfonso X, is one that guaranteed a sleep filled with sweet and pleasant dreams. If ever it is identified it will prove a boon to those users of LSD who have experienced bad trips. Still one more of the unknowns is the anaesthetic stone, which is very likely a late medieval version of the tale about the memphites stone that rendered a body immune to the pains of torture. Until the middle of the 19th century most surgical procedures were painful affairs, although scrapings of mandrake root in wine *did* offer a means of bypassing the agony, for both the ancient people and those of the Middle Ages possessed an effective anaesthetic in the judicious use of that medicinal plant.

It was probably administered more than once for the operation called "removing the stone of folly," an undesirable lithic growth in the forehead that had to be excised to restore the sufferer to his or her senses. Two prime candidates for that surgery were the Countess of Lupfen and the Countess of Saarbrucken. The Countess of Lupfen set the peasants on her estates to the pleasant task of gathering all the snail shells they could find and then winding yarn upon them for her needlework. The Countess of Saarbrucken surpassed that degree of nonsense when she visited her manor at Folkelingen, where there seems to have been a large resident colony of frogs. On her arrival at the manor house all the serfs were ordered to keep the frogs silent at night, so that the sleep of the Countess would be undisturbed. With social attitudes of that sort one did not need a crystal ball to foretell the peasant's revolts in the early 1500s, but crystal balls were constantly pressed into service, nonetheless.

Mankind has always had a hankering to know what will happen before events actually occur. Generally they bring nothing but disaster when they do come along, but people are eternally optimistic that the catalogue of evils and errors that they have always known will somehow suddenly terminate, and the lovely land beyond the rainbow will be theirs to enjoy forevermore. And because of that recurrent wish thousands of man-hours of labor have been expended on shaping rock crystal into exquisitely rounded spheres.

Clear rock crystal is the prime material for making crystal balls, but sometimes they are formed from crystal that has been penetrated by numerous inclusions of rutile, that is, long, narrow, needlelike crystals of black or white coloration. The effect is that of a mass of needles and thread frozen into a ball of ice. For most crystal-gazers such a stone would offer nothing but difficulties, as the object is generally to concentrate on the points of light reflected from the sphere. Continued for any length of time, that procedure will gradually induce a state of self-hypnosis, and then the act of crystal-gazing can properly begin. Most accounts state that the gazer, or skryer as he is sometimes known, suddenly finds that the globe has disappeared, and has been replaced by a veil of mist upon which visions come and go. Much the same can be done with a mirror, a piece of flat, polished stone, such as obsidian, or even with a pool of ink spilled out on an impervious surface.

Generally the conduct of crystal-gazing sessions requires two people, one being the skryer, who should be approaching adolescence, and of a sensitive, nervous disposition. The other should be the diviner or interpreter, who waits quietly until the skryer has entered a trance, and then, after suggesting images to him, puts a series of questions to the gazer, and interprets his replies if there is any need to do so. Behind the hocus-pocus atmosphere some very real psychological forces are put into motion, releasing a flood of subconscious images and memories that combine with the suggestions of the diviner.

The act is often very convincing, and has, in the past, deluded such otherwise sensible people as Elizabeth I of England, and her minister, Lord Burghley. Dr. John Dee of Mortlake was the man who accomplished the harmless hoodwinking of her majesty, and actually performed a charitable act for her, after naming an auspicious day for her coronation. On one occasion the entire court and the Privy Council were in a panic after one of their number found a wax image of the Queen lying on the grounds of Lincoln's Inn Fields with a pin stuck through its heart. Dee was instantly summoned to Hampton Court to deal with the matter, and pleased the Queen greatly with his pronouncement that the image "in no way menaced her Majesty's well-being." Coming from such an authority on the occult arts as Dee was reputed to be, Elizabeth must have felt a great sense of relief.

At a later date Dee fell in with a somewhat younger man who had pretensions of being a genius in alchemy. He professed to be able to make gold, even producing a square of the metal on one of the royal cooking pots, also much to Elizabeth's delight. But chiefly he acted as skryer to Dr. Dee, who had an impressive array of crystals at Mortlake, some of them being of smoky quartz or cairngorm, one of the favorite stones of the Scots. He also had plaques of obsidian, or "show-stones" as he called them. In these, with the help of his skryer, Kelly, he conjured all sorts of visions, but none that foretold the obvious eventual fate of that young trickster. He prevailed upon Dee to accompany him to Prague where he intended to make a name for himself as an alchemist at the court of Rudolph II, Emperor of the Holy Roman Empire, and erratically subject to mild bouts of insanity. During one of his more intelligent periods Rudolph ordered Kelly imprisoned (Dee had already left for England), after Kelly had repeatedly failed to make gold as he had prom-

Above: *Pope Clement VII, who quite literally ate up a treasure.* Opposite: *Avicenna, or ibn-Sina, the greatest physician of 10th-century Islam, placed very little reliance on stones as healing agents, greatly preferring remedies from the plant kingdom. He did not, however, object to receiving gems as a fee for his services.*

ised. Rudolph, it seems, spent a great deal of money and had amassed an art and jewelry collection that eventually furnished the nucleus of three major European museums. Disappointed in Kelly's performance, it is highly possible that Rudolph had him dropped from the tower in which Kelly had been locked away.

There were other famous people with a penchant for crystals, among them Childeric, the father of France's first king, Clovis. The Duchess of Portland garnered five of them, which were sold in England in the aftermath of the French Revolution, and the Green Vaults at Dresden, capitol of the royal house of Saxony, boasted an enormous one weighing about fifteen pounds, and almost seven inches in diameter. Even Napoleon consulted a French seeress, though history does not record whether she warned him about Russia and Waterloo. Her grandson kept the art alive in the family, and he was fairly accurate in his predictions of the assassination of King Humbert of Italy and the attempt on the life of Alfonso XIII of Spain while returning from his wedding.

But for all the wonderment that arises around the lights and shadows that cross the minds of crystal-gazers, the crystals themselves sometimes offer even more. Anyone who has ever held a perfect hexagonal piece of rock crystal in his hand cannot but admire its purity of form, the beauty of geometry made visible. At times the quartz seems to surpass itself by containing a number of other similarly shaped crystals within its own body. These exactly repeat every angle, face, and point, looking for all the world like diminishing echoes of its form receding endlessly in space. Something similar also occurs in opaque quartz, with successive layers of crystal nesting one upon another. Another phenomenon, not very often seen, is the production of "cap" or "stilt" quartz in which the crystal is interrupted in its formation and creates a bulbous growth atop a slender vertical one. John Ruskin, the Victorian art and social critic, likened the contortions of one such aberrant crystal to a parasite causing sickly decay, exhibiting an image of decrepitude and dishonor. Not exactly a fair appraisal of a mineral that had met unexpected difficulties on its way to perfection, it is encouraging to know that the laws of physics, even as you and I, occasionally slip up.

123

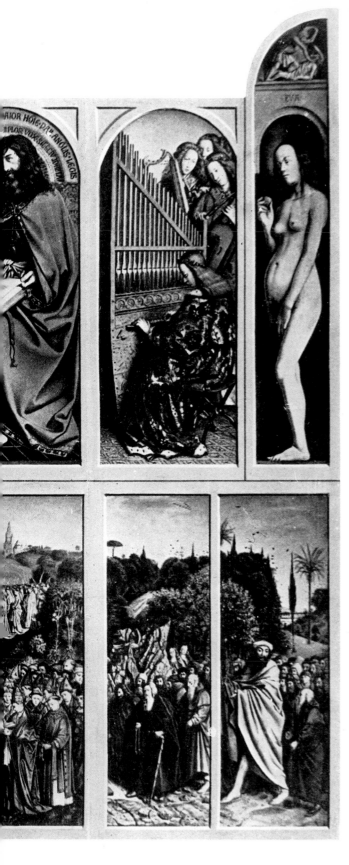

6

Chapter 6
STONES OF HEAVEN

From time to time there have been cynics who have questioned the Creator's wisdom when he included gems among his productions. Still others shift the blame of their creation entirely to Satan, who is given full credit for bringing them into the world. It seems, according to an old legend, that when Satan found that nothing useless had been created he became greatly disturbed. Things that were idle, vain, and sterile were the chief weapons in his arsenal of temptations, but finding none at hand with which to beguile newly created man Satan had to set about inventing some. He soon observed that Eve took great delight in the colors and shapes of flowers, and, following that lead, took some earth and fashioned it into clear, sparkling stones, such as diamonds. Then he extended the range of color and made rubies, emeralds, sapphires, and precious stones of every hue, all of which appealed so strongly to human covetousness, greed, and envy that ever since they have been the cause of much sin, crime, and sorrow. Whatever personal view one may take of Satan, it must be admitted that he has always been a superb psychologist, and a salesman with an unerring knowledge of how to motivate the market.

Nonetheless the gem and ornamental stones found their way into the scriptures of many faiths, and we find the celestial realms completely paved, piled, and plastered with them. At first there is very little or no mention of precious stones, although as time wore on everything became more and more elaborate and bejeweled. This, of course, is understandable, for the early hunting and agricultural societies put a very high premium on food rather than precious stones, and rightly so; they would have perished without it. A ragout of rubies does not nourish the stomach, and no more does a side of emerald, nor yet a tankard of crude oil to supply us with drink. Modern technology, in its haste to provide us with a free lunch,

seems to have overlooked those facts, and insists on serving us a plenitude of minerals, metals, hydrocarbons, and other indigestibles.

The earliest great civilization to emerge from the murk of barbarism was Sumer, and its repertoire of jeweled splendor was rather limited. Generally it revolves about lapis lazuli which, despite its sparse distribution throughout the world, is readily accessible in those areas where it is found, and has been mined for over four thousand years in Afghanistan. According to one of Sumer's legends, Inanna, goddess of the heavens and of love, descended to the underworld with the idea of taking its control from her sister, Ereshkigal. The route to that gloomy realm led through a mountain of lapis lazuli to a palace of lapis lazuli wherein Ereshkigal presided over all the dead. To gain entrance through the seven gates that barred the way, Inanna had to divest herself of her jewels and garments, giving up something at each gate until she came, naked and helpless, into Ereshkigal's judgment hall. Along the way she lost her measuring rod of lapis lazuli, a necklace of the same stone, and two other gems called *nunuz* stones, which even today remain unidentified. Their existence does inject some small variety into the otherwise monotonous catalogue of Sumerian gemstones; a monotony that resulted from the region's general lack of building stones and jewels.

Lapis lazuli also appears in the Gilgamesh legend, where that hero comes to the Garden of the Gods in his search for immortality. Although the questionable boon he is seeking is not there, he does find a tree with precious stones strewn about its trunk, leaves of the ever-present gem, lapis lazuli; and fruits made of jewels, pleasing to the eye but anything other than toothsome.

Farther to the west, midway between ancient Byblos and Baalbek, is Afqa where there was once

Preceding pages: *Jan van Eyck's* Adoration of the Lamb. *The panel of the Virgin shows her crowned with stars, represented terrestrially by jewels.* Above: *A genre painting by Petrus Christus of a Flemish couple presenting themselves to St. Eligius, a lapidary and pawnbroker. Their parents, who appear in the mirror at lower right, are approaching to stop the marriage. The saintly pawnbroker is shown surrounded by touchstones, examples of rings and pendants, gold and silver vessels, and seed pearls. He is weighing a ring.*

127

Specimen courtesy of The Collector's Cabinet

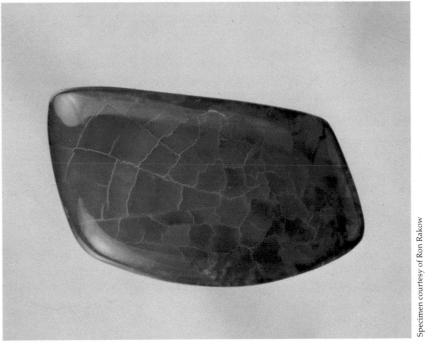

Specimen courtesy of Ron Rakow

Specimen courtesy of The Collector's Cabinet

Opposite: *A cube of Spanish pyrite, or "fool's gold."*
Actually, pyrite never contains true gold. Top: *Hematite's*
name comes from the Greek word for blood and refers to the stone's
internal color. Hematite is widely distributed throughout the
world. Above: *This 93-carat opal comes from one of the*
world's major sources of opals: Lightning Ridge, Australia.

129

a sanctuary to Astarte, the Phoenician Aphrodite. Nearby is the source of the Nahr Ibrahim, and the place where Tammuz, the Adonis of the Phoenicians, was slain. In proof of that the stream runs red with his blood every year. A seemingly supernatural occurrence, the phenomenon owes its appearance to an abundance of hematite in the area. Conditions at one season of the year cause minute particles of the stone, which is actually an oxide of iron, to flake off and be carried down into the stream, dying it a blood-red color. Occasionally mythology and metallurgy do meet.

With the rise of the later religious systems, beginning with Judaism, greater prominence was given to precious and semi-precious gems in regard to ritual, symbolism, and association. Five out of the seven Moslem heavens, for instance, are made of such stones; there being the House of Rest or Peace (Da'r al-Salam), formed of rubies and zircons; followed by the Garden of Eternity (Jannat al-Khuld), of yellow coral; the Garden of Delights (Jannat al-Na'im), all diamond; and the Garden of Eden (Jannat al-'Adn), which is of red pearl. And in Hinduism there is Vaikuntha, Vishnu's heavenly city, with walls and streets of gold, and palaces built entirely of precious stones. There one finds the Devas, or other deities, wearing jewels whose fire lights the sky like a hundred suns.

Even the essentially ascetic religions of Jainism and Buddhism make some slight reference to gems when describing the lives of their founders. Jina, who revealed Jainism to the world, chose to leave heaven in order to enlighten mankind. He descended as an embryo into the womb of Devananda after showing her fourteen favorable omens in a dream—one of them being a heap of jewels. For some reason, however, the gods decreed that he was to be born of another woman, Trisala, wife of King Siddhartha, and so transferred him to her. (That such sophisticated implant techniques were then available is, of course, entirely the result of divine abilities, for nothing is impossible to the gods.) On the night of Jina's birth Siddhartha's palace was miraculously showered with sandalwood, fruits, flowers, gold, silver, pearls, nectar, and diamonds; thereafter jewels do not figure in the story.

Buddhism, too, makes only a passing or occasional mention of gems, and, as in Jainism, it is chiefly a matter of poetic imagery. Buddha, in his final enlightened state, is spoken of as being enthroned on a giant golden lotus with a diamond stem formed by the Naga kings. Since the Nagas were snakes, usually cobras, perhaps this story is related to the myth of the guardian serpents of the valley of diamonds. Elsewhere there is the tale of Buddha's ascent to heaven so as to expound on his law to the gods. He remained with them for three months, finally returning to earth by means of a ladder whose sides were of gold and silver, with fixed rungs of coral, ruby, and emerald. Because materialism had no place in a creed that valued neither possessions nor power, but spiritual attainments instead, gemstones otherwise receive no attention in Buddhism.

In China the national passion for jade gave that stone much the same preeminence that lapis lazuli had in Sumer. There was Yu-ti, the Ancient One of the Jade, sometimes called the August Personage of the Jade, and he lived in a palace of jade fashioned in the same manner and with the same number and types of officials as could be found in the Imperial Court at Peking, its earthly counterpart. The realms over which he presided, heaven and the earth, were symbolized respectively by a disc of jade pierced through its center, the *pi,* and a square-sided length of jade bored from end to end with a circular tube, the *ts'ung,* or emblem of the earth.

The August Personage also had a wife, the Lady of the West, and she, too, lived in her own palace of jade, a structure nine stories high. It was surrounded by a garden in which the Peach Tree of Immortality grew, and in which the Eight Immortals dwelt and strolled. Somewhere else in the west, at its outer limit, was the Land of Extreme Felicity where K'un-lun rose, Mountain of the Immortals, site of the paradise and palace of Amithaba Buddha. In a lake with gold sands and shores of shining jewels just outside the palace there were lotus buds that opened eventually to release purified souls that lived forever within the paradise and palace itself. The garden about it was built on seven terraces, each with seven rows of trees, all with branches and leaves of precious stones that sent forth music when stirred by the gentle winds, bearing an echo from the Sumerian

Garden of the Gods where leaves of lapis lazuli gave the same effect.

One of the few places in China where lapis lazuli does take precedence over jade is in the Temple of Heaven, where all the ornamentation of the Emperor was appropriately made from that blue stone, although he stood on a disc of green jade while officiating. At the nearby Altar of Earth there was an octagonal tablet of yellow jade, and yellow jade adornments; while the Altar of the Sun called for red coral; and the Altar of the Moon demanded white jade. The four magnetic directions each had an altar as well: east being marked with a pointed piece of green stone, west with a white one, north with a semicircle of black stone, and south with an oblong of red jade.

In Japan the primal god, Izanagi, had a necklace of precious stones that he gave to his daughter, the Sun Goddess Ameratsu, who was also made ruler of the heavens. These gems became five male deities after Ameratsu's brother, Susanoo, crushed them between his teeth, and then breathed forth a newly made quintet of gods. Perhaps some fertility clinics should be set up in quiet precincts of our jewelry stores, but the patrons will certainly have to measure up to a stringent standard of dentition.

The only other gem-related connection with Japanese divinities seems to be that of the two jewels of the God of the Sea. Precisely what his precious stones were remains unmentioned, but he used them to regulate the tides—one for high, the other for low.

The rituals and literature of Judaism and Christianity give slightly more prominence to the existence of gemstones than can be found elsewhere, but even they do not exactly overdo it. The Book of Job lists six gemstones and speaks of mines, while other references occur in Exodus, Isaiah, Ezekiel, and the Apocalypse of St. John in the New Testament. Reading any of those texts in English translation gives the impression that all problems in finding exactly equivalent words have been fully resolved, and that rubies are the same stones as are now found in jewelry shops under that name, along with topaz, emerald, sapphire, and a few more. Unluckily nothing so simple is the case, since the original Hebrew texts have been either lost or destroyed. The earliest

version of the Old Testament that can be approximately dated is the Septuagint, compiled in Alexandria, Egypt, about 250 B.C., and that was a Greek dialect translation, *not* from Hebrew, but from Aramaic. Whoever ventures into that linguistic swamp, covered with a blanket of historical fog, is apt to lose his reason before emerging with enough facts to have made the journey worthwhile. Furthermore, he must be thoroughly conversant with at least nine ancient languages, plus Latin, and the histories and customs of all the people who spoke them. Nothing of that sort will be attempted here, to the vast relief of the author, editor, and all but the one or two readers passionately fond of exquisite accuracy.

Since Exodus provides us with the most famous list of precious stones, those in the breastplate of the High Priest, it is perhaps best to first examine that item, especially since echoes of it carry over into the imagery of the Apocalypse. The breastplate was made in response to divine command by one Aholiab, a lapidary of the tribe of Dan. He, incidentally, is worthy of more commentary than he generally receives, for he was the one who had to follow the complex instructions issued by Jehovah, and to do so under very trying circumstances. The Sinai desert, after all, is not an optimum location for a workshop.

First Aholiab had to obtain fourteen gemstones, each about two by two and one-half inches, according to the estimates of Biblical scholars, and, after shaping and setting them in golden mountings, he had to engrave each with the name of a tribe of Israel. There were, of course, twelve tribes, making a grouping of stones about seven and one-half inches wide by eight inches deep, and these were attached to a specially woven cloth that covered the chest of the High Priest. However, there were also two shoulder stones upon which were engraved the same tribal names—six to each shoulder—requiring Aholiab to exercise particular care in order to retain clarity and legibility. Undoubtedly his fingers, skilled as they may have been, were tired and cramped long before he finished his almost interminable task. It is noted, though, that Moses wrote the various names with ink, and then had a *shamir* passed over them in order to engrave the letters. While that may sound as though Aholiab was saved much

Specimens courtesy of The Collector's Cabinet

Figure courtesy of Jamie Androde

labor it really comes down to a lengthy process of abrasion, for *shamir* is simply emery, and, unless an exception was made in this instance, it would have had to "pass" more than once or twice.

As to the stones that Aholiab was instructed to use, there is some understandable difference of opinion concerning them. Both the Septuagint translation and Jerome's Latin Vulgate agree on the order of the first ten stones. They list sardius (our carnelian); topazius (our peridot); smaragdus (a green stone, often, but not always, emerald); anthrax or carbunculus (a glowing coal, usually considered to be garnet or ruby); sapphire (the old name for lapis lazuli); iaspis (our jasper); ligurius (generally regarded as amber); achates (our agate); amethystus (purple or amethystine quartz), and chrysolitus (citrine quartz). Number eleven according to the Septuagint is beryllion (modern beryl), and twelve is onychion (onyx); but the Latin Vulgate reverses these two, making the eleventh onychinus (onyx), and the twelfth beryllus (beryl). To round things off, the 1611 Authorized King James version, still reprinted, gives the following order of stones, without noting that any of the names may have indicated different gems in earlier times: sardius, topaz, carbuncle, emerald, sapphire, diamond (not in any previous translation), ligure, agate, amethyst, beryl, onyx, and jasper. Other authorities would add zircon and jade to the roster, but there seems to be little reason for adding any further ingredients to the puzzle, particularly since not a single stone is assigned a symbolic, historic, or religious significance. That task was left for later commentators, especially those of the medieval era, who constructed elaborate systems of symbolism based on connections between the stones of the High Priest's breastplate, and the foundations of the New Jerusalem in the Apocalypse.

Much controversy has raged over two items included in the description of the breastplate, the mysterious Urim and Thummim. Likening them to lenses or spectacles that enabled him to make an English language version out of the strange, graven characters his eyes beheld without them, in the 19th century Joseph Smith said that he used them to translate the golden plates of the Book of Mormon. In Exodus they were not used in that manner, but were worn over the heart as part of the ritual garment. One ingenious explanation had it that duplicates of the twelve stones were held within the Urim and Thummim, and would deliver an oracle when called upon to do so; the idea being that the stones were to be shaken about until three of them became visible through small openings, and thereupon the combination would provide a message for interpretation. It all sounds vaguely like a Las Vegas slot machine with its three bars, bells, or cherries, but much less expensive to operate.

Obviously something less elaborate was intended, and when the text of the passage from Exodus is read carefully a simpler explanation does emerge. It will be recalled that the names of Israel's tribes were engraved not only on the stones of the breastplate, but also on those that the High Priest wore on his shoulders. He customarily wore them in that manner when in full regalia before the public and when with his priests in the sanctuary, called "the holy place." Yet when he went "before the Lord," that is, into the Holy of Holies, where he alone might enter, he was required to place the names of all the tribes on his heart within the breastplate. Clearly the inscribed stones resting on his shoulders would have to be lifted from their settings and moved to a new position if that command was to be carried out. Hence the Urim and Thummim are likely to have been those same two stones under special ritualistic names, names applied to distinguish between the jewels of the right and left shoulders. That theory may or may not solve the mystery, but if it does not, there will be no lack of others in the future.

Rabbinical traditions, which never entered the Bible itself, were constructed about the stones of the breastplate and the visions of some of the prophets, and were elaborated upon in ever-greater detail. That practice was adopted by the Christians as well and accounts for the many commentaries that eventually appeared in Biblical texts, especially during the Middle Ages. The Apocalypse of St. John, since it listed the kinds of stones that formed the foundations of the New Jerusalem, was a particular favorite for that purpose. It permitted all manner of speculation about the colors, order of placement, and other properties of the various gems; and the amount of symbolism and allegory any one medieval author could attach to a single given word or phrase was staggering. Their minds were so delicately tuned to such convoluted modes of thought, so skilled at detecting similes and parallels, that they make the thinking processes of modern bureaucrats seem simplistic by comparison. If their methods had been applied to our tax forms the incidence of insanity would have risen sharply, but luckily it remained confined to literature and art where it produced masterpieces instead.

Two ecclesiastics who wrote on the topic of the New Jerusalem were the 9th-century archbishop of Mainz, Hrabanus Maurus, and Marbode, bishop of Rennes (A.D. 1035–1123). While both works are in general agreement, there are some differences between them, and Marbode's version, set in verse, undoubtedly benefited from the enormous popularity of his book *Of Stones.* Over 125 Latin manuscripts of it have survived, plus translations into seven other languages, and it is now in print in English as well.

The New Jerusalem was a celestial city that St. John had been shown while he was descending to earth during the Apocalypse. Its twelve gates were each shaped from separate large pearls, sawed in half by angelic carpenters, and they opened onto streets of gold so fine that they were as transparent as glass. The foundations of the city itself were made of twelve precious stones, arrayed in the following order: jasper, sapphire, chalcedony, emerald, sardonyx, sard, chrysolite, beryl, topaz, chrysoprase, jacinth, and amethyst. Each foundation bore within it the name of one of the twelve Apostles, who were considered the base upon which the heavenly city was built, and twelve, as a symbolic number, was sometimes used to represent the entire Church, that is, its saints, martyrs, clergy, and all its flock of the faithful. The similarity to the names of Israel's tribes inscribed on the separate gems of the High Priest's breastplate is immediately apparent; this occurred because everything in the New Testament was believed to parallel and expound on what had been said in the Old Testament.

Hrabanus and Marbode agreed that the primary stone, jasper, signified faith, which is why it was placed first, since nothing further could be erected in religious matters without its presence.

Hrabanus says nothing more, but Marbode further identifies the stone as green jasper, an appropriate color for something that retains eternal vigor and freshness. The second stone was sapphire, which was blue, the color of heaven and of hope; while the third was chalcedony, which conceals its beauty save in the bright light of day, and supposedly attracted chaff when warmed by the sun. That represented the hidden inner flame of charity, whose warmth was welcomed even by sinners.

That trio, of course, represents the three major theological virtues, upon which all else rests. Hrabanus likened emerald, the fourth stone, to faith in adversity; Marbode elaborated on this symbolism by recounting the myth of the one-eyed Arimaspians, who guarded against the maurauding of griffins and their attempts to steal the jewels from their place of origin. The griffins, of course, represent demons, and the Arimaspians those whose singleness of vision betokens a steadfast, unswerving purpose that keeps their spiritual eyes fixed on one master to the exclusion of all others. Besides the aerial attacks of the griffins, lions with the wings and beaks of eagles, the poor Arimaspians lived in desolate arctic regions of deepest cold, suffering an endless existence of adversity with never so much as two weeks in the Caribbean.

Sardonyx was the fifth stone and was of three different-colored layers; red on top, white in the center, and black at the base. Hrabanus said that red signified the suffering, and white the pure humility of saints, who saw themselves blackened by sin despite the virtues others attributed to them. Marbode repeats the same notion. Saintliness, it seems, has its own disadvantages, among which is a tendency to a guilt complex. Sard, the sixth stone, we now call carnelian. Its red color stood for the blood of martyrs. The seventh stone, chrysolite, we have renamed topaz. Hrabanus compares its clear golden color to true spiritual preaching together with the presence of miracles. Here the reasoning seems a little murky, but Marbode informs us that chrysos, meaning gold, should be understood as that combination of wisdom and charity that is more perfect than all the virtues, surpassing them as gold does all other metals.

Top: *The name of lapis lazuli means "stone of the color of the unclouded sky," and one can easily see why lapis lazuli has been chosen so often for sculpture of idealized terrains.* Above: *A Chinese* pi, *symbol of heaven.* Right: *Chinese vase of spinach-color jade.* Opposite: *A Chinese* t'sung, *symbol of earth.*

136

Object courtesy of Rare Art, Inc.

These Sumerian amulets of lapis lazuli and
agate were found in the tomb of Queen Shub-ad.

With beryl, the eighth stone, both Hrabanus and Marbode seem to be struggling in deep waters. Hrabanus speaks of beryl as representing the perfect operation of prophecy, but quite understandably does *not* say why. Marbode, somewhat more venturesome, compares it to water warmed by the shining of the sun, and says it represents those struck by the light of the true sun, that is, Christ, and who warm and aid others about them by reflecting that luminary. About the ninth stone, topaz, Hrabanus is quite arbitrary, saying that it symbolized the ardent contemplation of the prophecies. Marbode ascribes two colors to it, one golden, the other "more clear." Perhaps he means a yellow jasper and a transparent topaz, but that is by no means certain. However, he does say that the stone signifies those who love both God and their fellow men (differing markedly from Hrabanus), and so alerts us that there may be future argument and trouble even in Paradise.

There is more accord on the tenth stone, chrysoprase, which is likened to the work of martyrs and their reward by one authority, and hardship and labor occasioned by charity, by the other. Marbode, however, calls the stone purple despite the fact that everyone else labels it golden-green, as even its name when translated out of Greek indicates. Perhaps that may be an unintentional revelation of color-blindness on Marbode's part, for later he describes amethyst as being completely rosy red. Both writers agree that jacinth (our zircon), the eleventh stone, represents those whose minds can soar to ecstatic heights of insight and understanding, but who also have the gift of speaking clearly to those of duller or more humble wit. Marbode said that jacinth was chosen because it mirrored the atmosphere in which it was placed. It appears flashing and bright under clear skies, as when among those of quick intelligence; lusterless when cloudy, as when accommodating those who are slow to perceive.

Amethyst was the twelfth stone, and Hrabanus, for reasons of his own, chose it as representative of those humble souls who constantly kept the idea of heavenly standards in their thoughts. Marbode adds the explanation that they are the souls who possess the supreme virtue of praying for their persecutors, grieving more that sinners will be denied heaven than for any harm done to themselves. They are rare at the best of times, and exceedingly so among those who must pay taxes. Marbode also says that the totally *red* amethyst (which doubtfully exists) glows like the rosy flame of charity within their hearts, a coloration that he cheerfully accepts on someone else's authority.

There were female experts on the subject as well. For example, the Abbess Herrad of Landesberg (c. 1125–1195) wrote of the splendor of Lucifer before his fall from grace. As his name implies, he was a glowing, radiant spirit, the very essence of light, and beautiful to behold. Herrad, a painter as well as a writer, depicted him in the robes of a Byzantine emperor—brocaded silk embroidered with pearls, and heavily studded with gems. Rows of carnelian, topaz, jasper, chrysolite, onyx, beryl, sapphires, rubies, and emeralds were strewn upon the borders and hems of his garment, and on his forehead he bore a diadem set with a large ruby framed by four huge pearls. All in all he was made so conspicuous that it is no wonder he became afflicted with pride, particularly since his attendant angels were rather modestly garbed.

Because Lucifer was so gorgeously arrayed while he was among the angels, it is only to be expected that other members of the heavenly host would also be ornamented with precious stones. St. Gregory the Great, who was also Pope, and who gave us Gregorian chant, drew up a list of these celestial beings in the order of their nine ranks, and named the gems that were appropriate to each. First among them were the Seraphim, those fiery, purifying ministers of the Lord, each with six wings. Their jewel was the carnelian. In medieval paintings they are sometimes seen as small winged beings with red or vermilion flesh. Then come the Cherubim, who possess only a head between two wings; their gem was topaz. Occasionally they are depicted as being completely blue in color. The third group are the Thrones, and they are represented as wheels of fire with wings filled with eyes; their stone is jasper. Together those three orders, whose place was always nearest to the divine presence, were known as Counsellors.

Another group of three, called Governors, all wore the same costume: a long white alb, a golden

Opposite: *Apophyllite crystallizes out of warm, mineral waters in the cavities of volcanic rocks, and when subjected to heat will open up in leaflike layers that detach from each other.* Above: *Carving of a mountain in blue topaz.* Above right: *Wulfenite is a lead-bearing mineral named for F.X. Wulfen, an Austrian scientist.* Right: *Cabochons and eggs of jasper.*

girdle, and a green stole, that is, a ribbonlike strip that is draped about the neck. Save for their great wings they looked like human beings. They were ranked as Dominations, whose stone was chrysolite; Virtues, whose gem was the sapphire; and the Powers, whose jewel was beryl. A final trio of angels were known as Ministers, and they were garbed in soldier's armor, with golden belts, holding short spears and hatchets. The first of them were the Principalities whose stone was onyx; the second the Archangels, who were given rubies; and last, the Angels, who were assigned emeralds. With such personages thronging the golden streets of the Heavenly Jerusalem nobody could ever call it dull, and it was in total contrast to the disorder of the infernal regions where the population lacked all ornamentation, had flesh that was either deep black or dull blue, often covered with matted hair, and was spattered with all kinds of mire and ordure. The medieval theologians, it seems, were every bit as adept at manipulating a desirable image as any of their later counterparts on Madison Avenue, although their motives were a shade less suspect.

Still another heavenly ornament was the Crown of the Virgin Mary. One version of its composition was that it held six stars (the authentic astronomical variety) and six flowers (unspecified, although roses, columbines, and lilies, all associated with the Virgin, must have been among them). Between these were set the twelve stones of the New Jerusalem. Jan van Eyck's *Adoration of the Lamb*, now in the Cathedral of St. Bavo, Ghent, does show the Virgin so crowned, but with additional stars and flowers. In painted examples, such as the 15th-century triptych in the Cathedral of Moulins, the stars become the usual five-pointed ones made of gold, but the circlet of the crown is adorned with large rubies, sapphires, emeralds, and other gems. Stefan Lochner's *Madonna in the Rose Garden* shows a crown whereon the blossoms are made of jeweled petals, and it has a naturally formed diamond crystal with eight sides. The crown also bears two arches of pearls, and is topped by a large sapphire, whose blue color is always a characteristic of the Virgin's garments. The northern Gothic style of the 1400s appears to have fixed, for once and for all, the standard method of depicting Mary's crown, for the three above come from Flanders, France, and Germany, respectively.

The stars of the Virgin's crown remind us that those bright jewels of the skies, together with the planets, were long believed to exert strong influences on the lives and deeds of men. The tradition of associating and linking planets, signs of the zodiac, colors, and gemstones has a long history that culminated in the creation of astrology. The association probably began with the tower constructed by Borsippa, just beyond the city of Babylon, which had eight levels, the bottom one representing earth, and the other seven, each of a different color, dedicated to the sun, moon, and the five known planets. The lowermost step was black and stood for Saturn, or the Babylonian god Ninib. Above that tier came one colored orange, which was sacred to Jupiter, or Marduk, and higher still a red layer for Mars, or the Babylonian Nergal. The fourth level was gold for the sun, Shamash, then considered a planet, while the fifth was colored yellow for Venus, or Ishtar. Mercury, or Nebo, was marked by a blue step, and the last of the pile was silver for the moon god Sin. At the apex of the entire structure was a small chapel into which only the king might enter to pray to the gods for his city. The arrangement is reminiscent of the Holy of Holies, and, while there were only seven planets in the system, each was assigned a

The symbol of the melding of Christianity and Mithraism: the Abraxas god.

jewel, much in the same way as the twelve tribes of Israel were memorialized.

Among the earliest pairing of stones with astronomical bodies is the gem that Abraham is said to have worn. It supposedly had the property of curing any and all illnesses whenever it was looked upon by those who were sick. Unluckily for Abraham, it was of no avail to him in his own final days, for it had been decreed that he was to go to heaven and there receive the souls of all the faithful within his bosom. As recompense to suffering humanity his wonder-working stone was placed in the sun. So, ever since, the pains and ills that increase during the hours of darkness are eased with the sunrise. King Necho of Egypt possessed a similar stone of green jasper, upon which was carved the image of the dragon, Agathodaemon, whose head was surrounded by rays of light shining forth like a halo. It must be admitted that its powers were extremely limited in comparison with Abraham's omnipotent stone, for this one was useful for digestive ailments only. And Galen, a famed Greek physician of the 2nd century A.D., further diminished the esteem in which that dragon was held by saying that it was only the stone, not its carven image, that held any value. He had bought a necklace of green jasper, made from plain pierced stones, and said that it benefited his stomach as much as if it had borne the likeness of the dragon-god on every stone.

Yet another talisman, worn as either a ring or an amulet, was the Abraxas god of the Gnostics. This strange little creature, who was first described at Alexandria by Basilides, was composed of a mixture of the many creeds and deities that flourished there among those who were not committed to either Judaism or Christianity of the orthodox variety. The Abraxas god is really not a god at all, but a symbol that weds some Christian doctrines to Mithraic ones. His head is that of a cock (symbol of vigilance) and of Mithra (the sun and also Christ's resurrection). In his right hand he holds a whip, signifying triumph; while on his left arm he bears a shield as a defense of his faith and soul. This notion of defense of his faith is further reinforced by his tunic and cuirass. These both symbolize the higher principles of man, and a means of defense against evil. From the hem of his tunic down, his legs become a twin-headed serpent, the amphisboena, symbolic of a balance of forces, representing the self establishing internal harmony by overcoming its own evil tendencies. The serpent, because it sheds its outer skin, thus renewing itself, is also a symbol of the resurrection. Accompanying the figure are the letters IOA, sometimes in Roman characters or sometimes in Greek—iota, alpha, omega—and thus acronymic of Iesus, Alpha and Omego, that is, Jesus, the Beginning and the End. Such a seal engraved on a gem was believed to confer spiritual protection against all evil and temptation on its owner. If the stone was a heliotrope, or bloodstone, it would stop hemorrhaging as soon as applied to the bleeding area. Giorgio Vasari, who wrote about the lives of the artists and architects of the Renaissance, was stricken in that manner while in a church at Arezzo. His companion, the painter Luca Signorelli, immediately took a bloodstone amulet from his pocket and placed it down Vasari's back, whereupon the flow of blood instantly ceased. Despite Mithra, Abraxas, and Christ, however, such a stone may not work today because the force of the stars upon any gem is said to lessen with the passage of years; so that weakness eventually necessitates a replacement.

Gemstones, because they were the hardest objects in creation, were supposed to retain the astral influences of the planets and stars much longer than any other substances, which is why they were so frequently graven into amulets and talismans. Great care had to be taken to choose the most propitious moment to begin and end the carving, as well as to match the proper stone and sign of the zodiac with the benefits that its future owner desired from it. Very often complicated calculations had to be made that took into account the purchaser's horoscope, the changing actual positions of the stars and planets while being formed, the nature of any spiritual beings linked to the stone, and a few other items necessary to bring all factors into perfect compatability. For instance, every planet had its own guardian angel, as did the days of the week, and if these happened to be opposed to each other or to the qualities inherent in the stone, the project might very well be scrapped. While astrology brought many a customer to the jeweler or lapidary, it also caused an immense amount of rigamarole, and computations that would boggle many a modern computer. Perfectly formed and flawless stones were also required, for any slight imperfection rendered the entire operation null and void, and, according to Hindu beliefs, could cause actual harm.

Specific cutting designs were prescribed for ring stones meant to be worn on the varying days of the week, and each day and planet was under the protection of a deity and a guardian angel as well. Sunday's god was Apollo, the sun god; the guardian angel was Michael; the preferred design was a lion; and the stone was to be a diamond. However, if the prospective client for such a stone had been born before the latter part of the 15th century, nobody could satisfy his Sunday birth requirements, since it was only after that time that diamonds could be engraved or faceted. Nor was that the only case where difficulties might be expected. Take Tuesday, which was consecrated to Mars and under the care of the angel Samael. It demanded the figure of a scorpion be cut on an emerald, which was a stone known to be under the influence of both Venus and Jupiter. Contradictions of that sort abound, and the more one attempts to reconcile the differences the greater the difficulties, somewhat like piling numbered balls in sequence—vertically.

The reason for the problems is not hard to discover, since one has only to look at the historical development of astrology, and the various cultures that had a part in constructing its traditions. In early Sumerian times, and in the later Babylonian era, individual interests were outside the area of consideration, while only the welfare of the state and its populace were sought. Even then, only five planets entered into the calculations, plus the sun and moon. Disregarding the obvious error that the latter were not planets, there remains the fact that three more planets, Uranus, Neptune, and Pluto, were not included in any of the computations made before 1781, when Uranus was discovered. For that matter, poor neglected Pluto had to wait until the 20th century to be found lurking outside everybody's horoscope, doing God alone knows what to the most exquisitely devised calculations. Nor does Pluto have any gemstone assigned to it.

Flaws of this nature, and the outright charlatanry of some astrologers, brought the entire art into disrepute beginning in the 16th century. In fact, one noted astrologer, Jerome Cardan, who was also a mathematician, physician, and a poet as well as something of a naturalist, grew quite disturbed at the state of decline that he witnessed. He was aware that such authorities as St. Augustine and St. Thomas Aquinas, with other members of the clergy, had not rejected astrology although they disapproved of its flirtation with magic. Thus, when casting his own horoscope, which predicted his demise in 1576, he is said to have starved himself to death in that year so as not to bring discredit on the "science."

In any case, astrologers in general did not include the signs of the zodiac in their figuring until about 700 B.C., nor did they establish the twelve essential divisions until about 550 B.C. About two centuries later the practice began to move westward to influence the course of affairs in Greece and Rome, and it was about then that the Greeks instituted the individual horoscope. Later developments in the Christian, Arab, and Jewish worlds gradually built up layers of superstition, compiling lists of stars, planets, signs, and supernatural beings that were attached to gemstones. Much of that astrological lore traces back to the writings of Censorianus, whose book, *Of the Day of Birth*, has permeated many of the usages existing to the present, despite the fact that it was written about A.D. 238. All in all astrology is not as ancient as some of its practitioners would have us believe.

The concept of the stones of Israel's twelve tribes became interwoven with the twelve signs of the zodiac. This, of course, became linked with the twelve months of the year, and that meant each acquired a special birthstone. Stones were also assigned to the twelve prophets, to the foundations of the New Jerusalem, as mentioned earlier, to each of the twelve Apostles, and, in medicine, to the twelve principal members of the body. The resulting combinations made hash of the systems so carefully worked out in simpler, less ecumenical times, and as the governing factors increased it became more and more difficult to reconcile their separate properties; they frequently canceled out one another. The number twelve, found repeatedly in those groupings, was regarded as a divine number by which all heavenly things were to be measured, and was esteemed as the number of grace, perfection, time, experience, and knowledge. Its connection with the zodiac is obvious, but much less so with such things as knowledge and perfection.

At this point perhaps a few lists and tables might be in order to show exactly what stones belong to what day, month, planet, or sign, and to what deities or angels they may be connected.

The gems of the weekdays are as follows: Sunday, Topaz or Diamond; Monday, Moonstone, Pearl, or Crystal; Tuesday, Jasper, Ruby, or Emerald; Wednesday, Crystal, Amethyst, or Lodestone (Magnetite); Thursday, Sapphire or Carnelian; Friday, Emerald; and Saturday, Turquoise.

Much of the below was changed in August of

Birthstone Table (Old Style)

Month	Stone	Sign	Guardian Angel	Angel's Stone
January	Garnet	Aquarius	Gabriel	Onyx
February	Amethyst	Pisces	Barchiel	Jasper
March	Jasper or Bloodstone	Aries	Malchediel	Ruby
April	Diamond or Sapphire	Taurus	Ashmodei	Topaz
May	Emerald or Agate	Gemini	Amriel	Garnet
June	Agate or Emerald or Cat's Eye	Cancer	Muriel	Emerald
July	Turquoise or Onyx	Leo	Verchiel	Sapphire
August	Carnelian or Sardonyx	Virgo	Hamatiel	Diamond
September	Chrysolite	Libra	Tsuriel	Jacinth
October	Aquamarine Beryl or Opal	Scorpio	Bariel	Agate
November	Topaz	Sagittarius	Adnachiel	Amethyst
December	Ruby or Bloodstone	Capricorn	Humiel	Beryl

1912 when the National Association of Jewelers, in solemn convocation assembled at Kansas City, Missouri, decreed the new order of birthstones to be as follows:

January–Garnet
February–Amethyst
March–Bloodstone
April–Diamond
May–Emerald
June–Pearl
July–Ruby
August–Sardonyx
September–Sapphire
October–Opal
November–Topaz
December–Turquoise

The Guardian Angels, either uninvited or not in accord with an unorthodox arrangement, remain unmentioned in this list.

For the ancient system of seven planets there was also a list of appropriate stones. To the sun was assigned the sapphire or the diamond, and to the moon, rock crystal. Mars was represented by emerald or jasper, while Mercury, probably be-

cause it symbolized trade and drew everything to it, was signified by the lodestone (magnetite) or by the almost mythical alectorius, an ordinary stone converted to value by the labor and rarity of its production. Jupiter was given either carnelian or emerald, and Venus had amethyst or pearl. The last, Saturn, was possessed of turquoise or onyx. The sign of each planet was, quite naturally, the best and most effective design to carve into its particular stone, but even that could be heightened by adding the image of a favorable god, or a combination of symbols that guaranteed more varied powers to the gem. Even the catalogued stars were granted stones of their own that were worn to direct the powers of that star to the person who carried the gem. Thus Aldebaran was paired with garnet; Asgol with diamond; Canis Major, or the Dog Star, with beryl; the Pleiades with rock crystal; and Ashaiot with sapphire, to mention only a few. Most of the named stars were labeled by the Arab astrologers, who were among the first to add them to the ever-expanding list of items necessary for their calculations.

Even the seasons were decked out with jewels: emerald for Spring, ruby for Summer, sapphire for Autumn (though topaz would seem more appropriate) and diamond for Winter. Those stones could readily be grouped and sometimes even combined to create a wardrobe of gems to be worn throughout the year. As for anniversaries—enough of them are marked by precious stones to keep a married couple only one step ahead of bankruptcy through all their wedded life. Between the twelfth and nineteenth anniversaries they are called upon to celebrate successively with agate, moonstone, moss agate, rock crystal, topaz, amethyst, garnet, and zircon. Thirteen more occasions over the years will find them back at the jewelers for sapphire (23rd), star sapphire (26th), pearl (30th), coral (35th), cat's-eye (39th), ruby (40th), alexandrite (45th), star ruby (52nd), emerald, (55th), canary diamond (60th), gray star sapphire (65th), purple star sapphire (67th) and finally diamond on their seventy-fifth, if they are still surviving the course. Nothing is programmed beyond that point. It is notable that the thirteenth stone is moonstone, marked with a line of light, and supposed to beneficially neutralize all bad luck connected with that number. The same is

The twelve signs of the zodiac, shown in this 15th-century Italian woodcut, marked the path of the sun's imagined orbit around the earth. They are seen here on one of the chief astronomical instruments of the Middle Ages, an armillary sphere.

true for all five multiples of thirteen on the list.

Further prescriptions for setting stones to ensure maximum efficacy consisted of putting them into specially selected metals. Onyx was to be placed only in lead, the metal of Saturn, to whom the stone was also subject. Copper was to be used for jasper; silver for carnelian and rock crystal; and tin for sapphire, amethyst, emerald, topaz, and jacinth, a directive that would break any self-respecting jeweler's heart.

Particular designs were also to be engraved on certain stones for special purposes. For instance, a dragon on a ruby guaranteed that the owner would be healthy, happy, and rich, and if he could afford the stone he was probably already in at least one of those states. A falcon on a topaz insured the goodwill of the rich and powerful, while a lion on a garnet guarded one's health, honor, and safety. These and similar designs added specific powers to an individual's arsenal of defenses against any unkind actions of fate that the heavens might try to impose.

In India, as might be expected, there was as much if not more interest in avoiding the harshness of the fates as there ever had been in the West. One method was to make offerings to the gods at their temples or shrines. Rubies offered to Krishna ensured that the worshiper would be reborn as an emperor; however, if his offering was only a single small ruby he could expect to be no more than a king. Emeralds brought perfect knowledge of the soul and of eternity. Diamonds opened the path to Nirvana, where eternal life in the highest heaven was assured. There was also the custom of offering birthday gifts to the divinities. On such occasions the image of the god was robed in the finest garments and jewelry from the temple's treasury. A worshiper might dedicate a gift of jewels to the god, and it would then continue to be worn for a fixed period of time until it lost its sacred religious character. Perhaps its association with humanity, even at a distance, caused it to become contaminated, bringing about its eventual removal. Such decorations were then sold to defray every kind of temple expense, and were eagerly purchased by pious believers who valued the fact that the stones had been in intimate contact with the gods. Although no longer sacred, they were believed to have acquired other characteristics valuable to humans by having been sanctified objects, and could become potent forces for bringing about good health, good fortune, and a happy destiny in future life for their new owners.

Among the jewels or ornaments used for that purpose was the nine-gemmed jewel called the *naoratna*. This consisted of nine stones set in a prescribed order that made a ring. Each element of the design was related to the seven planets and to the ascending and descending nodes of an astrologer's chart. The sun was represented by a ruby and was placed in the center. Around it to the east was a diamond for Venus (who is often skilled at obtaining them); to the southeast a pearl for the moon; and to the south coral for Mars. Set to the southwest was a zircon to signify the ascending node; to the west a sapphire for Saturn; a topaz in the northwest for Mercury; then a cat's-eye to the north for the descending node; and finally a topaz in the northeast for Jupiter. In the Orient the nodes are frequently called the Dragon's Head and Dragon's Tail, both important factors for astrological calculations. The entire *naoratna* ornament was designed to bring about the most favorable influences of all the heavenly bodies, and generally worked even before it was owned, since only the very wealthy could ever afford it.

Such a valuable instrument might have come to the aid of Western astrologers in 1524 when a second deluge was foretold. All of the planets were foreseen to gather in the sign of Pisces in that year, a sure indication of a devastating flood. One gentleman in Toulouse took the prediction seriously and built an Ark in preparation for the event. Unfortunately, 1524 was a year of record drought, and how he floated his craft no one will ever know. As for the astrologers who lost their reputations because of a bad forecast, they had the consolation of remaining alive and undrowned. No doubt the three ignored planets, Uranus, Neptune and Pluto had something to do with the great miscalculation, especially Neptune. However, the discomfited prophets of doom had no way of getting the full and correct data for another four centuries, when knowledge of the missing planets would allow their consideration in astrological calculations.

7

Chapter 7
THE ROYAL COLLECTORS

The modern museum, with its carefully classified and arranged exhibits of related materials, is a concept that the Middle Ages never envisioned. Despite the outpouring of masterpieces in medieval times there was never a notion that works of art could serve any purpose apart from lavish display or of providing sumptuous additions to luxurious living. The idea that they might have historical importance did surface occasionally, but never consistently, and certainly never with the intention of aiding the cause of learning by providing collections for study. The unlucky result of that lack of concern was that many items, invaluable for their association with great personages or great events, have been lost beyond recall.

One such example is a gift of four jeweled rings made by Pope Innocent III to King John of England. All that survives is a letter in which the pope enjoined John to consider what each of the separate jewels represented, and to be guided in his future conduct by the virtues they represented. Those were the practice of faith, hope, charity, and good works as symbolized by an emerald, sapphire, ruby, and opal, and they were to be worn as lasting reminders of what the pope expected of the king. The occasion was the end of a quarrel about the choice of a new archbishop of Canterbury, in which John was forced, under threat of interdict and a crusade, to submit to the pope's decision. No doubt John wished the rings out of his sight as soon as possible, and probably hastened to convert them into cash without a thought of their historical value. Had there been a suitable repository for permanently lodging such items they might have been preserved, but in those days usually only holy relics were thought to be worth keeping, and King John, by common consent, was not considered to have a scrap of holiness in any part of his physical or spiritual

constitution—being a thorough rotter.

With the beginning of the Renaissance, however, even the crowned heads of Europe became caught up in the quest for learning, and many of them established curio cabinets, art chambers, and treasure rooms within their palaces. Much of this activity took place north of the Alps in those countries that were then becoming the new centers of power. England, France, and Germany were in the forefront of a shift away from the former economic and military leadership of the Italian and Byzantine regions, and they suddenly found themselves creating vast new wealth through improved commerce, technology, and conquest.

Mineral-rich Saxony, where silver and lead were mined in great quantities, became wealthy on its proceeds, but wasted many of the gains in the religious and political wars that swept central Europe after the Reformation. Even so, its rulers maintained an extravagant style of living for over two centuries, and were among the first to create the ancestors of our present art and natural history museums. At Dresden, Maurice of Saxony and his brother and successor, Augustus, established a collection that was later to become one of the most notable in the world. While it is true that those two princes furnished the money and necessary approval for the project, it is highly doubtful that they were as aware of its necessity as was their advisor in the matter, Georgius Agricola, their appointed Historiographer of Mines, the so-called Father of Mineralogy.

Since 1170, after their initial discovery at Freiberg, silver and lead had been extracted from the mountains of Saxony. From then on, until the collection at Dresden was brought together, numerous other ore samples and gemstones had poured forth in profusion, and Agricola was the first to realize the importance of bringing some

Preceding pages: *King John during one of the many unhappy moments of his reign—signing the Magna Carta. Although Pope Innocent III sent him a gift of four rings, he also placed an interdict on England, excommunicated John, and negotiated with John's enemies for an invasion of England.* Above: *This portait of Henry VIII captures the "frugality" of the king's attire.*

order into their study. He circulated among the miners, amassing and recording all kinds of data, and informed his royal patrons that their subterranean wealth far exceeded all else that they had on earth. In 1550 he finished his book *De re metallica (Of Things Metallic)*, dedicating it to both Maurice and Augustus. It did not issue from the press until 1556, some short time after Agricola's death in 1555. Although it was the first attempt to classify minerals, the work is still valuable and remains in print today; it is a monument to the perceptive ability and accuracy of its author. It is particularly useful for its information about early mining methods and techniques of removing and refining ores, much of which can still be seen clearly in its 269 woodcut illustrations.

Agricola's continued search for prime geological specimens was bound to influence the course of the collections at Dresden, and finally evolved into the famous Green Vaults, the Grünes Gewölbe, one of the world's most spectacular displays of jewelry. At first a rather heterogeneous mixture of minerals, scientific instruments, books, and objects of art, combined with the workshop of the Elector Augustus I, it was housed within only seven rooms of the palace. As Saxony's silver mines provided an expanding source of revenue, a similar expansion occurred in the number and kinds of objects collected, finally requiring eight extensive locations, some in buildings specially constructed for the purpose of displaying all of them.

Within a period of about one hundred years the Electors of Saxony gained an enviable reputation for the quality and extent of their artistic holdings. New luster was then added to that fame when Augustus the Strong succeeded to the throne of Saxony in 1697, for he carried on and enlarged the collecting tradition already in action. His designation as "The Strong" was no idle bit of flattery since he did possess great physical strength, and on at least one occasion broke an iron horseshoe in two with his bare hands. It was under his patronage that the great goldsmith and jewel designer Johann Melchior Dinglinger established a workshop in the Grünes Gewölbe. There he created a stream of masterpieces, becoming known at last as the Benvenuto Cellini of Saxony. And if his name sounds suggestive of a ringing

bell it is fully in keeping with his abilities, for his designs and craftsmanship were cause for celebration almost every time he created jewelry.

Although he made many objects, only a few were ever signed by him, and all of those are to be found in the Green Vaults where they originated. For a time his workshop was a family enterprise, comprising his two brothers, Georg Christopher and Georg Friedrich, as well as himself. There he carved and signed a chalcedony vase, which became known as the Bath of Diana; created the Obelisk Augustalis, made of gold, enamel, and jewels; a Temple of Apis; a golden coffee service for Augustus; and a composite piece, the Birthday of the Great Mogul. This last was a fanciful bit of Orientalia showing the royal court at Delhi paying tribute to their ruler, Aurangzeb. It consisted of 132 movable pieces such as costumed courtiers, horses, elephants, soldiers, and the Great Mogul himself seated upon his throne. All were of gold liberally studded with gems, and the entire assemblage was a dazzling procession, equally as gorgeous in its imagery as the actuality in India must have been. In a sense it was a royal plaything not unlike the maneuvering of toy soldiers on parade, but instead of lead and bright paint there were emeralds, rubies, sapphires, and diamonds encrusting masses of gold.

Augustus the Strong had not been the first to surround himself with a blaze of jewels, for his immediate predecessor, John George IV, had elaborate caparisons for the horses that drew the royal coach. There were at least three sets of harness and trappings, the most modest of which carried some 500 pearls, while the other two each displayed 550 rubies and 700 diamonds. They were all exhibited in the saddlery of the Johanneum Museum, separate and apart from the Green Vaults where the crown jewels of Saxony were to be seen. The Crown owned a green diamond of 48½ carats set in a hat clasp, and a 59-carat brilliant-cut diamond to ornament a shoulder knot. A bow containing some 662 diamonds, and the royal regalia of Poland, were also shown with the other precious stones, as well as a large collection of cups and vessels made out of agate, jasper, onyx, rock crystal, and lapis lazuli.

The treasures at Dresden continued to grow, thanks to the undiminished output of the mines,

Above: *Jane Seymour, Henry VIII's third wife.* Right: *Frederick the Great inherited his armies from his father, Frederick William I, who traded gems and precious objects for the dragoons and grenadiers of foreign princes.*

153

VICTORIA

and were further augmented by the production of superb porcelain. With wealth the acquisition of art gradually took precedence over efficient administration of government, and one of the earliest signs came with Augustus the Strong's decision to trade a regiment of Saxon dragoons to Prussia in exchange for some porcelain vases. With the accession of Augustus III luxury triumphed, for not only did he neglect his duties as a ruler in favor of his collections, but left the economy of Saxony in bankruptcy at his death in 1763 after losing the disastrous Seven Years' War to Frederick the Great of Prussia. Apparently nobody had told Augustus III that countries needed revenue every bit as much as princes, perhaps even more, and that power politics put greater reliance on cannons than on connoisseurs.

One ruler who never needed instruction in that regard was Henry VIII. Although he thoroughly enjoyed collecting, and was a patron of the arts, Henry never impoverished his treasury on that account. A survey of portraits done of him will quickly show that, while he was as fond of making a rich display as any other king, he also possessed a certain frugality in the matter of purchasing gems. Twenty-nine jewels consistently decorated his doublet, the sleeved garment directly beneath his outer surcoat. All were step-cut rubies, or possibly even garnets or spinels, but since it is impossible to subject their painted images to mineralogical analysis there is no certainty about them. Each was set in a gold clasp, suggesting that they could be moved from garment to garment as necessity might dictate, or as the cloth wore out. His collar, draped over both shoulders, held fourteen stones, a pendant another four, while his plumed and velvet cap carried an additional eight. Customarily Henry also wore three rings, and had several small jewels set into his sword hilt and guard, for a total of sixty-one. Not many people could find the room to exhibit that many gems on their person, nor to bear up under the weight, but Henry had amplitude enough for all of it and more. In his latter years he achieved such monumental girth that a specially designed surcoat became necessary to keep his corpulence under wraps. At first it bore only six more gems than the total on his doublet, but as Henry expanded twenty-two others were added. Fortunately for

England he died at the age of fifty-six, before it became a prohibitive expense to cover him. That, in any case, was as hopeless a task as making an elephant inconspicuous, or eligible for a list of the well-dressed.

Quite noticeably in Henry's time, stones were no longer restricted to the cabochon style, but were varied in form and sharply cut. That difference resulted from the use of diamond dust in shaping the harder gemstones such as ruby, sapphire, topaz, and emerald. A prime example can be seen in a pendant brooch belonging to Henry's third wife, Jane Seymour. In that jewel the stones are cut to present her initials on either side of a crucifix, an appropriate device for the wife of the "Defender of the Faith," as Henry was somewhat inaccurately called.

Jane Seymour, whose family changed its name from St. Maur in the 14th century, had a liking for jewelry with religious overtones about it. She had a Cross of St. Anthony Abbot, in the form of a T, which was made from sapphires, and a pendant that symbolized the three persons of the Holy Trinity. God the Father was an oval-cut sapphire, God the Son a rectangular ruby, and the Holy Spirit was a drop-shaped pearl. The Court painter, Hans Holbein, who had been trained as a goldsmith, reputedly designed the piece that Jane wears in the wedding portrait that he made of her. If that *is* the case then both Holbein and the jeweler commissioned to execute the work had to produce it in a hurry, and because of Henry's well-known temper, they had to do it well. Wedding, portrait, and jewel all came about in the spring of 1536, the year that the artist entered Henry's service, and there is little doubt but that Holbein extended himself to ensure a favorable outcome. Unluckily for Jane Seymour the talisman that was to shelter her from harm did not offer any protection when she gave birth to the future Edward VI, for she died shortly after, and he was sickly for all of his brief life.

In many of the portraits of that age subjects can be observed wearing a multiplicity of rings, for they adorned every finger of both hands, and sometimes even the thumbs. Today that would create a rather gaudy, vulgar effect, but the rich velvets, silks, brocades, and gold thread of Tudor costumes outshone any display that mere rings

Opposite: *A youthful Queen Victoria, wearing one crown and standing beside the Imperial Crown.* Below: *Rudolph II's updated version of the crown of the Holy Roman Empire.*

155

could provide. Besides, the rings had to compete with gem-studded collars, chains, pendants, clasps, sword and dagger hilts, and more, since almost every Tudor aristocrat looked like a perambulating jewelry shop and would not have passed unmolested for the length of one of our modern city streets.

Such a collection of precious stones, particularly those belonging to the king, required special housing and an efficient inventory and keeper. For centuries they had been kept in the Jewel House at Westminster, which acted as the king's wardrobe and personal treasury. In 1532 Thomas Cromwell became Henry VIII's Master of the Jewels, which seemed at first like setting a hungry hound to guard a butcher shop, for Cromwell had helped Cardinal Wolsey to strip more than one monastery of its wealth. Not being even faintly stupid he refrained from letting any of Henry's wealth slide into his own pockets, especially after seeing Wolsey's fate when that ill-advised man tried to outshine the king. Cromwell was discreet, commonly wearing, at most, only one or two rings; he was more interested in power than in baubles. His craftiness soon advanced him to the post of lord chancellor and the title of Earl of Essex; then he finally made the fatal error of persuading Henry to marry Anne of Cleves. The ceremony over and the wedding yet to be consummated, Henry contracted a violent case of loathing-on-first-night, for Anne had brought him a goodly number of warts with her dowry. Within the year Cromwell was tried on charges other than the real one, and lost his post, title, and head on the executioner's block. It obviously did not pay to present Henry with a flawed jewel of any kind, and it was plain that Cromwell's otherwise shrewd and penetrating vision had not penetrated deeply enough.

A little over a century later another Cromwell named Oliver, great-great-grandnephew of Thomas, also became involved with royalty and the crown jewels. In his case, however, it was not to provide care for either, but to destroy them. As much of the royal regalia as Cromwell could lay his hands on was put under the hammer and smashed, showing the keen sense of history customary among fanatics of whatever persuasion. And like many others of that ranting breed, he was still careful enough in his outbursts against the sin of luxury to determine the cash value of the overthrown sinner's possessions. At the time of the Commonwealth the ancient crown of St. Edward, dating back at least to his coronation in 1043, was valued at £248, and consisted of gold filigree set with a variety of stones. Queen Edith's crown, as consort to King Edward the Confessor, was much less valuable, being estimated at no more than £16. No doubt that infuriating discovery led to more vigorous destruction of other objects, for the only value the crown had was in its silver-gilt, all of the gems being imitations. Nonetheless Cromwell had no real complaint, for what he lost through Queen Edith he more than made up for through Edward, since duplicates existed of both. One set was kept at Westminster in the Jewel House for use at coronations, and the other at the Tower of London for wear on state occasions. Much the same situation exists today, with the coronation items on display at the Tower, perpetually crowded with visitors, and a far less packed and inconvenient exhibit of facsimiles in the crypt of Westminster Abbey. Both sets are eye-filling, to say the least, and, given the traditional duplicity of governments, who can say which set, if either, is real?

Although the original royal regalia was destroyed, some fragments of it did survive, notably the spinel known as the Black Prince's Ruby. As for the jewels of Henry VIII and Elizabeth I, all have disappeared without a trace save for those commemorated in their portraits. Holbein has already made us familiar with Henry's treasury of jewels, and has portrayed them with an eye that was almost microscopically accurate. Elizabeth never had the fortune to be painted by as great a master, and her imperious will and vanity may very well have prevented that from happening. Her official painter was Nicholas Hilliard, an able goldsmith and miniaturist, as Holbein had also been, but never a master of the same rank. Deft enough at decorating her gowns with a profusion of gems, Hilliard never quite succeeded in making Elizabeth's face take on the same degree of reality as he did her costumes. In one of his portraits of the Queen, now at Hatfield House, some of the jewels that cascade down her dress, bedizen her coiffure, and border the tops of her puffed sleeves, have a familiar look about them. A number of the gold-bordered rubies and sapphires seem to have been made over, with but little if any modication, from the clasps worn on Henry VIII's doublet. A comparative survey of Elizabeth's portraits and those of her father might very well establish some similarities.

Elizabeth seems to have been partial to pearls to a far greater extent than her father, for they are liberally distributed over the fabric of many of her gowns and headdresses, in combination with lengthy, many-stranded necklaces. One such painting in London's National Portrait Gallery shows her standing before her crown and sceptre wearing a long string of pearls with only a few rubies bordering the stomacher of her dress. The crown in that picture is partially obscured in shadow, making it difficult to see all details clearly, but it seems to be of a slightly different design from that of Edward VI or of James I. Still another painting at Hatfield House, a decidedly allegorical and symbolic one, shows the same enormously long necklace; to it are added pearl drops in her hair, pearl earrings, still more in an elaborate headdress that seems to represent a basket of plenty, and circlets of pearls hanging from her wrists. A few rubies and sapphires, enough to guarantee a lifetime income for most people, are also visible, but the pearls are the most prominent items, probably because they seemed emblematic of a virgin queen. Much humor has been expended on that virginity, and it could even be said that her favorite palace, Nonesuch, was named in honor of it; Elizabeth lived and died in loneliness, isolated by her position and the need to keep her nation from any alliance by marriage.

Although the Commonwealth under Cromwell made no use of a crown, Cromwell's own coinage shows one surmounting the arms of the Commonwealth itself, an odd and anomalous circumstance that brings his intentions into question. There was no question, though, but that the destroyed regalia had to be replaced for the coronation of Charles II at the Restoration in 1660. An attempt was then made to replicate St. Edward's crown, but upon what basis is not clear. Nothing, however, was skimped in the process for the crown weighs five pounds and, mercifully for the sovereign who has to bear it, is removed after the opening ceremonies and replaced by the lighter Imperial State Crown. It is set with faceted diamonds, step-cut rubies, amethysts, sapphires, and emeralds, the largest of which has additional triangular facets, and is a total anachronism. That kind of lapidary work was impossible in the 11th century when the original crown was made.

Eleven years after the crown, orb, and staff of St. Edward had been recreated they fell into an adventure of their own. In 1671 Colonel Thomas Blood, a landed Irishman who was something of a 17th-century hit man, made an attempt to steal all of them from the Tower, and very nearly succeeded. He and his two accomplices tricked the Keeper of the Regalia, an elderly man named Talbot Edwards, into giving them access to the treasures and then overpowered him, leaving him for dead as they tried to flee the scene. Blood clutched the crown under his cloak, one of his partners put the orb in his pocket, but the other member of the trio was saddled with a ninety-pound staff, which was nearly five feet long and could not be concealed easily. In panic he tried filing its length of gold in half, but the process was interrupted by the return of Edwards's son who came to investigate a suspicious noise. In the skirmish that followed the orb rolled out onto the stone pavement, the staff went clattering as well, and Blood dropped the crown in order to defend himself. Although caught red-handed in the act of stealing Crown property, King Charles II nonetheless freed Blood from prison, pardoning him in full and restoring his Irish estates as well. Ever since then historians have speculated that the incident occurred at Charles's request, for he was perpetually in need of money, and the jewels offered a handy way to obtain some without paying ruinous interest. Blood's remark when he was captured adds a bit of weight to the supposition for he said, "It was a brave attempt, for it was for a crown," a statement that can be interpreted to have dual meaning, depending on the capitalization or noncapitalization of the word "crown." There is no doubt that the royal finances *were* in serious trouble, for Charles's brother and successor, James II, had to hire diamonds from a jeweler in order to provide his consort with a crown at their coronation in 1685.

Several stones that disappeared when the regalia was first destroyed resurfaced at the Res-

toration, but how and from whence they came are questions that will get no answers. One was the Black Prince's Ruby, one the Stuart sapphire, and a third, the oldest crown jewel of all, another sapphire from a ring of St. Edward himself. No doubt interested Royalists safeguarded some of them, but things do have a way of going and returning in large collections as witness the royal sceptre made for Mary II, then misplaced and forgotten on a back shelf in the old Jewel House at Westminster for well over a century. With all his faults old Thomas Cromwell would never have been guilty of that oversight.

All those recovered stones plus some 2800 diamonds and 300 pearls were fashioned into the present Imperial Crown of State. Victoria chose to be crowned with it at her coronation, and it has been a permanent part of that lavish ceremony ever since, being much lighter than the St. Edward crown; it is now worn throughout the major part of the proceedings immediately after the so-called Recess. Still later additions to the crown jewels were the Kohinoor, a 162-carat diamond called Mountain of Light, and a 530-carat diamond that crowns the Sovereign's Sceptre. Yet with eight crowns already on hand George V had to requisition a ninth when he attended the Durbar in Delhi in 1911. It seems that a centuries-old law forbade *any* of the royal crowns from being transported overseas, and *how* could a king uphold the law of the land if he himself broke it? As a note of interest the value of the crown jewels, before the Cullinan diamond and its progeny (about 1060 carats in all) were placed on display in 1908, was estimated to be £3,000,000. What the current price would be is anybody's guess, but something in the order of £35,000,000 would not be out of line.

Among the greatest of all the royal collectors was a ruler of whom very little is heard today, the Holy Roman Emperor Rudolph II. He gathered a little bit of everything from everywhere, a massive accumulation centered in Hradcany Palace at Prague until its dispersal after the Thirty Years' War, when its holdings provided the nuclei for museums in Vienna, Munich, and Stockholm. His taste for such omnivorous collecting was probably acquired during his education at the Escorial where his uncle, Philip II of Spain, had a vast library, innumerable works of art, tapestries, gold-

Opposite: *Charlemagne, whose crown (not to mention his title and spirit) inspired Napoleon.* Above: *Cardinal Wolsey, who looted monasteries for the king.*

smith's work, gems, and curiosities. One item that must certainly have touched his imagination was a feather, fully three feet long, of a delicate, blushing rose color. Reputedly it came from the wing of the Archangel Gabriel, who must have suffered some uncelestial periods of moult.

The less angelic Rudolph also had his moments of physical misery, not, however, from any organic cause but from pure hypochondria. During his better days he often occupied himself with discussions with astrologers, astronomers, alchemists, and physicians, vainly seeking nostrums to improve his health, which would have done much better if left alone. He also painted, tolerably well by most reports, and always enjoyed polishing and shaping stones in the workshops he had established in the Belvedere on the palace grounds. Agate and jasper and semiprecious stones were cut by him, and eventually made into an ornamental tabletop which his personal physician, one Dr. Guarinonius, proclaimed as one of the wonders of the world, and valued at one thousand ducats. If, indeed, it was such a wonder, then the price seems quite reasonable; but the good doctor's judgment was not always the best. He fully accepted such things as mermaids' teeth, unicorns' horns, phoenix feathers, and nails from Noah's Ark that found their way into Rudolph's collection through the ignorant innocence of the times, and generally at the exorbitant prices that 16th-century swindlers placed upon them.

Rudolph was not deceived in his artists and lapidaries, however, and gave them precedence over ambassadors and ministers in his own government on almost any occasion. This was habitual with him, and his motto ADSIT, which supposedly stood for *A Domino Salus In Tribulatione* (From God deliverance in troubled times), might as easily have meant, "After diversion statesmanship is tolerable." He delighted in skillful productions, such as the *pietra dura* work his Florentine craftsman made in decorating cabinets with landscapes contrived of colored marble sections. Others counterfeited tulips and other flowers, carving them out of colored jasper—stem, leaves, blossom, and all—and then arranging them as bouquets in rock crystal vases. They also carved cameos for him out of agate, sardonyx, chalcedony, and other stones suitable for the purpose,

placing them in pendants, chains, and collars as sumptuous ornaments to wear. Platters made of carefully chosen and matched cross-sections of semiprecious stones set in gold or silver, and studded with gems, poured from the workshops, many of them items worthy of a king's ransom. And as a mark of the high regard in which he held his artists and their director, Jacopo di Strada of Mantua, Rudolph fathered three boys and three girls by Jacopo's own very attractive daughter. While Rudolph had a reputation for suffering from melancholia, for which he was given copious doses of lapis lazuli, it seems that his case was improperly diagnosed, and that treatment for satyriasis would have been more in order. In fact it was long rumored that his involvement with a young lady was the reason that he left Spain before he was supposed to.

Never a student, Rudolph nevertheless learned by practical means, and could speak German, Bohemian, Spanish, Italian, French, and the obligatory Latin, because his subjects did. He acquired skill as a lapidary from his craftsmen and that eventually led him to seek a 17th-century modernization of the crown of the Holy Roman Empire. Until 1602 that state had never changed the design of its crown, first made in the 10th century. Both crowns are preserved to this day in the treasury of the Hofburg in Vienna.

The earlier crown is encrusted with cabochon amethysts, sapphires, cushion-cut emeralds, and pearls, all set onto plates of gold; it is a Carolingian masterpiece. The other, with faceted sapphires, rubies, and diamonds, has an imperial look that thoroughly justifies Rudolph's commissioning of it. No doubt it was lighter, more comfortable, and more suitable for wear on court occasions than the medieval crown used until Rudolph's time. Its higher crest, achieved by means of hemispheric plates of gold, added stature to the Emperor's modest height; he was only about five feet five inches tall. Though slight of build he had a puffy face with sagging pouches beneath his beard, giving him the look of having stuffed his jowls with billiard balls. But for all of his unprepossessing appearance he had more spirit than could be assumed on first sight. Watching him stroll through his gardens made one quickly aware of that fact, for he was always accompanied on those walks by his lifelong pet, Ottokar, a lion that Rudolph had raised from a cub. Luckily for the courtiers, Ottokar had a gentle disposition. Nevertheless, a small emperor accompanied by a large lion somehow becomes a rather formidable object. After 1612, however, the court officials breathed a little easier, for in that year both Rudolph and Ottokar died, and before long the castle, gardens, workshop, and collections passed away with them.

Vienna's Kunsthistorisches (Art History) Museum still holds many of Rudolph's treasures, and ironically also preserves the crown of his enemy, Istvan Bocskoy, Prince of Transylvania. Its gold body, rather like two-thirds of the pope's tiara, and topped by an acorn-shaped emerald, holds 188 gems and about 214 pearls, all distributed in rows. It is of 17th-century Turkish workmanship, and it is interesting to note that all but a few of the stones retain their natural forms save for the kind of smoothness that tumbling action would give them. Emeralds, amethysts, rubies, spinels, topaz, garnet, and turquoise cabochons are all deeply set in gold mounts, giving the crown an appearance midway between Oriental and medieval styles. Since it comes from the beginning of the 1600s there is little chance that the prince wore it very often, for he died in 1606, the year he exacted a treaty of religious freedom after leading a Protestant rebellion against Rudolph II. Some historians voice the suspicion that he was poisoned, but at this distance in time, and remembering that Hungarian soil was well laced with arsenic the matter will have to remain in doubt. In any event kingship would seem to be a highly risky occupation, scarcely worth the perquisites it briefly offers.

In Turkey, where the crown had been fashioned, the mortality rate of sultans, pashas, and beys was generally rather high, with an almost steady splash of bodies being dumped into the Bosporus. But while the potentates and their ministers remained alive they were apt to be rather acquisitive, as witness the gems that have found their way into the Topkapi Palace (formerly the royal seraglio) at Istanbul. About the most spectacular item in that collection is a dagger and sheath that was intended as a gift from Sultan Mahmud I to Nadir Shah. Nadir was the conqueror of Delhi, and carried off the Kohinoor diamond and the Peacock Throne from there. In 1747 Mahmud I sent him a dagger decorated with emeralds, green being a color associated with the Prophet Mohammed, but it only reached Baghdad when Nadir was assassinated, and the gift-laden convoy turned back to Istanbul. One bead-shaped emerald tips the dagger's sheath, upon which some one hundred cut and polished diamonds are set; but four more huge stones, each about one-and-one-half inches long, are mounted on the hilt. The topmost is the only one that is faceted, and it has been given an octagonal shape, being hinged to reveal the face of a watch placed beneath it. No doubt assassinations had to be closely timed in those days.

Still another item on display is the Throne of Shah Ismail, which may have originally belonged to Tamerlane, the 14th-century Mongol conqueror who was known, with good reason, as the Prince of Destruction. The throne is Indian, and is inset with jade, pearls, rubies, and emeralds, and came to Iran in the 18th century as part of Nadir Shah's booty. To curry favor with the Turkish Sultan Mahmud I the throne was sent to Istanbul as a gift in 1746 and has remained there ever since. And, as though one throne was thought to smack of roughing it, an extra was listed among the royal possessions. It is called the Holiday or Golden Throne, since its metal was derived from melting down 80,000 ducats, and its golden hue is reinforced by the presence of some 954 topazes. Sultan Murad received it in 1585 from his Grand Vizier, Ibrahim Pasha, who was either very fond of his employer, or was salving his conscience after some particularly expert bit of diddling.

Almost as dazzling as the emerald-hilted dagger is the eighty-six-carat Spoonmaker's Diamond, mounted amid some forty-nine large diamonds of the first water (the clearest form of diamond). Its spoonlike shape is one reason for its name, but it is also said that a fisherman, who had no idea of its value, traded it to a merchant in exchange for three spoons. Its history is a little clouded, quite unlike the quality of the gems that compose it, but it is highly likely that its story began in India in 1774 when a French officer named Pigot bought it from the Maharajah of Madras, the locale from which the 410-carat Pitt diamond had come. When Pigot returned to France he apparently sold it, initiating a chain of buyers and sellers that culminated in an auction at which it finally came to rest in the hands of Napoleon's mother, Maria Letizia Bonaparte. When her son finally fell on bad times she sold the diamond to benefit him, and it was purchased by the Turkish governor of Morea, Tepedelenli Ali Pasha, for 150,000 pieces of gold. He soon had it confiscated by Sultan Mahmud II on grounds of having fomented rebellion in the Grecian domains of his master, and so it joined the gathering at Topkapi. It possibly acquired an additional forty-nine stones at that time, but there is no record as to who made that addition. It is, and will remain, as mysterious as any benefit that Napoleon may have derived from the stones his mother sold.

Before Napoleon reached that point, however, he had become a collector on a truly imperial scale. In 1796 he inaugurated the policy of looting Italian wealth and art while commander-in-chief of the French army in Italy, and a member of the Directory. In short order the coffers of Lombardy were stripped of 20,000,000 francs; 12,000,000 from Modena and Parma, and 35,000,000 each from Tuscany and the Papal States. The Italians gave him still another title, *Il Gran Ladrone* (The Great Thief), and he appointed officials whose only duty was to pack works of art for shipment to Paris. In 1815, when a portion of these were restored to their rightful owners, some 5233 masterpieces of painting and sculpture were confiscated by the Allies. Many others could no longer be returned because their original owners, whether states or individuals, had ceased to exist.

As for Napoleon himself, he had a crown made in imitation of the one supposedly worn by Charlemagne, but its gems, all antiques, were decidedly real. It still rests in the Louvre very near the thoroughly fake facsimile of Louis XV's crown, together with the 136-carat Regent diamond, one of the few royal gems that remained after the 1887 sale of the French crown jewels. Accompanying it are the Mazarin or *Fleur de Pêcher*, a rose-colored diamond, and a dragon cut from a ruby by Mme. Pompadour's favorite jeweler, M. Guy. The Napoleonic crown was especially designed for his coronation on December 2, 1804, an event that ended in a rebuff to Pope Pius VII. The pontiff had been invited to attend the ceremony at Notre Dame, no doubt to lend an air of official approval and sanction to the act, but found the crown snatched from his hands at the last moment by Napoleon, who then proceeded to crown himself. Anyone capable of such a breach of conduct was also capable of any other kind of reprehensible act, and Europe soon had ample proof of that fact. One old Jacobin, one of the Revolutionists who had hoped to give France a more democratic government, when hearing of the incident said of his new emperor, "Only one thing is now missing—the million men who died to put an end to such pomp and nonsense." Perhaps those who decided to bury Napoleon's body in a massive sarcophagus of Siberian porphyry may have been making reference to the burial of his power that began in Russia in 1812. Or, like the Italians who had experienced how much his fingers could grasp, they wanted to ensure that he would be securely weighted down, and calculated that nearly thirteen hundred square feet of stone would serve that purpose.

Before the excesses of Napoleon there had been those of the Revolution, and those of Marie Antoinette. She had acquired a passion for luxuries and gambling after her arrival in France, rather like a convent-trained girl eager to make up for lost time. Much of her reputation, however, is not entirely deserved, but stems from her desperate efforts to compensate for a condition over which she had no control. It is true that she made enormous expenditures for jewelry and dress, buying gems worth as much as 360,000 *livres* from the court jeweler, Charles Böhmer, in one year. She wheedled Louis XVI into giving her a collection of rubies and diamonds that cost 200,000 *livres*, and that after having received numerous gifts of precious stones costing 100,000 *écus* or more. The *livre* is estimated to have been worth four 1981 dollars; the *écu* about fifteen of the same. Marie Antoinette lost fortunes on gambling; and her expenditures on gowns were astronomical, one season accounting for some million dollars worth of clothes. These stupendous sums and her reckless pursuit of pleasure stemmed mainly from one unfortunate fact, namely, that her husband suffered from a painful disability that prevented their marriage from being consummated. Everyone, of course, urged upon her the necessity of having

162

*A very impressive parure, or matched set of jewelry, said to have belonged
to a member of the Bonaparte family and dated 1815–1825. Included are a comb,
pair of bracelets, brooch, earrings, and necklace in gold set with amethysts.*

163

children, something that did not occur until 1778, after Louis had submitted to a painful circumcision. The undeserved abuse that was poured on the Queen, sometimes even to her face—as happened when some marketwomen and fishwives harassed her for her barrenness—did nothing to lessen her extravagance. By the time the physical side of her marriage had been put in order she had acquired an unremediable taste for jewels, and never tried to control it. A magnificent set of diamond earrings, shown to her by the jewelers Böhmer and Bassenge, became a necessity, and she concealed the purchase and its tremendous cost from the king.

That incident led to deep suspicion of Marie Antoinette's part in the notorious affair of the diamond necklace, which sounds like a story out of Sherlock Holmes, but is, nonetheless, part of history. It began with the accumulation by the court jewelers of a number of diamonds that they made into a necklace for Mme. Du Barry, but had to retain when her patron, Louis XV, died. By 1778 they had almost persuaded Louis XVI to buy it as a gift to the queen after the birth of their first child. Some say that she refused to involve Louis in the expenditure of 1,600,000 *livres*, about $6,400,000 in current terms, advising him to build a man-of-war instead. It does not sound at all like Marie Antoinette, and there is another version in which Louis, having second thoughts on the matter, changed his mind. In any case no sale was made, but Böhmer and Bassenge tried again in 1781 when the dauphin was born. They were no more successful than before, so they put the necklace back in their vaults to await a better day.

Apparently destiny had been trying to deliver them a message that went unheeded, and if the jewelers had only listened they would have broken up the piece immediately and sold the diamonds separately. As it was the fate of the necklace became something far different from anything that Böhmer and Bassenge had ever imagined, and developed into one of the great mystery stories of the 18th century, one that remains unsolved to this day. It also produced a juicy scandal and a sensational trial that involved some confidence artists, the charlatan Cagliostro, and Cardinal Rohan, who Marie Antoinette heartily detested on several grounds.

The end result was the theft of the necklace, which was never recovered, the jailing of a so-called comtesse, and the ruin of Cardinal Rohan despite the fact that he was acquitted of all wrongdoing, and was recognized as an innocent dupe. He had, however, been most unclerically intimate with the charmer who had engineered the whole plot, and had been convinced by her that the queen had reversed her opinion of him, and now desired receipt of something more than advice and absolution. None of that did his ecclesiastical reputation any good, and he was exiled from the court with loss of his revenues. Nor did Marie Antoinette emerge unscathed, for suspicions swarmed around that unpopular queen. Although she had disposed of an objectionable member of the court on justifiable grounds, many believed that she had hired the plotters to accomplish her separate ends, the downfall of Cardinal Rohan, and the secret acquisition of the necklace. Nor were those suspicions lessened when the comtesse, the only person to be jailed, soon made a clean escape from her supposedly escape-proof prison. Whatever the case, only one thing is certain—that the diamonds survived somewhere, somehow, after being rearranged or recut. Let those jewelers who seek royal patronage be forewarned.

The course of monarchy was rapidly running out in the West after centuries of absolute monarchy, largely because of the abuses most rulers had visited on their subjects. Matters were, if anything, even worse farther east where the tradition of tsardom had been set by Ivan the Terrible. He *did* attempt something for the arts in Russia by establishing workshops in the Kremlin, and had various jeweled gifts produced there for monasteries, cathedrals, and the like. One such item was a pearl-bordered cross that he presented to the Solovetsky Monastery in the far north of Russia. It contains a turquoise, carnelian, and amethyst in addition to eight sapphires (Ivan's favorite stone), which ranged in color from blue to a nearly transparent state. Since they were shaped in 1562, a year that saw some problems for Ivan, there is little doubt that the gift was something in the nature of spiritual insurance. He was fortunate enough to die in holy orders in 1584, assuming the habit of a monk on his deathbed. All of that following an exemplary life in which he had murdered some of his boyars, St. Philip of Moscow, his son Ivan, and the population of Novgorod, having taken a full five weeks to accomplish the latter task.

Through the end of the 17th century the workshops that Ivan had created in the Kremlin continued to set gems in deep mounts, very much in a Byzantine or medieval style, using cabochon-cut stones for most pieces, but also faceted stones in the time of Peter the Great. His Cap of Monomach, a sable-bordered cap made of golden plates bearing jewels and pearls, was made about 1682–1684 in the Silver Chambers of the Kremlin and contains several gemstones, sapphires, emeralds, and the like, which are either faceted or cut to octagonal, oval, or cylindrical forms not possible with the former cabochon style. Another item that showed the immense progress made between the times of Ivan and Peter is a pectoral cross, about four by six inches, that belonged to the latter. It contains four faceted white sapphires, four round-cut diamonds, and ten emeralds cut in rectangular or triangular shapes, one of which carries an engraved representation of the Crucifixion.

Peter the Great hoped to give the Russia of his day more prestige with Western nations by encouraging technology, and also by hiring Western architects. He brought an Italian architect and sculptor, Carlo Bartolomeo Rastrelli, to Russia to work for him, and commissioned a palace at Tsarskoe Selo (Tsar's Village) from him in 1724. It was somewhat theatrical when finished, containing a rich assortment of varicolored marbles, mother-of-pearl inlays, lapis lazuli, and a room covered with plaques of amber. He had first seen it in Prussia a few years before, and then persuaded Frederick William I to give it to him in exchange for fifty tall grenadiers. Augustus the Strong of Saxony had worked a similar deal with Frederick, giving him dragoons in return for huge porcelain jars. Frederick did not care for esthetics at all, his idea of a nice present being a regiment of cannoneers, cavalry, or the like. He could not read, had no interest in anything that was not practical, or could not be used for military purposes. As for Peter and Augustus, they were confident that they could rear sufficient soldiers for their needs, but could never have too many objects of art. As a footnote, the amber plaques are still around and so are the porcelain jars, but the dragoons and grenadiers have long since gone, along with their military usefulness.

When Catherine the Great finally came to the throne in 1762 she made further strides in improving the quality of Russian palaces. At Tsarskoe Selo, some fifteen miles south of old St. Petersburg, now Leningrad, she set a Scottish architect named Cameron to work. One of his masterpieces there is the Agate Pavilion, so-called because that stone is prominent in every facet of the decoration of its round dressing room. Another room in it, the study, is of jasper, while the salon mingles white and rose marble. All parts of the pavilion, which is a separate building, are done in the classical Adam style that has the restrained elegance Catherine delighted in. For that matter much of the interior of the main palace was redesigned along the same lines, and the same rich but understated ornamentation was even carried out along the floors. Some are wooden parquet, but many others are polished inlays of colored marbles. For those who may have trouble in putting down linoleum squares those floors provide a liberal education in what the hand of a craftsman can do. At the Royal Palace in Madrid there is an even more spectacular use of inlaid marble wherein it is treated as freely as a woven or painted design. Ten or more colors are combined in swags, swirls, arcs, and circles giving the effect of an Aubusson carpet.

Catherine's greatest efforts, however, were directed toward transforming the Winter Palace, and providing a retreat there, which she named the Hermitage. At every turn great columns of marble support staircases with marble treads, and polished balustrades and panels abound on every hand. All those ornamental stones were cut and polished in the huge 18th-century imperial shops at Ekaterinburg in the Urals, and then transported some twelve hundred miles to their place in the Hermitage. Priceless columns of malachite came from the Urals, along with others made from jasper, porphyry, and marble, becoming decoration for rooms where Catherine conversed with the French encyclopedist Diderot. As a result of those animated talks the empress often became as colorful as her surroundings, for Diderot always

emphasized his remarks with resounding bangs on Catherine's thighs. She finally installed a table between them to "preserve her members," since she continually emerged from those sessions pummeled black and blue.

One other interesting feature of the Hermitage is also to be found in its throne room—a map of Russia about eighty-eight square feet. No ordinary chart this; it is made from semiprecious stones such as jasper in a variety of colors, carnelian, agate, and still others found within the country's borders. Cities and rivers are marked by rubies and emeralds, adding to the splendor of the effect. A similar map, probably inspired by the one in the Hermitage, was exhibited in the Soviet Pavilion at the 1939 World's Fair. All the member countries of the Soviet Union were shown, each made of a different colored stone, and with the cities marked by gems such as sapphires, topazes, emeralds, and diamonds. It returned to the Soviets just in time for World War II, so we may hope that it survived, perhaps as a decorative mural in Moscow's ornate subway system, though the odds are greatly against that happy ending.

One thing that the throne room map did not point out was the road to revolution, but, whether or not its route was made clear, it arrived at the Winter Palace on schedule just as it had at Versailles. Nicholas II was the one unlucky enough to be in its way, and consequently became the last royal collector. Ironically the craftsman whose work he chiefly patronized was a jeweler who had kept alive the goldsmith and lapidary skills of prerevolutionary 18th-century France, the renowned Peter Carl Fabergé. Fabergé's shops in Moscow, Odessa, Kiev, St. Petersburg, and London poured forth a stream of exquisitely designed baubles for Alexander III and Nicholas II, the last two tsars, work that the commissars judged in category AAA of the nonessential.

But from 1881 until 1917 Fabergé made full and imaginative use of every kind of precious and semiprecious stone to be found in the Russian mines. In addition to the Easter eggs, for which he was famous and which usually contained jeweled clockwork toys such as roosters that beat their wings and crowed, he produced numerous other miniatures, statuettes, and highly ornamental objects for daily use. Their variety can only be hinted at in a summation such as this, but includes such whimsies as light switches of onyx shaped like swimming goldfish, with white jade eyes as the push-buttons. Small peasant figures combine agate, carnelian, and jasper to simulate the colors and forms of faces, hands, and costumes. Plants were imitated with leaves of nephrite, bearing fruits or flowers or buds of ruby, coral, amethyst, topaz, or pearl, all set in a rock-crystal vase that seems to be partly filled with water. Furthermore the flowers could be removed from their carefully drilled sockets, and then be worn as jewelry. Minute models of Louis XVI furniture were made with aventurine quartz simulating gold ormulu mounts on grained wood "counterfeited" by sardonyx; and animals and birds were fashioned from just about every stone that was either rare or precious. Many of the objects are reminiscent of the microscopic perfection achieved by Dinglinger for the court of Saxony, and, being the works of art that they are, they will continue to delight the eyes for centuries to come.

There is little doubt that such things will never again be made in an age that has placed its head in the machine's mouth, nor should they be at the cost they once exacted. But a world without its dash of playfulness and beauty is a pretty barren bargain no matter how it is offered. Besides, the gems and those who work with or use them have at last become reformed sinners, dedicated to the service of science, as the next chapter will explain.

Two important figures in the westernization of Russia. Opposite: *Catherine the Great.* Left: *Peter the Great. Peter began work on Tsarskoe Selo with an Italian architect; Catherine continued the work with a Scotsman.*

8

Chapter 8
THE RISE OF TECHNOLOGY

Mankind's debt to stone is past all imagining, for stone was the first material that permitted man to amplify his powers. Through its use we became a technological animal capable of making tools, fire, and architecture. Because of its presence we have acquired the means to expand our knowledge, reading the history of our past and that of our universe in the record of the rocks. Gemstones have become instruments of communication instead of mere ornaments, but they have also kept us alive to the laws of beauty through their color, fire, and purity of form. And as we have probed deeper into their being we have learned that, while they may lack the power of animation, they are an ultimate result of movement, being the contained force of untold numbers of atomic particles whirling in constant motion. Each is a dancer in dimensions that transcend sight, and each offers a microcosmos of many worlds yet to be explored. What gifts stones have already given us we may yet find will be given tenfold more.

In a sense our knowledge of stone first grew when we became quarriers, seeking workable flints or building blocks of limestone and marble. Ancient sites with their scarred hillsides from Ethiopia to the Appenines testify to our unending search for usable stone, an activity that still goes on in places such as Carrara, Vermont, Algeria, Canada, and India, among many others. In earlier times there was much confusion about what was and what was not marble, with the result that many formations such as alabaster, basalt, porphyry, and serpentine came to be called by its name. As a consequence, ancient descriptions of marble used in architecture need very careful checking, particularly when restorations or reproductions of former structures are undertaken.

The primitive methods used at the earliest quarries met with scarcely any improvement until the advent of steam power at the beginning of the

19th century. Stone, whether marble, granite, or limestone, was broken up by several methods that relied on tools such as spikes, chisels, or wedges that were driven in by repeated hammer blows. One method, called gadding, split the rock with spikes. Feathering, a second technique, involved metal plates, curved in opposite directions, that were inserted into fractures and then forced further apart by driving metal wedges between them, thus splitting the stone. Channeling, a third method, was accomplished by cutting out grooves, or fluting, and then cutting a block loose along the line so made.

Once steam power became available, rock could be parted by broaching, which meant that a series of closely spaced holes was drilled and the intervening web of stone was parted with broaching tools. Sawing was also employed, using wire cables, as much as 16,000 feet in length, in combination with abrasives and water, running them over pulleys that stretched them over the line to be cut. Chisels that traversed the rock face, pounding out a cut by pneumatic pressure, were also used; and lastly, jet-drilling, in which a mixture of fuel oil and oxygen burns out a mass of expanded rock along a drill bit that has become immovably wedged.

Cranes now move forty- and sixty-ton blocks as easily as a child's toy, hoisting huge masses for loading onto trucks. Cables also swing large pieces about, enormously lightening work once entrusted to horses and oxen guided by their drivers. Despite all the improvements resulting from the use of power equipment, accidents are still of sufficient frequency to put quarrying into the category of a hazardous occupation. When cables snap there is not only the danger created by the falling stone but also from the whiplash action of the cable itself, as well as its weight when it lands. After all, 16,000 feet of triple-stranded wire can-

Preceding pages: *The work of building the Cathedral of St. John the Divine
in New York City goes on, with modern stonecutters learning the arts of the
ancients.* Above: *For over 2000 years the quarries of Carrara, Italy,
yielded high-quality marble brought out by muscle power rather than by machines.
The oxen can be easily distinguished because they aren't goring anyone.*

not be regarded as so much soapsuds. Blasting accidents do occur, and chips dislodged by pneumatic hammers sometimes fly in unexpected directions. Last, but not least, quarries hold and reflect heat, becoming ovenlike in summer, creating numerous cases of heatstroke.

While there are many marble quarries around the world, some producing material of excellent quality, the region around Carrara is probably both the oldest and best-known, having been worked since Caesar Augustus transformed Rome from a city of brick to one of marble in the 1st century A.D. In 1518 Michelangelo worked stone in the Altissimo quarries, which is one of the numerous towns about Carrara. These include Ceraglia, famous for ochre-colored marble; Luna, the old port from which marble was shipped to Rome; and Querceta and Pietrasanta, the respective centers of commercial and modern sculptural production.

About 600,000 tons are cut annually from the mountains around Carrara, utilizing some 170 quarries, and about 3000 workmen whose skills range from blasting to trucking, though only 80 are actually quarriers at the present time. At the turn of the century over 1000 quarriers were employed, for during the 19th and very early 20th centuries there were many monumental projects

Statuette courtesy of Rare Art, Inc.

Three views of rose quartz. Opposite: *A rose-quartz egg and a specimen of rose quartz on smokey quartz. Above:* A specimen of rose quartz. Right: *A Japanese statuette of carved rose quartz.*

173

with granite, which resists the effects of corrosion much better when used in an architectural setting. The chemicals in our air are decidedly hazardous, not only to our fragile and irreplaceable lungs, but also to any artistic statement couched in marble. For that reason granite, although five times as costly, is being used with increasing frequency by architects as facing material for the decoration of buildings. Granite is also much harder, offering greater resistance to wear and damage. While a twenty-ton block of marble may be cut into sixty slices within eight hours, it takes one week to accomplish the same division with granite.

Throughout the 19th century marble was a very popular building and ornamental stone, figuring in steps, sills, panels, columns, and capitals, while also being used for tabletops, mantelpieces, and tombstones. Marble was fashioned into slabs for those purposes at steam-powered mills in almost every city in the United States during the 19th century. At Vergennes, Vermont, where they had access to water power, the mill had 65 saws capable of cutting 20,000 feet of slabs worth $11,000 per year. In 1809–10, when that statistic was compiled, the dollar had a purchasing power in excess of fifteen 1981 dollars. So marble was not an entirely cheap product at that time; in fact some varieties were enormously expensive. Consider *griotte* marble (colored like the brownish French cherries of that name), a variety used in some of the ornamentation of the Arc du Carousel, and which cost 200 francs per cubic foot, or $750 in modern currency. There would have been a reason to produce marble artificially even then, and in 1806 such an attempt was successfully carried through. Sir James Hill packed limestone into a cannon barrel, sealed it, and then brought it to an exceedingly high temperature to drive off carbonic gas through the touch-hole. Afterward, when it was allowed to cool slowly, the result was pure, crystalline marble. Today, even in our shrinking market, some ten million square feet of thin marble slabs are still turned out annually at the Henraux Mills in Querceta, Italy, so it is obvious that our taste for marble has not entirely disappeared, nor is it likely that it will in the near future.

Colored and patterned marbles have always commanded a premium price on the market, and

underway. One of these, the Roman Victor Emmanuel II monument, which is irreverently referred to as "The Wedding Cake," because it looks like one, took twenty-six years to build, from 1885 to 1911. Workmen, of course, came cheaper then, but even today a 40-hour week of dangerous labor nets only about $200, which does not amount to as much as bus drivers or garbage collectors are accustomed to earn.

Skilled craftsmen, working in the shops where sculptures are enlarged, probably earn somewhat more, but millionaires are not common in the hills around Carrara. While the area seems blanketed in snow, even in summertime, both because of a pervasive layer of marble-dust and the swaths of exposed marble on the hillsides, the industry is having difficulties. One stems from the cost of transporting large sculptures, without even taking into account the care needed to keep them free from chips and scratches, for it often costs more to move a sculpture from the dock or freight station to a gallery than it does to buy the block and carve it. Additionally there is the heavy competition

The Stonecutter, *by Jost Ammon. This woodcut from 1568 shows a worker, seated by a window, operating a polisher driven by a foot treadle.*

accordingly some artificial methods were devised to either imitate or outdo nature. By using vitriol, bitumen, and other fluids commonly employed to color marble, plain slabs could be turned into rare and colorful varieties. The trick was to paint the desired pattern on paper, then place it between two pieces of marble and seal all the edges with wax. The resulting sandwich was then buried for a month or so in damp soil, after which time the design would be found to have penetrated clearly and sharply from front to back on both halves.

Ingenious methods for cutting columns were also devised, including one that cut hollow columns of progressively smaller diameter from a single large one. Not only did more columns result, but the structural weight of each was reduced without any loss of strength. Ordinarily, turning solid blocks into columns is a slow process calling for ample supplies of water power. Such a condition existed in the Ural Mountains at Ekaterinburg (Sverdlovsk) where Catherine the Great established the large mills to shape and polish columns for her many building projects in St. Petersburg (Leningrad). Similar facilities exist at Idar-Oberstein in West Germany where such mills have been in operation on the river Nahe for centuries.

Marble, of course, is still a costly material, and even the ancient Romans referred to it as the noble stone. Hence very little of it is wasted wherever it is processed; wastage from blocks is used for slabs, while the remains from the slabs are turned into tiles, and accumulated dust and chips find a use, like plaster of paris, in molds. Because of its cost, no sculptor starts hacking away at a monolithic block in order to hew out a great statue. Usually he shapes his design in clay and then takes it to a workshop replete with jackhammers, pneumatic chisels, hydraulic lifts, cranes, and turntables where the piece may be scaled up to as much as twenty times its original size. This entails a horde of measurements obtained by calipers of all sizes, and requires very fine judgment by the sculptor and his assisting artisans in making all necessary adjustments as work progresses. On some rare occasions it is even possible to dispense with the three-dimensional model and work from a drawing instead.

At a rough approximation, granite is about twenty-one times harder than marble, and would seem to be one of the most unalterable items on earth. Rocks in general have become synonymous with changelessness, but that is somewhat of an illusion, since it is now well known that even the bedrock of continents is in a continuous process of movement. Earthquakes occur with varying degrees of severity along weak spots in the earth's mantle almost every day, which means that enormous masses of rock are involved in fractional motions, shifting about and creating new areas of pressure. What was once an ocean floor has often been lifted up to the mountaintops. Futhermore, there is great movement within the materials that compose the rocks themselves, with elements constantly being replaced through chemical alteration, weathering, or recrystallization caused by heat, pressure, or a combination of both. Nothing ever stays the same, and nothing ever will.

In fact, if earth movements did not exist and if pressure was not released by weathering of the rock overburden, quarrying of granite might well be an impossibility. But because minute fractures develop in the rock, usually parallel to the earth's surface, and these strata then extend in sheets for considerable distances, granite becomes somewhat like so many layers of onion skin to be peeled away. Those fractures are called joints and, if too closely spaced, that is, making very thin slabs, or if they intersect at right angles, the granite becomes unusable. More often than not, however, nature proves helpful, and this hard and useful stone will continue to be quarried, cut, and polished for millennia to come.

Despite its common occurrence granite is something of a mystery, its process of formation being one of geology's major problems. It may result from the slow crystallization of molten rock buried deep beneath the earth's tremendous pressure, or it may be formed by means of recrystallization through heat of a volcanic order, pressure, and volatile elements that completely alter volcanic or sedimentary rocks into granitic masses. A third possibility is that elements may be introduced or replaced by others, such as alkalies or silica being substituted for calcium or iron magnesium. In any case it is fortunately abundant, and its massiveness and durability aid many of the geological processes, acting either as a bar-

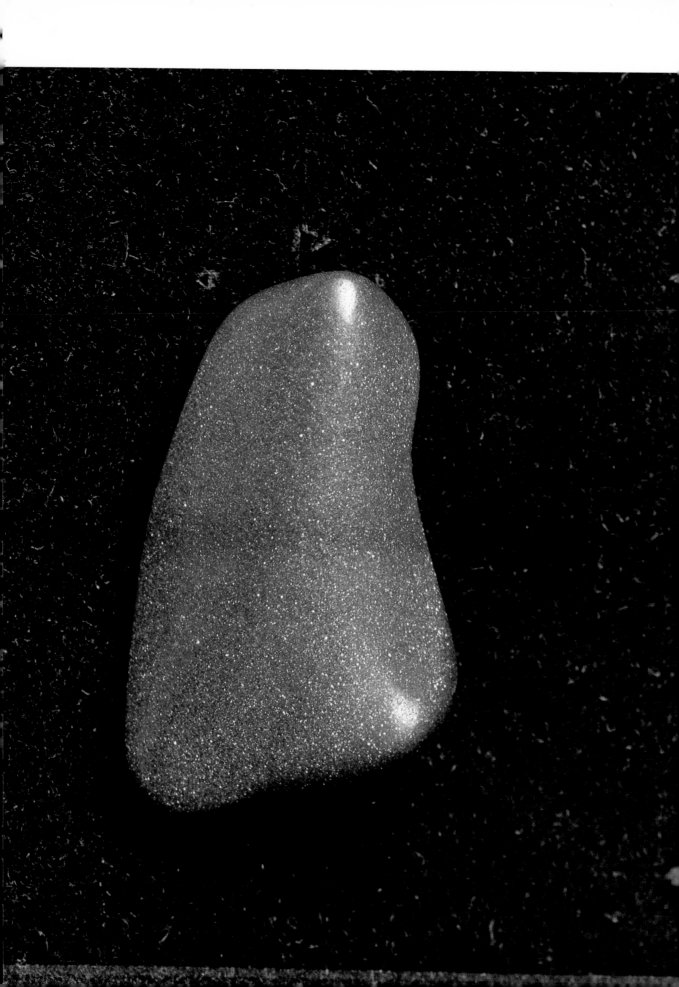

Opposite:
Aventurine.
Above left:
Fluorite melts easily and derives its name from the Latin verb fluo *("to flow"). It pops and crackles when heated; is a major source of hydrofluoric acid; and its crystals, if clear, form lenses for optical instruments.*
Above: *Siderite.*
Left: *Calcite.*

177

Above: *The
Rutland Marble
Company's mills
in West Rutland,
Vermont.* Right:
*Using a machine
drill deep in a
tunnel. This
idealized vision
depicts a worker
completely
unprotected from
sound and flying
stone.*

rier, or a creator of pressure, or both.

Granite often contains substantial amounts of quartz and alkali feldspar, the latter being chiefly responsible for the coloration of the stone. While it is usually a light gray imbedded with crystalline flecks, granite can also be rather white, or of a pinkish hue, like the rocks along the Massachusetts coast. Still another type is called "graphic" granite because it contains quartz that is distributed in an angular pattern resembling some ancient alphabets. All types, when highly polished, give a most decorative appearance and withstand wear and corrosion particularly well.

Monolithic columns of granite were often shaped and polished at the turn of the century, but facilities for so doing have become rarer with each passing year. What the ancient, Renaissance, and 18th-century technologies could accomplish with stone is fast going the way of hand craftmanship, surviving here and there in pockets, always dangerously close to extinction. Machines were once the tools that helped us achieve higher levels of perfection, but now their limitations are setting boundaries that we have become reluctant to cross and soon will have lost the skill to do so.

As a basis of comparison the column that stands in Leningrad as a monument to Tsar Alexander I has a monolithic shaft fifty-five feet high and six feet thick. It was shaped by 18th-century workmen with 18th-century tools and techniques, but a column of the same dimensions, shaped by 20th-century techniques in the United States, had to be made in two sections since no equipment was available to work a single piece of that size. The Alexander column was moved over twelve hundred miles to its final site, the bisected American one a little less than half that distance. Some comfort can be taken in the fact that there was more than one American column involved, for the architectural project required eight of them.

Still another building stone of great importance is limestone, now rapidly being displaced by glass sheets hung upon steel skeletons. It has other uses as well, being the mainstay of cement production, a purifier of iron in the smelting process, and was the basis of lithography, which was discovered through the use of Solothurn limestone.

Because of the relative abundance and ease of quarrying such materials as marble, granite, and limestone there has been little incentive to synthesize them. Now and then, however, compositions of a stonelike nature have been invented, chiefly for the purpose of producing molded architectural ornamentation or sculpture. One highly successful formula was devised in the 18th century with the creation of Coadestone, a secret that has been lost since its manufacture ceased in 1837. It was made in a factory at Lambeth where the material was used to fashion a seven-ton lion, now to be seen on the Lambeth side of the Thames just south of Westminster Bridge. In its earlier, livelier days it stood proudly atop the Lion Brewery, resisting then, as now, the sophisticated pollution bred out of London's atmosphere. While other artificial stones were made, Coadestone was acknowledged to be superior to all others, for it could be cut or molded, had a smooth finish that seemed soft to the touch, and weathered extremely well. Chemical analysis of surviving examples has failed to reveal the elements of and means by which it was made, so perhaps it depended upon either heat, a volatile catalyst, or an exact progression in the mixture of its components. One possibility is that selenite and marble dust, a combination that becomes hard and will take a polish, may be part of the formula. It would prove a worthwhile defense against present atmospheric conditions if ever its secrets can be unlocked again.

The greatest activity in regard to artificial stone has always been the production of imitation gems. Methods were known and used even in antiquity, but the 18th-century techniques were far and away the best ever devised, and the most deceptive in their finished state. Anyone who has seen the *carnets du bal*, which were given away as souvenirs of the court balls at Versailles, knows to what extravagant lengths luxury could go, even when using substitute materials. Gold was washed over copper, and elaborate enameled designs often surrounded miniature portraits, all being decorated with a profusion of sparkling stones that counterfeit cut jewels. At first sight, and very often at second and third, these gems give the appearance of being the real thing, a deception that is maintained by the difficulty of removing them from their mounts for closer inspection. A closed mount, rather than an open one that reveals the

179

Above: *Carved figure of
steatite (soapstone).* Right:
Diamond cutting in Amsterdam.
Opposite: *The original of
this medieval bas-relief,
now in the cathedral museum
of Notre Dame, has been
replaced in the structure
by a reproduction.*

180

Courtesy of the author

181

bottom of the stone, is usually an indication of an imitation. The closed mounts concealed a layer of foil, almost always of very high quality and untarnished brilliance, since the mount protected it from exposure to air and any consequent yellowing. One very clever trick was the use of an "air foil" in which the ring-mount was lined with a highly reflective foil put down over faceted metal. Above that came an empty space, containing nothing but air, and at the very top a wafer of cut gemstone, or colored crystal, held tightly in an air-tight frame. Still another method was to place a black dot in the very center of the metal foil under a piece of cut crystal, for that procedure stepped-up the refraction of light, making the stone seem brighter.

Jewel thieves were as common in the 18th century as they are now, perhaps even more so, and the wealthy owners of gems soon adopted the expedient of wearing fakes whenever they traveled the highways. The material from which their imitation jewelry was made was known as "paste," and was very similar to modern lead crystal, although an extra degree of hardness was achieved in some examples. As early as the 16th century Gian Battista Porta of Naples wrote descriptions of the entire process of manufacture, and it was not new even then, for ancient Roman law had forbidden such topics from being discussed in manuscripts.

As Porta (and later writers in the 18th and early 19th centuries) explained the necessary steps, the chief ingredients were patience and unremitting labor extending over several days. Flintstones of good quality were gathered, preferably from riverbanks, and were then calcined in a kiln prior to a quenching that caused numerous internal fractures in their structure. Afterward they were repeatedly pulverized and washed until all trace of impurities had been disposed of, and then they were melted in a crucible.

Since flint is a silicate composed of silicon oxide, it needs only the addition of an alkali and some lead oxide to turn it into a heavy, highly refractive glass when it is melted in a furnace. Because the workmen who created the paste were painstaking in their procedures, grinding the powder exceedingly fine, and taking great care to remove any foreign matter introduced from the mortar and pestle by the very act of grinding itself, they achieved a quality of the highest order. Even during the melting the degree of heat was gradually increased, being held for hours at a constant level until further intensification was needed, and every stage was carefully timed.

Further refinements came in the 18th century when it was realized that superior color could be obtained only from bases that were compatible with the coloring substance. In the 16th century it had been sufficient to create blue through the use of calcined brass beaten into powder, or to add manganese to melted crystal to obtain amethyst. But by the 18th century, when gems of good color and quality were more commonly seen in Europe, the standards of excellence became more demanding. It was then that at least five separate bases were employed for the manufacture of paste. These called for such items as red or white lead, rock crystal, flint, borax, arsenic, niter, and salt of tartar in varying quantities and combinations. There was also a great deal of pulverizing, heating, melting, boiling, washing with nitric acid, drying, mixing, etc., etc., until the recipe grows wearisome, but the end result justified the labor with a remarkably fine crystalline composition, much like a colorless sapphire.

All of that was so much preparatory work for the coloring, and the colors were derived from gold, silver, copper, iron, tin, and other minerals such as cobalt, manganese, and antimony. Emeralds were made by the use of copper verdigris, while yellowish-green or red resulted from the use of iron. Silver was employed in making canary diamonds or opals, while cobalt created sapphires. Antimony made a respectable topaz, while manganese could be used in the production of either rubies or amethysts. One kind of crystal from Bohemia, which contained a high proportion of lead, was originally yellow, but on being subjected to heat sufficient to redden but not melt it, became a fine ruby color. Usually red of that quality is the result of mixing gold into the crystal, but this material had nothing more than lead as a part of its composition.

One of the great perfecters of paste was the court jeweler to Louis XV, a craftsman named Georges Frédéric Strass, who came to Paris in 1719 and gained his official recognition from the king in 1734. At the time he created his pieces, paste diamonds held a distinct advantage over the real ones insofar as design was concerned. Although the art of diamond cutting had been known since 1476 lapidaries still found it difficult to exercise tight control over the shaping of small stones. The result was that most cut gems tended to be somewhat too large to be spaced closely together, thus causing an awkward effect rather like a mouth set with teeth that are drifting apart. Paste jewels, softer than diamonds, were more readily cut and accommodated themselves better to jewelry designs, allowing the creation of effects that were both delicate and elegant. Strass's formulas for paste became as famous as the designs in which his artificial gems were set, and eventually stones of that nature came to be known as "Strass," a term still used in Europe today.

One anomaly in the production of paste was that the substance that seemed to promise the best results, crystalline quartz, actually had less luster than lead crystal. Lead crystal resulted from the experiments of an Englishman named George Ravenscroft, who lived in 17th-century London and actually made glass in that future hotel, and Gilbert and Sullivan landmark, the Savoy. The addition of a flux of either white or red lead to the melt gave his glass a refractive index only slightly less than that of diamond, and Strass was among the first to see its advantage. Their remote and accidental collaboration finally led to the establishment of the costume jewelry industry, which is still flourishing, now to a lesser extent than in the earlier decades of this century. Perhaps modern young women no longer care to rival Indian maharanis and the Empress Josephine, or else effects of the revolution have arrived at last, and jewels will be cast in the gutter for the swine to eat—at peril to their digestion.

Once it became possible to imitate diamonds passably well, only one thing remained—to learn how to make them. People had been tantalized for years by the fact that they knew coal and diamonds were made from the same material, carbon, and that it was simply a matter of reorganizing its crystalline structure. That, however, was not as simple as it might seem, for nobody had any idea about the necessary heat and pressure that the transformation might entail. To add to the

frustration, it was also realized that every human being was a walking, breathing diamond mine who exhaled enough carbon in one hour, in the form of carbonic gas, to create one hundred carats of diamonds.

Nature puts no premium on diamond production as we humans do, so she makes relatively few of the gems. She also conceals their inherent beauty under the outward appearance of a somewhat unattractive, greasy pebble, making any diamond rather inconspicuous to the untrained eye. The first diamonds ever to be discovered in the Brazilian gem fields turned up as counters in a card game, a service they had performed for some time before someone realized that the counters were worth more than any of the stakes that had been wagered. And in South Africa one huge diamond began its career under the guise of a child's plaything.

While diamonds are the hardest of all known natural substances, they are also capable of being cleaved evenly along certain planes. This characteristic, which makes diamond cutting possible, can pose a problem for the jeweler who must set the stones into rings. If, for any reason, the mount is made imperfectly, and does not permit the stone to be seated evenly, then either fracturing or outright cleavage can result from a light blow in normal wear. Hardness is one thing and fragility is another, as witness the old and erroneous legend that a diamond can split an anvil if struck with sufficient force. The inevitable result, as anyone who ever tried the experiment learned, to his regret, was always a little pile of diamond dust.

One of the first experimenters to claim that he had created diamonds in the laboratory was J. Ballantyne Hanny, from Glasgow. Specimens that he submitted to the British Museum in support of his claim were accepted as genuine, but, on later reconsideration, were judged *too* genuine, being recognized as natural rather than synthetic fragments. That event took place in 1880, but it was not until December of 1954 that a successful attempt was achieved by H. T. Hall working in the General Electric laboratories at Schenectady, N.Y. From that day forward mankind became free from reliance upon the natural supply of industrial diamonds, and can, in fact, make a stronger, more durable product. However there is no need to rush

out and sell your stock in diamond mines, for the natural material remains quite competitive with the synthetic, and gem-quality stones are not yet even faintly in the running, particularly sizable ones. To the present, nothing larger than an uncut one-carat diamond has been produced, but research continues and may crack that barrier at any time if, indeed, it has not already done so. As a note of interest, the world's largest owner of diamond mines, the De Beers Company, purchased rights to produce the stones by means of General Electric's patented process. They now manufacture them in Ireland, Sweden, and, unbelievably, in South Africa, which is something like building an icehouse in Antarctica. In any event, they have been foresighted enough to provide for the future when their natural supply does run out.

Shock waves passed through the jewelry trade once it became known that diamonds had been synthesized at last, and the usual dire predictions were made. They had, however, as little foundation as before, for the end result was a preference for the real thing. Our age, which is almost completely permeated with synthetic products, from plastic veneers on wood to artificial turf to analogs of meat products made from soy beans, is in an excellent position to grade the worth of such substitutes directly from its own experience. In almost every instance, and especially in the matter of gems, the natural product has consistently received the accolade of consumer preference. One after another gemstones have been synthesized since 1885, and each time the same pattern has been repeated: initial fear by those with a heavy stake in the matter, followed by a return to normal once distinguishing tests have been established.

In the case of diamonds, production of gemstones on a commercial scale has been unfeasible economically, and they have been limited so far to an upper limit in size of about one carat. Until more stones are produced and the experimental nature of the process is eliminated, proper standards for distinguishing the real from the synthetic cannot be determined. But anything else that approaches the genuine can easily be weeded out by testing its degree of heat conductivity. Diamonds transmit heat faster than any other gem, faster by far than highly efficient copper metal, and that is why the recently devised heat-

probe test works so well. When the needlelike probe is applied to any surface of a diamond, regardless of size, it will instantly give an accurate reading of the stone's degree of thermal conductivity as registered on an electronic meter. A simpler version is accomplished by breathing on the stone, for the condensed vapor of the breath will vanish more rapidly from the suface of a diamond than from any other substance.

Presently, industrial diamond grit is the chief synthetic product, and has established itself as a major competitor to Brazilian carbonado, a polycrystalline form of diamond used for drills and other tools. Two-thirds of the world supply now comes from manufactories, and about 45,000 pounds of the precious abrasive is made in the United States each year, with every prospect of a continuing increase in output. This type of diamond has an extremely tough structure since the orientation of the crystals is randomly distributed, canceling out any tendency to propagate such cleavage as occurs in single crystal stones. The necessary carbon is cheaply and readily obtained, utilizing many substances such as sugar, paraffin, or even those as unlikely as mothflakes or peanuts! While carbonado is relatively simple to make, single-crystal diamonds are another matter. These are industrially essential for such things as laser windows, and semiconductor heat sinks in high-power electrical installations, for diamond is five times as efficient as copper in transmitting heat. Eventually the gem-size ones will come, but for the moment the more practical grit for rock drills, or wire-forming dies, takes priority over the engagement ring.

Diamond production has taught us a great deal about crystal formation, knowledge that will eventually help in the creation of other synthetic gemstones and which may yet lead to creation of stones that have never before existed even in nature. We now know that crystals obtained at pressures of about 900,000 pounds per square inch and at temperatures of 1600 degrees centigrade will take on the characteristic octahedral shape of diamond crystals. Other pressures and other temperatures produce other effects, but that information remained in the realm of theory until equipment was devised that would withstand such stress. The great problem was that, aside

Diopside is a fairly hard silicate (5 to 6 on the Mohs scale) that produces some transparent, prismatic crystals that may be cut as gemstones. Green diopside is often associated with kimberlite, a diamond-bearing rock, in the Siberian and South American diamond fields.

Above: *Grinding agates in
a workshop in Baden, Germany.*
Right: *Diamond cutting.*

from diamond itself, all known materials crumbled at or near the required pressure. Thanks to research developed during the attempt to create synthetic diamonds we can now contain pressures of 6,000,000 pounds per square inch, and where that capability will take us is still to be seen.

The synthesis of gems did not begin with an attempt to make diamonds, but rather with ruby, the chemical nature of which had been properly analyzed in 1817. Nearly a century of research and experimentation was to pass before a French scientist named Auguste Victor Louis Verneuil announced his discovery of the ruby-making process in 1902, followed in 1904 by full publication of all the details. He had already received a gold medal for producing a superior glass for telescopes (in 1900 at the Paris Universal Exposition), and had successfully duplicated a lost, ancient black glaze used on Greco-Roman pottery. Naturally it would be assumed that he would be laden with honors and be famed throughout the entire civilized world; but the assumption would be incorrect. His doctoral thesis won a prize and he published a number of scientific papers, but apparently his diplomas and degrees lacked some cachet of approval from academia for he is barely mentioned anywhere. In most standard biographical reference works he is not noticed at all, although an obscure namesake in paleontology gets a mention, as does the Marquise de Verneuil, sometime mistress to Henri IV of France. Science, of course, is scarcely competitive with sex, but still it is a little shabby to begrudge genius a name, particularly one whose work made fortunes for others, a common occupational hazard in the genius business.

The Verneuil process used aluminum oxide passed through the flame of an acetylene torch in order to grow a bullet-shaped ruby crystal known as a boule. Rodlike boules of seventeen inches and weighing forty-five hundred carats could be obtained by Verneuil's method. Early trials had often terminated through shattering of the crystals so formed, until internal stresses that developed in the growing boule were relieved by making the contact point between the seed crystal and the growing one as small as possible. Much of the production went into jeweled bearings for watches, but electronic watches, which eliminate the need for bearings, have greatly reduced the demand. Still further the increased use of lasers calls for crystals of higher optical properties than can be obtained with Verneuil growth. That fact, in combination with present higher costs of manufacture, brought about the end of Verneuil ruby production in 1974, at least in the United States.

Other processes have been developed, however, one of which is the Czochralski pulling technique. Aluminum oxide is brought to its melting point of 2050 degrees centigrade and a small piece of ruby crystal, the seed ruby, is touched to the upper surface of the molten mass, called the melt. The temperature of seed and melt must then be kept within a range of no more than one to two degrees apart throughout the process. If too high the seed will melt; and if too low the molten material will solidify. When everything is right, however, the bottom edge of the seed fuses with the upper surface of the melt, and when lifted upward very slowly will draw more and more of the melt with it, forming a rod. Rates of growth can proceed at from one-quarter inch to one inch per hour, the slower rate favoring the formation of larger, longer crystals. These can be a bit more than four inches in diameter by sixteen inches in length. This process has largely replaced Verneuil's, resulting in crystals with superior optical qualities that are ideal for lasers.

However, when such crystals must be cut and faceted, as in making gems for jewelry, the labor cost of cutting reduces much of their price advantage. In fact, a synthetic diamond, particularly when cut and polished, is ultimately *more* expensive than the natural product. Loss of material ranges between 75 and 85 percent of the rough stone to shape the final jewel. Another limiting factor is the slow rate at which some kinds of crystals form and grow. Opals, which result from the settling of elements held in solution, can take one year to form, while emeralds increase their size by only one millimeter per month. Should you plan to present someone with a birthday ring or necklace you had better start early in the year. These mineral crops take somewhat longer than beans or wheat to harvest.

While synthetic stones will never fully replace the natural product they do fill a genuine need. With each passing century the natural supply dwindles by an unknown amount of irreplaceable carats, at the same time that new demands for the remainder increase. We are fortunate to be able to synthesize them, but now and again possession of any man-made stone could be a disadvantage, as the following story from the gem world will demonstrate through the realities of the marketplace.

Shortly before World War I a housemaid in the employ of a German industrialist was about to retire from service and rejoin her relatives who had emigrated to New York. She was asked what she would care to have as a retirement gift, and, being of a modest disposition requested the privilege of a discounted purchase from her employer's stock of synthetic rubies. As part of his many operations he made the stones by the Verneuil process, under license, and made them available to all employees of his organization for a few marks. The request was readily granted, and on the next day a trayful of the gems was submitted for her choice. The selection was made, the nominal price paid, and the maid left happily for America. The stone, however, was unset, and wishing to have it made into a ring she brought it into Tiffany's in order to have it set in a simple mount. The jeweler in charge of the transaction, after a casual glance at the stone, praised its clarity and asked if she would like to sell it. Thereupon she told him it was a synthetic, worth only a very small sum, much less than the cost of the setting, and that she preferred to keep it as a memento of her working years. The jeweler excused himself for a moment only to return shortly with Tiffany's gem expert, George F. Kunz, who examined the stone through his loupe and promptly offered the bewildered woman $5000 as a purchase price. Her old employer had very generously tricked her by offering her a selection of real rubies in place of the man-made ones.

At other times common and nearly valueless stone, such as steatite, which we call soapstone, can become the basis of a profitable home industry. Eskimo communities in Canada, particularly those around James Bay and on Baffin Island, were badly disrupted by economic and social changes as they were increasingly affected by 20th-century influences. Some outsiders who saw the profusion of steatite available and had observed the skill with which Eskimos could carve almost anything,

The quarrymen chopping and lugging this New Hampshire
granite have no amenities and very few "modern" aids, only a
few horses and oxen and a lot of cables and pulleys.

189

put those elements together and created an industry. Not only did it bring in much-needed income, but it provided a new creative outlet for people who were losing much of their old life. Spears, ivory fishhooks, all manner of household and hunting gear that had been lovingly shaped by hand, had lost much of their usefulness, for game had decreased, and modern political and economic policies were bringing the old, nomadic way of life to an end. Traditions and folk tales that were in danger of being lost were given a new life through sculpture and prints pulled from incised blocks of soapstone. The superb sense of design and the profound feeling for form of the Eskimo artists made a tremendous impact upon a world that had hitherto ignored them. Their sculptures and prints flow directly out of the life-process itself, and make the overly intellectualized product of so-called civilized artists seem anemic by comparison.

It was not simply a matter of giving them stone and tools with which to create art, for it was also a matter of teaching new and unfamiliar concepts of art. The old Eskimo sculpture was always small, rather like Japanese netsuke, and was most often worn as a personal ornament. Therefore a piece had no base, but could be readily swung about so as to be seen from every angle. It was difficult to alter this original form of construction; but it was even more difficult to alter the original Eskimo system for making graphics. In the old days designs were woven or stitched onto parkas or boots, whereas drawing was a matter for mapmaking, or decorating the shaman's trappings. Originally, images and areas of prime importance were always made larger, with all others subordinated, corrections being made verbally. Add to that the fact that an Eskimo sees and understands an object or picture equally well from any position or angle, and it becomes clear that these "primitives" had to shift into low pictorial gear to communicate with "cultured" viewers who insist on an unalterable upside and downside.

A far cry from soapstone carving, in fact from any other type of sculpture, are those works that take entire mountainsides of solid limestone for their realization. Stone Mountain in Georgia is one, the Chief Crazy Horse monument to an American Indian warrior is another, and Gutzon Borglum's colossal portraits of four presidents cut across the face of Mount Rushmore makes a third, giving the United States quite a lead in what has to be called the "Megasculpture Derby." Hammers and chisels are secondary sculptural tools in all those instances, since most of the work is done by means of precisely calculated explosive charges located in places chosen with the greatest of care. A bit of roughness is left to retard the effect of weathering and to prevent uneven changes in scale as erosion does occur. To see the carvings at their best may require a few more centuries, or even a millennium or two. In the interim those who fancy large-scale sculpture may be better off visiting Grand Canyon—before it levels out.

Equally as staggering as the man-made or natural modeling of geological features is the masonry work of the great medieval cathedrals. Even more astounding is the fact that the skills that put together those towering examples of craftsmanship have not perished, but are being practiced to this day, and in one of the great cities of the modern world, New York. Young masons are being taught how to fashion such strange-sounding architectural members as gablets, crockets, quoins, and internal angle stones, all from raw, unshaped blocks just as was done at Chartres, Cologne, and Canterbury. The cathedral, which may be finished in 1992, one century after its beginning, is that of St. John the Divine on Morningside Heights in Manhattan, an all-masonry structure built in an age of steel and glass. To visit its stoneyard, where the blocks are cut by hand right at the site, is a unique experience that takes the viewer back in time to the atmosphere of the Middle Ages, but free of the innumerable disadvantages of that era. One of its most valuable features is that a skill, which was teetering on the edge of being lost forever, has now been restored to life. New generations of craftsmen will be formed to restore the fabric of these great buildings as they come to need repair, for cathedrals need continuing maintenance as much as paintings or other works of art. Granite, limestone, jasper, marble, and all the other building stones yield their secrets only to trained hands and eyes, and that training can only be obtained through building from the ground up. In a sense it is only just that a Gothic structure, such as those that intro-

It is remarkable how few tools are required to convert a mountain of hard, rough stone into a soaring cathedral.

duced extensive use of glass in building, should now become the vehicle that is restoring the stone framework to its former importance. The idea of the glass-curtain wall has been done to death, and now serves only expediency, or to provide transparent coffins in which the embalmed spirit of our age may be viewed.

It is not only cathedrals that can exemplify mass, transparency, and the beauty of design, for all of those qualities may be found in crystalline quartz as well. Always a source of joy to the beholder, the clarity, color, and form of quartz crystals, clustered like forests of solidified light, have exerted tremendous appeal for the lapidaries who carved and shaped them as objects of art. And while quartz may be common it does possess many properties and characteristics that give it tremendous value in our civilization.

Until recent years the state of Minas Gerais in Brazil has been a major source for the supply of quartz crystals to collectors, lapidaries, and industry. From its mines have poured such varieties as rose quartz, one of the rarest kinds; citrine, which approaches the beauty of topaz; smoky, a brownish gray; blue; and amethyst. Other kinds are aventurine, which has either a golden or greenish spangled appearance; tiger's eye, caused by fibrous bands; red rutilated, containing minute reddish needles; and some that form enormous crystals, such as Siberian milky quartz, that has occurred in a mass of thirteen metric tons. But, as with industrial diamonds, the laboratory is coming to be the main source of this material, for there its synthetic growth can be tailored to specific scientific needs.

Quartz is one of the most versatile substances known, and without access to its many capabilities the work of the scientific community would grind to an abrupt halt. Its crystals contain several properties that absolutely guarantee that fact, for quartz is piezoelectric, pyroelectric, and can rotate the plane of polarized light. Piezoelectric means that the crystal generates minute electrical currents when subjected to pressure; pyroelectric means that temperature changes acting on the crystal will induce polarity in electrical currents flowing through it; and polarization means that normal incoherent, undisciplined light rays can be marshalled into a single direction. Our technol-

ogy could not operate without the capabilities those effects offer us in matters of control and accurate measurement. Without quartz oscillators tuned to keep a wavelength within definite limits, broadcast signals from radio and TV stations would be a matter of endless search as they varied with changes in the atmosphere, magnetic conditions, electrical interference, and other disembodied gremlins. With them we can confidently turn our tuning controls to a chosen position, and unfailingly receive the same station that we did yesterday or the year before. Control oscillators keep a wavelength fixed by harnessing a quartz plate and an alternating electrical current to operate in perfect, unalterable unison. Such crystal plates must be totally free of cracks, bubbles, flaws, and the twinning habit that most quartz is subject to when produced under nature's sometimes untidy conditions. After all, the American poet Emerson did remark that everything God made is a little crooked or has a crack in it. Those characteristics are what help the world to hang together, of course, and technologies that eliminate them may not prove, in the end, to be the brightest of bright ideas.

Among the many instruments that rely on quartz crystals for their efficient action are special pressure gauges, resonators, wave stabilizers, polarimeters, spectrographic lenses, and a host of other bits of sophisticated gadgetry that surpass the understanding of the average nonscientist, while making life a little more orderly and pleasant for him. More mundane uses for quartz include its employment in making glass, paint, abrasives, and fire-brick for high-temperature furnaces in the ceramics industry. It is even utilized to make a special insulating paper than can withstand strong electrical fields and temperatures of up to 3000 degrees Fahrenheit before it breaks down. That product is made by melting the quartz, which is then spun and mixed with clay to obtain the final result, and while invaluable in certain electrical installations it is scarcely worthwhile for use as stationery.

One of the most familiar uses for quartz glass is in the manufacture of infrared heat lamps or ultraviolet sunlamps. Quartz glass, unlike ordinary window glass, is transparent to those wavelengths of light that lie outside the visible spectrum.

While you may practically roast by basking in a greenhouse, sunburn will never result, since regular glass blocks off all the ultra-violet rays. Another desirable feature of quartz glass is its exceptionally low coefficient of expansion and contraction, which makes it extremely useful for laboratory purposes where precise measurements must be carried out regardless of changing ambient temperatures. One of the most colorful uses of quartz glass is its ability to produce "black light," which induces a glow in fluorescent materials, thus pointing out the presence of certain minerals that could otherwise pass undetected. These "black light" tubes contain mercury vapor and a filter of dyed glass that screens off all ultra-violet and visible light, emitting only rays that excite molecular activity in many materials. That invisible radiation when reflected from an object is converted into visibility, and takes on highly diagnostic coloration in the process. Art museums make good use of these lights in analyzing varnish formulas on paintings, detecting restored areas on wooden panels and furniture, and even repairs or fills in marble statuary. Art forgery, though still practiced, is becoming a more perilous occupation every day, and is gradually being forced to imitate contemporary works and artists.

Still another use of crystals, undreamed of in the early years of this century, is the generation of the laser beam. The word "laser" is merely an acronym for light amplification by stimulated emission of radiation. A typical laser generator consists of a ruby crystal, although fluorite and scheelite may also be used, a sapphire coating about the ruby, and a xenon arc lamp. The ruby crystals presently in use are formed by the Czochralski process, which insures an optically perfect crystal, and these are covered along the length of their rodlike shape by a sapphire coating. The function of the sapphire is to pass the light from the xenon lamp through the sides of the ruby crystal, and at the same time its high reflectivity prevents any of the absorbed light from escaping, effectively trapping all rays within the ruby rod. Additionally, the rod has a reflecting plate at one end, which stops contained light from escaping in that direction. Its other end has a partially reflecting plate through which the sped-up light will eventually escape in a flash of radiation. What occurs is that the light trapped in the crystal excites the chromium atoms of the ruby, causing them to organize the light into a continuous, coherent beam of high intensity. When it builds up sufficient force and speed it bursts through the transparent area of the partially reflecting plate as a microscopically narrow, tightly focused light beam of one wavelength. It will then carry for immense distances without the loss by dispersion that occurs with ordinary light, and because it is intensely hot it can vaporize whatever it touches.

As a consequence of those properties, reflected laser beams assist geologists, astronomers, and other scientists in making minute and precise measurements in both laboratory and field. The great power of lasers will soon be stepped up a thousandfold through use of a magnetic field, as is now done with masers that amplify sound signals to that strength, making feasible radio telescopes and communication satellites in space.

Laser beam reflections from a gemstone reveal a unique "fingerprint" pattern for each, one that never alters until the stone is repolished. Lasers have also been added to the arsenal of tools used to detect art forgeries. Their intense heat, in a beam only 1/2500 of an inch wide, can be used to vaporize undesirable inclusions that flaw diamonds, and in fact can also drill those stones for wire-drawing dies. Best of all, that heat can be employed in surgery, since it affects only the direct area upon which it is focused, thus making it possible to excise individual diseased cells in the body, or to spot-weld torn or displaced retinas.

In the years to come the technological use of gems will probably exceed their ornamental use by far, opening possibilities not yet imagined. Every technical advance breeds still others, some of even greater consequence than the original one. Holographs, those photographic images that create the illusion of solid objects suspended in space, showing every surface from every angle, may yet revolutionize sculpture. Holographs, lasers, and computer projections may be combined to create and modify three-dimensional images of objects that have not yet become realities. The world of ornamental and gemstones may yet gain us a paradise greater than any we have ever lost.

9

Chapter 9
WHAT, WHERE, HOW:
The Basics of Collecting

The collector of rocks and minerals is more fortunate than most other collectors for much of the material that he gathers is free for the taking. It is also of international distribution; virtually no locality on earth does not offer specimens. Moreover the equipment needed to pursue the interest is minimal and may be bought at very little cost. The following suggested items should meet the needs of the beginning collector, and should be added to only after conditions warrant further investment. Equipment that may have invaluable properties for the professional or the specialist may also prove to be a burdensome waste to the amateur collector. For example, we have all seen amateur photographers carrying so many accessories with them that they miss a prime photographic opportunity before they can get all their gear sorted out.

Of primary importance is a good field guide. It should be accurately and amply illustrated, preferably in color, and should contain all relevant data, such as general classification, specific chemical content, Mohs scale of hardness rating, usual locations, and associated materials. Regarding the amount of information given for each kind of stone or mineral: the more the better, for in that matter there can never be too much. What may seem at first an excessive amount of information will soon become less formidable as you gain in expertise, so it is best to begin with a book that you will not outgrow.

Of almost equal importance is the purchase of a hammer for field use. Do not skimp here; obtain the best you can afford, for the prices, in any cases, are not great. The face of the hammer should be square, and the head and haft should be forged from a single piece of metal, for wooden hafts have a habit of splitting. The haft should be covered with a handle of either composition material or of rubber, whichever feels most comfortable, and offers a firm, reliable grip that will permit full control when you are shaping a specimen. The rear of the hammer should have an undivided, chisellike edge, and should be curved in a flat and shallow arc. Add a good cold chisel, obtainable from almost any hardware or ironmonger's shop, to complete your set of necessary tools. (You may wish to add a more slender pick or probe at a later time.)

Other items essential for field collecting include a sturdy knapsack with broad, comfortable straps that do not cut into your shoulders or chafe after the sack is well filled, and strong work gloves. A 10x lens is also a handy addition, one with a protective cover; as well as a compass, a notebook, a container (either a metal canteen or a plastic bottle) for drinking water—which may not always be available in the field— and some sheets of folded newspaper in which you can wrap specimens. All of the above should fit easily into the knapsack, leaving ample room for any collected material; and these implements should weigh only slightly more than three pounds. Lightweight packs are a positive blessing in the field, especially in hot weather or in difficult terrain, two conditions that often accompany rock collecting.

In earlier times many collectors gathered fairly large specimens, something still rather difficult to resist, especially when faced with those of exceptional appeal. In the modern world of fairly cramped quarters, however, the trend is now in the opposite direction, and thumbnail-sized specimens have proved increasingly popular for a number of reasons. First, they do not pose a weight problem after they have been gathered, and, when they are catalogued after returning

home, a far more extensive collection results, for it requires relatively little space. Additionally, small specimens make the work of preparing thin sections for microscopic examination that much easier, should the collector wish to pursue that particular line of interest. Such specimens when viewed by polarized light are often astoundingly beautiful, revealing an infinite variety of colors and patterns and providing perfect subjects for microphotography.

The flakes or chips, when carefully cut from the living rock, exhibit all the characteristics neces-

Preceding pages: *Some of the rock hound's tools include a field guide, broad chisel, safety goggles, knapsack, hand lens, water container, and folded newspaper for wrapping specimens.* Above: *Marking a specimen.*

sary for full identification and classification. They can even make it somewhat easier to put together gradations or series that show the geological or mineralogical features of a specific area. Specialized collections can also be made of examples of every kind of quartz or limestone or feldspar or any other stones peculiar to a given area. Smallness of size does not always indicate the degree of interest inherent in any particular specimen. A micromounted group of crystals, viewed under a 10x or 20x hand lens, can easily offer more to the eye and mind than a featureless slab of sandstone. Such micromounts are much smaller than the thumbnail specimens, and are usually set into bits of cork or balsa wood to prevent loss, and to make viewing more convenient.

Not all collectors will care to confine themselves to miniature specimens, and some pieces, in fact, will demand a larger size. Geodes, for instance, should be kept intact after being opened to show the special characteristics of their formation. It is also a matter of some importance, both esthetically and scientifically, to retain some of the matrix that usually surrounds crystals. The matrix will provide them with a base upon which they can stand solidly, and will also serve to show materials with which they are normally associated or from which they grow. Uniformity of size may seem a worthwhile goal for a collector, but in practice it is very difficult to achieve. As long as nature and human nature retain their variability, collections will continue to be as mixed as they have been in the past. After all, that which is of primary importance to most collectors is the enjoyment that comes from gathering, arranging, and studying chosen materials, while maintaining an enthusiastic growth of interest that is always seeking fresh discoveries and approaches.

As to where specimens may be found—some of the most productive areas are located on ridgetops, cliffsides, along riverbanks, or on steep hillsides, anywhere that the natural forces of erosion are at work in exposing outcrops or fresh material. It makes a great deal of sense to let nature do most of your digging for you. Other locations that often provide fine items for the collector are in and around highway or railway cuts, gravel pits, quarries, excavations, and mining dumps. Before entering such sites it is always wise to obtain any

necessary permission, and to be advised of any hazards peculiar to the specific area. If operations are being carried out by workmen it is probably better to wait for slack periods, such as lunchtime, to conduct your own activities. Danger is always present wherever rock is being worked, and such danger can easily be released whenever amateurs are heedless. Minimize risks to yourself and others, for the exercise of a little caution can pay great dividends.

When actually taking specimens make good use of your notebook, writing down the location for future reference, describing all particulars of interest such as the geological formation, and other mineralogical forms that are present. In time all of that accumulated data will make it possible to spot likely areas for exploration, or to save time and effort where nothing is apt to be found. Give each specimen a number in the notebook and write it on the outside of its protective newspaper wrapping as well. Later the identifying number can be attached permanently to the item by painting a small dab of lacquer, nail polish, or white correction fluid such as typists use, onto the stone and writing on it after it is fully dry. The numbered piece can then be properly filed and indexed.

When a desirable sample of stone is found it is always a good idea to use your hammer to expose a fresh, unweathered area. Generally a sharp, glancing blow will suffice to remove any weathered or discolored portion, though sometimes a chisel may be required, particularly with very hard rocks. Then strike off the specimen you are collecting from the main piece of rock, reducing it afterward, if necessary, with light blows that trim and shape its edges and thickness. That is where the back portion of your hammer will prove most useful, as will your heavy work gloves, for more often than not trimming is best done while holding the stone in hand. A pair of safety goggles for eyes is a sensible addition to your kit; rock splinters can fly in the most unexpected directions.

The next step is to wrap the specimen in the newspaper that you have brought along. It may seem foolish to give hard pieces of stone any additional protection, but if left to rub against each other while loose in your knapsack, scratches or disfiguring chips could easily destroy a prized

198

specimen. Always fold the paper so that both ends are closed, while several layers prevent the stone from emerging along a center fold, or possibly breaking out through a single thickness. If you anticipate gathering more delicate items, some pieces of tissue paper and rolled cotton are necessary before the final wrapping. If the specimens possess needlelike formations or fragile crystals, they should be placed in separate cardboard boxes before putting them in your knapsack. Once at home, they can be set into compartmented trays, boxes, or shallow drawers that you have purchased or improvised. A wide variety of storage and display cabinets is available from scientific supply houses, but remember when purchasing them that their main purpose is to keep your collection in order and easily accessible, nothing more.

If you have occasion to open many geodes, or to split concretions, or even to break off sizable fragments of rock, then a good cracking hammer will prove a useful addition to your basic tools. The hammer should be flat and square at both ends, like a sledgehammer, and should weigh about two pounds (one kilo). That amount of weight, when swung forcefully against stone, will usually achieve the desired effect, and, if it doesn't, then its force can be more sharply and directly applied by combining its use with a broad chisel.

To recapitulate, here is a checklist of essential items: field guide, geologist's hammer, broad chisel, safety goggles, knapsack, 10x hand lens, compass, work gloves, water container, notebook, folded newspaper. To that list you may wish to add a cracking hammer, but keep things simple, few, and versatile, saving weight and leaving more room for specimens.

Once you have your specimens safely at home you can do many more things with them than just look at them. For instance, you may wish to arrange your collection systematically, grouping items according to their mineral content, placing all representative micas, garnets, feldspars together. Or you may elect to order them by their ratings on the Mohs scale, or their chemical structure, such as silicates, carbonates, oxides, halides, and other basic classes. Specialized collections can be made demonstrating the varieties

of crystalline and cryptocrystalline quartz, or setting forth the characteristics of igneous, sedimentary, or metamorphic rocks. Hundreds of themes are available at no greater trouble than the use of your imagination, and each of them will give you greater insight and understanding as to how the earth was put together. During the course of field work you may even discover linkages with other areas of scientific inquiry, such as fossilized plant and animal life, or learn how to distinguish underlying minerals through the plant materials that draw nourishment from them. All in all the possibilities are endless.

If sufficient funds are available your horizons can expand in many other directions with the purchase of specialized equipment. To analyze rocks and minerals, much can be established visually in the field by means of matching descriptions in your guide book to the basic visible properties of your specimens. The luster, hardness, magnetism, color, streak, habit of cleavage or fracture, will usually lead to positive identification without further tests. In some cases, however, specific gravity will need to be determined, or flame tests will have to be carried out, using an inexpensive blow-pipe. Powdered specimens can be heated in closed or open tubes, that is a regular test tube or one open at both ends, while other tests can be made with acids, water, or application of heat to drive off fluid contents. A good mineral guide will describe a variety of these procedures in detail, and the presence or absence of such information is, in itself, a good indication of the worth of the guide you choose. A basic knowledge of chemistry will be helpful if you do conduct these analyses, but lack of it is not necessarily crucial since most guides will usually tell you what to expect under varying circumstances and what to look for.

A petrographic microscope with a polarizer and analyzer will, at about the cost of a good camera, open an entirely unexpected and generally invisible world to your eyes. Low-power magnification, usually about 20x, is ample to examine most materials. When a camera is attached for microphotography, the results can equal some works found in art galleries, certainly as far as color, form, and design are concerned. For this type of examination of specimens, it is necessary to grind each of them down to extreme thinness, to the point that permits the passage of light, rather on the order of translucent marble or alabaster. Motorized grinders and buffers will accomplish that chore with their belts or disks that carry various grades of abrasive from coarse grit to jeweler's rouge.

Here we begin to enroach on the lapidary's territory, and very often the mineralogist finds that geology allied to craftsmanship can be infinitely rewarding, and possibly a source of revenue to support the hobby. That final step, however, can be a treacherous one to take, because once you get caught up in doing work for pay you are apt to end by doing little or none for your own pleasure. In my opinion, hobbies and professions should be kept in separate bins.

The lapidary's equipment can be quite expensive, and it also requires a fair amount of electrical power, an item that needs to be carefully considered in times of fuel shortages and rising costs. High-speed, heavy-duty saws using diamond dust fixed in a notched rim or fused to their cutting edges are needed in order to begin the work. This is normally followed by grinding, using both coarse and fine grit alternately, then lapping, which is done on a horizontal disk using three grades of abrasive, progressively finer. Next comes smoothing with a sanding cloth mounted on either a disk or belt, and finally the polishing or buffing.

Using this kind of equipment allows easy formation of either oval or pillow-cut cabochons, and, with the addition of mechanical aids, faceting can be achieved, although that requires a fair degree of skill. Simpler and less expensive tumblers or rockers will polish roughly cut pieces into smoothly finished free forms that can be made into necklaces, bracelets, earrings, and other simple jewelry, and will probably satisfy the demands of most amateurs, particularly those with limited budgets. Remember, though, that the tumbling or rocking equipment runs on electricity and often must be kept in motion for at least two full days. One convenient method of sampling the practice of lapidary work is to purchase what are known as "pre-forms" in local shops that cater to the rock and mineral collectors. These are partially shaped stones on which most of the heavy

work has already been done; they have reached the point where only finishing touches are needed to bring them to completion. That final, additional work, however, can range from simple shaping and polishing to skilled design engraving, so there are unlimited possibilities if you decide to make use of pre-forms.

Rock-shops, as they are commonly called, can be useful places to fill out the gaps in your collection, especially when they provide pieces from remote locations. When travel costs are taken into consideration, specimens from central Africa or Australia may well be more reasonable at two hundred dollars when purchased than the expense involved in going to the site. It may not be as much fun—bought specimens never have the associations that personally collected ones do—but they do offer you *something* to work with. Very often rock-shops do give the amateur collector a wide range of material for study at rather low cost, especially if he is willing to forego gem quality. Cabochons, beads, or disks of practically any kind of stone and mineral are obtainable for very low prices, and can add great interest to the pursuit of your hobby at a minimum of cost.

To round out sources of information about rocks, minerals, and everything connected with them, it is useful to search out whatever mineralogical or rock-hobbyist publications are available in your local library, evaluate them, and then subscribe to those that interest you. The articles and advertisements will keep you abreast of current developments, and often make you aware of new or different approaches to your hobby. You might veer off in search of fluorescent or radioactive materials, unusual combinations of ores, or seek out traces of algae or diatoms in ancient rock, for anything is possible once an interest in collecting specimens has been aroused. In any case, you will find an ever-expanding group of sources that will keep your interest alive and growing, an interest that is beyond possibility of exhaustion.

Just as "diamonds are forever," so it is with the study and collection of rocks and minerals, a study that will unfailingly bring you a host of jeweled moments to ornament the rest of your life.

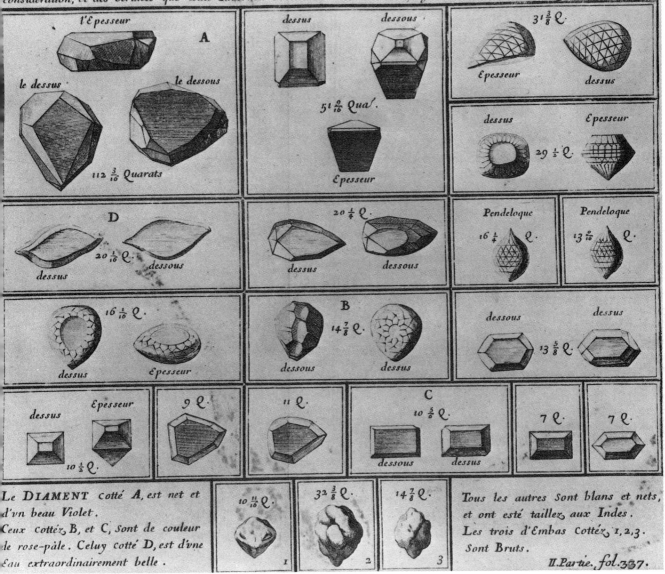

Some 20 of the diamonds that J. B. Tavernier, jeweler and explorer, brought back from India to the royal court of Louis XIV at Versailles. The illustration tells us something of the ways jewels were marketed in the 17th century, either raw and uncut, as at the bottom of the picture, or partially or fully cut and faceted. The engraving comes from Tavernier's book Six Voyages to Turkey, Persia, and to the Indies, published at Paris in 1676–1677. Tavernier's seventh voyage remains unrecorded, since he died in Russia while attempting to reach India by an overland route.

201

GUIDE TO MINERALS AND STONES

This list of minerals and stones mentioned in the text is not intended to substitute for a complete, analytic treatment. That would require another book all by itself. It is merely intended to provide a few of the highly visible characteristics of the various minerals and the countries where they may be found. Detailed and diagnostic descriptions (which resist any attempt to combine abbreviation with accuracy), may be found in many of the good field guides and mineralogical handbooks now available in natural history museums, rock-shops that cater to hobbyists, or by order from publishers who specialize in scientific works.

Actinolite—A tough, dark-to-light-green stone found in regions rich in magnesium and iron. The Nephrite variety is often confused with, and sold as, more expensive Jadeite. Comes from Austria, Italy, Germany, Poland, Central Asia, Canada (British Columbia), U.S. (Wyoming), and New Zealand. Used in jewelry.

Adularia—See Orthoclase.

Agate—See Quartz, Chalcedony var.

Alabaster—See Gypsum.

Alectorius—A medieval name for a Quartz particle sometimes found in a capon's gizzard.

Alexandrite—See Chrysoberyl.

Almandine—See Garnet.

Almandite—See Garnet.

Amber—Fossilized resin. Transparent-to-translucent, color varies from orange to yellow to brown. Light in weight, easily carved. Baltic Sea area, also USSR, Romania, Italy, France, Spain, Dominican Republic, and Canada. Used in jewelry, formerly in incense and varnish.

Amethyst—See Quartz, Crystalline var., and Corundum.

Antimony—Soft, very heavy, bright and metallic mineral, mostly derived from its ore, Stibnite.

Comes from Borneo, Italy, Germany, Portugal, Canada (New Brunswick), and U.S. (California). Used in metal alloys, formerly as a purgative.

Aquamarine—See Beryl.

Arsenic—White veins in rock, exhibiting dull, opaque, saltlike crystals. When heated in flames gives off aroma of garlic. Often found with arsenides and sulfides of nickel, silver, or cobalt. Comes from Siberia, Czechoslovakia, Romania, Italy, Germany, France, U.S. (Arizona). Used in some industrial processes, and medicine, but chiefly as poison for pest control.

Aventurine—See Quartz, Crystalline var.

Azurite—A bluish mineral, either in nodules or crystals, associated with copper and malachite. Once used as a substitute pigment for lapis lazuli. Comes from France, U.S. (Arizona), southwest Africa, and Australia (New South Wales). Sometimes cut as a cabochon for jewelry despite its relative softness.

Basalt—Color is dark gray to black, often brown or reddish. An igneous extrusion that flows from surface or submarine volcanoes. Sometimes forms hexagonal columns, as in the famous Giant's Causeway, Ireland, but more often forms extensive beds. India's Deccan, the Columbia Plateau in the northwest U.S., Hawaii, Iceland, and South America's Parana Basin are typical sites. Common, of wide occurrence; used for paving, ballast, building, or for making rock wool and fiberglass.

Beryl—Very hard, just below Corundum in hardness; forms hexagonal crystals from a fraction of an inch to thirty feet in length. It provides the gemstones Aquamarine (blue), Emerald (green), Heliodor (yellow), and Morganite (pink), but most are off-white or pale bluish-green, and range from transparent to opaque because of numerous internal fractures and inclusions. Provides Beryllium for a variety of technical and scientific uses, and for jewelry.

Bezoar—A medieval name, from Arabic, for carbonate of lime concretions that form in the gastrointestinal tracts of animals, especially deer. Once highly valued as an antidote for poison.

Bloodstone—See Quartz, Chalcedony var.

Breccia—Fragmented bits of rock, usually quite angular, held in a matrix of clay, or of siliceous, calcareous, or limonitic materials. Occurs in Limestone and dolomite, often associated with Marble. It is found in France, Italy, England, and the U.S. Used for interior paving and as a decorative stone.

Cairngorm—See Quartz, Crystalline var.

Calcite—Highly variable in form, color, and degree of light transmission, transparent to opaque. Over 300 known forms, and distribution is worldwide. Germany, England, Iceland, Mexico and the U.S. are prime sources. Used in optics, cement, metallurgy, fertilizers, the chemical industry, and as polish and filling material.

Calcophonos—A medieval name for phonolite, a light gray igneous rock, commonly associated with basalt. Found in the USSR, Czechoslovakia, Germany, Italy, England, Brazil, western U.S., and such volcanic islands as the Azores, Canaries, and Marquesas. Very limited use as building material, and as a fertilizer.

Carbuncle—A medieval name that designated *any* transparent red stone, such as Ruby, Spinel, or Garnet. It supposedly glowed like burning coal; *Carbunculus* in Latin.

Carnelian—See Quartz, Chalcedony var.

Cat's-eye—See Quartz, Crystalline var., and Chrysoberyl.

Chalcedony—See Quartz, Chalcedony var.

Chelidonio—A medieval name for a stone believed to be found within a swallow; called *Chelidonius* in Latin.

Chelonites—A medieval name for a stone thought to be found in a turtle or tortoise; *Chelonia* in Latin.

Chert—See Quartz, Chalcedony var.

Chlorite—A kind of light-green schist, derived by metamorphosis from lava and tuff. Found in the western Alps, central Scotland, and the U.S. (New Hampshire, Vermont, North Carolina, California). Used as roofing tile, or can be turned on a lathe, and is also used for decorative carving. Known as "potstone."

Chrysoberyl—Often forms pseudohexagonal crystals that are colorless, gray, green, yellow, or brown. Provides the gemstones called "Alexandrite" that are green in daylight, red by artificial light; and Cat's-eye, a honey-yellow stone that exhibits a band of light that shifts as the stone is turned, a property called chatoyancy. It comes from Sri Lanka, the USSR, Norway, Italy, Brazil and the U.S. (Connecticut).

Chrysolite—See Forsterite.

Chrysoprase—See Quartz, Chalcedony var.

Cinnabar—Soft, very heavy, red masses, occasionally in crusts, very rarely in crystals. Always in areas that have had volcanic activity. Chief ore of mercury. Found in Spain, Italy, and Yugoslavia, the principal sources, but also in China, USSR, Algeria, U.S. (Arkansas), and Peru. Was once used as vermilion pigment.

Citrine—See Quartz, Crystalline var.

Conglomerate—A sedimentary rock containing many rounded pebbles in a matrix of calcareous clay and sand. Widespread occurrence. Fine examples in Scotland, England, eastern U.S., and South Africa. Used as building stone.

Coral—Calcareous skeletons of marine polyps. Found in the Mediterranean, and tropical waters of the Atlantic, Pacific, and Indian Oceans, where it forms atolls, reefs, and islands. Red coral is used in jewelry.

Corundum—An extremely hard, hexagonal, barrel-shaped crystal, exceeded only by Diamond in its hardness. The dark granular variety is known as Emery, and is used as an abrasive. The gem varieties are Ruby (red), Sapphire (blue or colorless), Topaz (yellow), Amethyst (purple), and Emerald (green), the last three usually being termed "Oriental" topaz, amethyst, and emerald.

Crapaudine—See Toadstone.

Diabase—A dark igneous rock, usually green to blackish, sometimes with brownish surface. Very hard and heavy. Widespread. Found in Germany, Scotland, Canada, U.S., South Africa, and Tasmania. Called Dolerite in England. Serves as building stone. Used in ancient Egypt for hammer-smoothing hard, rough stone.

Diamond—Hardest known substance. Industrial uses of great value ranging from wire-drawing, through abrasives, to diamond-edged saws. Found in USSR, South Africa, Zaire, Sierra Leone,

Ghana, U.S. (Arkansas) and Brazil, all yielding high-quality gemstones. Industrial grades come from Brazil and Zaire, which is now the leading supplier. No typical site, but is associated with kimberlite, a diamond-bearing rock, in South Africa and Arkansas, U.S.

Diorite—An extremely hard stone with a medium to coarse grain, dark to blackish gray in color. Great masses of it are found in mountainous regions around the world, especially in Romania, Italy, Corsica, France, Germany, Finland, Sweden, Scotland, and the U.S. (Minnesota). Used as building stone and polished facing slabs.

Dolerite—See Diabase.

Eagle-stone—A medieval name for geode formations.

Emerald—See Beryl and Corundum.

Emery—See Corundum.

Feldspar—A green variety of microcline feldspar was formerly called "Mother of Emerald." It was used first in ancient Egypt in jewelry, and also at later times. Feldspars of various sorts are major components of most rock formations, and are internationally distributed.

Flint—See Quartz, Chalcedony var.

Fluorite—Cubic crystals, colorless and transparent if pure, but may be yellow, pink, blue, green, purple, or black. Makes a popping sound when heated. Often associated with lead, zinc, and silver sulfides, also quartz and barite. Heavy, fragile, almost hard. Widespread occurrence with excellent crystals found in Switzerland, Italy, England, and U.S. Used for optics, metallurgy, and chemistry, especially manufacture of hydrofluoric acid. Often called fluorspar.

Forsterite—Hard, olive-green crystals, like stubby prisms. Sometimes yellowish or brown. They are abundant in basalts, and other igneous rocks. They are found on Zebirget Island, Egypt; the Ural Mountains, Burma, Italy, Germany, Norway, and the U.S. (Arizona). Used in making refractories or as the gemstone Peridot. Also called Olivine.

Galacia—A medieval name for a stone that supposedly produced milk in females.

Garnet—Very hard, many-faceted crystals, of bright to dark red, sometimes with a brown or purplish tint. Used as an inexpensive gemstone, and as an abrasive. Found in southern Australia, Sri Lanka, Malagasy Republic, Italy, Austria, Sweden, Greenland, U.S. (Alaska), and Brazil. Varieties are Almandine, Almandite, Grossular, and Pyrope.

Geode—A sedimentary rock, usually rounded in form, with an internal cavity lined with crystals, though it may contain sand or liquid. Good specimens come from the Mississippi Valley in the U.S. and from Uruguay, but any region where sedimentary rock can be found will produce them. They were called eagle-stones in earlier times.

Granite—An igneous rock visibly laden with granular crystals, and one which makes up the major percentage of continental rock formations. Color ranges from white, through grays, to mottled shades of pink. Very hard, resists weathering, takes a high polish, and is much used for sculpture and building purposes. Present in USSR, Scandinavia, Germany, Italy, Switzerland, France, England, Scotland, U.S., Canada, Brazil, Africa. Only trained geologists and mineralogists can distinguish true granite from allied and very similar forms, called granitoids, without specimen analysis.

Granodiorite—Very similar to true Granite, medium to fine granularity, light to dark gray. The west coastal ranges of North America from Canada to Southern California contain the world's largest deposits. Other areas include Japan, Yugoslavia, Romania, Austria, and Norway. Used as building stone.

Graywacke—Hard, sedimentary rock containing much Quartz, Feldspar, and rock fragments in a claylike or chloritic cement. Color gray to brown, occasionally green. Found in Japan, Italy, Germany, England, Wales, U.S. (West Virginia), and is used as a building stone.

Grossular—See Garnet.

Gypsum—A soft, light sedimentary stone. Often translucent to transparent, granular and compact. Color ranges through white, gray, cream, yellowish, to brown, and is often banded. Hardens on exposure to air, but is greatly altered by heat of flames. Used in making plaster of Paris, in cement, pottery, fertilizer, and for flooring or sculpture. Comes from Pakistan, Iran, USSR (in Asia and the Ural Mountains), Italy, France, Nova Scotia, much of the U.S., as well as Mexico and Chile. Common in areas once covered by seas, and in present or former volcanic areas.

Heliotrope—Synonym for Bloodstone. See Quartz, Chalcedony var.

Hematite—Stubby crystals of black color, often granular masses with iridescent surfaces. Heavy, fragile, hard, opaque, but always gives a reddish streak when drawn across other rock or a piece of white, unglazed tile. Common among igneous rocks. An important ore of iron, used as a pigment, polish, and occasionally in jewelry. Found in USSR (Ukraine), Switzerland, island of Elba, England, Canada (Quebec and Nova Scotia), U.S., Venezuela, and Brazil.

Hiddenite—See Spodumene.

Hornblende—Hard, heavy rock with short, prismatic crystals, needlelike or fibrous, color dark green to dark brown, and black. Has a glassy quality. Very common throughout the world, especially in Finland, Germany, Norway, Greenland, Canada (Ontario), and the U.S. Building and curbstone use.

Jacinth—See Zircon.

Jadeite—A precious stone that is found in compact, felted, and waxy masses. Very tough, heavy, and hard. Color varies from white, yellowish white, to green, and black. Most often found in Burma, Japan, southwest China, Tibet, rarely in northern Italy, also in U.S. (California), and Guatemala. Used in jewelry.

Jargon—See Zircon.

Jargoon—See Zircon.

Jasper—See Quartz, Chalcedony var.

Jet—A compact, hard variety of lignite coal. Black, shiny, has a glassy fracture. Found in England and Spain. Was popular for Victorian jewelry.

Kunzite—See Spodumene.

Labradorite—Found in igneous rocks, strongly crystalline structure, variable in color, colorless, white, yellowish, green, pink, or somewhat red. Quite often has bluish iridescence. Some kinds, such as Sunstone, have a play of color below their surfaces, the result of inclusions of Hematite. Sunstone comes mainly from Norway, USSR, and Canada. Labradorite comes from Labrador, although it is also found in Japan, USSR, Italy, and Norway.

Lapis lazuli—See Lazurite.

Lazurite—Generally in compact masses, dark blue, spotted with white calcite and yellowish pyrites. Fairly hard, opaque, fractures unevenly. Most important source is Afghanistan, but is also found, in small masses, in Burma, Pakistan, Siberia, Italy (Vesuvius and the Alban Hills), Angola, Labrador, U.S. (California and Colorado). Gemstone, decorative ornamental stone, formerly used to make ultramarine pigment, though Azurite was more often ground for that purpose.

Ligurius—A medieval term for Amber.

Limestone—A sedimentary rock with fine-grained, compact texture. Stratification rarely visible, fractures like flint or glass. Color is variable, usually white or light gray, but may be yellowish, pink, or reddish, even black, because of pigmentation present. Fossils abundant in some varieties. Common in Australia, Germany, England, and the U.S. Used as building stone, manufacture of lime, and lithographic stone.

Lodestone—See Magnetite.

Magnetite—Hard, very heavy, with variably shaped crystals quite evident. Associated with Emery and other forms of Corundum, often in alluvial and marine sands, also skarns and extrusive rocks. Black colored, strongly magnetic. Found in USSR, Sweden, Switzerland, Austria, Italy, South Africa, and the U.S. Rich iron ore, also yields phosphorus and vanadium, makes very hard steel.

Malachite—Semihard, heavy, strong green color, sometimes in needlelike crystals, generally in masses having a banded structure. Found with copper deposits. Large masses come from the USSR; other sources are Romania, Italy (Sardinia and Elba), France, Germany, Namibia, Zambia, Zaire, U.S. (Utah and Arizona), Chile, and southern Australia. Formerly crushed to make pigment, copper ore, now chiefly as a decorative stone for architecture and ornamental objects.

Marble—A metamorphosed form of Limestone with a crystalline structure. Color highly variable, ranging across the spectrum. Internationally distributed. Decorative stone for architecture, sculpture, and ornamentation.

Marcasite—See Pyrites.

Memphites—A medieval term for a stone with fabulous properties. Unidentifiable today.

Moonstone—See Orthoclase.

Morion—See Quartz, Crystalline var.

Moss Agate—See Quartz, Chalcedony var.

Mother of Emerald—See Feldspar.

Myrrhine—May have been a kind of Chalcedony, but no positively identified specimens have survived from Roman times.

Nephrite—See Actinolite.

Obsidian—Volcanic glass, black, shiny, always gives a circular fracture. Common in recent lava flows in Japan and Java. Also in Italy (Lipari Islands), Hungary, and western U.S. Used in prehistoric times for cutting tools and weapons, presently for making rock wool.

Oligoclase—See Labradorite.

Olivine—See Forsterite.

Onyx—See Quartz, Chalcedony var.

Opal—Compact earthy masses, often resulting from concretionary or stalactic deposits. Fairly hard, light, fragile, becoming more so as it evaporates its internal water content. Precipitates out of silica solutions. Comes from Turkey, Romania, Hungary, Italy, western U.S., Mexico, and Australia. Its pronounced play of colors has made it a highly favored gemstone, and has given us the term "opalescent" in English.

Oriental—This adjective when prefixed to any of the various Corundum gemstones indicates the hardest, most precious kinds from the Orient, such as Sapphire, Topaz, Emerald, Ruby, Cat's-eye, etc.

Orthoclase—Has prismatic, columnar, or tabular crystals in compact, granular masses. Often opaque, but in some varieties, such as Adularia, Moonstone, or Selenite, can be translucent and mildly opalescent. Fairly hard, colorless, white, gray, or pale yellow, pink, or blue. Found in a wide variety of intrusive rocks. Worldwide distribution. Used in porcelain, scouring powders, dental products, ceramic glazes, and in jewelry.

Pearl—Results from an organic secretion in oysters, clams, and similar shellfish. Used in jewelry.

Pegmatite—An igneous rock with large crystals, the rock often containing crystal-lined cavities. Color light but variable, generally associated with granitoid rocks. Important sources are USSR, Malagasy Republic, Brazil, U.S. (New England, Colorado, and South Dakota). Used chiefly for extraction of its mineral contents.

Peridot—See Forsterite.

Porphyry—A granitelike stone of dark gray, greenish, or reddish coloration. Found in association with granitic formations. Crystals of somewhat larger than fine to average proportions. Very hard, takes a high polish. Used in blocks or slabs for facing material, and was anciently fashioned into sarcophagi and statues. Classic locations in Egypt, also Scotland and Italy.

Prase—See Quartz, Crystalline var.

Puddingstone—A conglomerate containing many rounded pebbles of mixed sizes and color. Found in glacially formed areas and glacial stream beds. Comes from Switzerland, England, South Africa, U.S., and Australia. Used as a facing stone.

Pyrites—Cubic or polyhedral crystals, opaque masses of dark yellow crystals, fairly hard, sometimes with brownish iridescent surfaces. Common name "fool's gold." Found in Japan, USSR, Sweden, Norway, Germany, Italy, Spain, England, and the U.S. Used to make sulfuric acid. Gives off sparks if struck with a hammer, and sulphurous fumes if heated. Marcasite is a variety of pyrites used in jewelry.

Pyrope—See Garnet.

Quartz, Chalcedony var.—Crystals are microscopic, causing opacity. Very hard, has waxy or glassy luster. Often makes banded formations of a variety of colors, sometimes uniform, sometimes layered. Varieties are: Agate (concentric bands of various colors), Jasper (massive, very fine-grained), Onyx (has alternating layers of black and white), Sardonyx (has red layer in addition to black and white, Carnelian (red to reddish orange, also called Sard), Chrysoprase (a translucent to opaque variety colored golden green, or bright green), Heliotrope and Bloodstone (opaque deep green with red spots, hence "Bloodstone"), Flint (whitish to dark gray or black, forms in chalk beds), Chert (synonym for Flint). All the above are used for ornamental carving and for jewelry. Found in Germany, Italy, England, U.S., Brazil, Uruguay, Australia, India, and USSR.

Quartz, Crystalline var.—Transparent to translucent with glassy luster. Very hard, usually prismatic or hexagonal in form. Extremely common, making up 12 percent of earth's crust. Ranges from pure colorless through many hues. Varieties are: Rock crystal (clear as water), Milky (white and opaque), Smoky (light to dark brown and black, known as Cairngorm and Morion), Blue (color due to inclusions), Citrine (yellow, often passed as Topaz), Amethystine (purple shades), Rose (very rare, turns black if heated), Tiger's-eye (bands of brownish yellow), Chrysoprase (leek-green color), Prase (synonym for Chrysoprase), Aventurine (contains particles of mica, and is usually brownish yellow or green), Rutile (needle-like black, yellow, or red crystals within the quartz itself). Brazil, Uruguay, Germany, USSR, Sri Lanka, Zambia, South Africa, Canada, and the U.S. produce gem-quality varieties. Used in precision instruments and gauges, as abrasive, in glass, lenses, refractories, paints, and ornamental carvings.

Rock crystal—See Quartz, Crystalline var.

Ruby—See Corundum.

Rutile—Needle-shaped crystals of prismatic form. Colors are yellow, red, brown, and black, often bent into elbow or twin-heart shape. Hard, heavy, fragile, and generally found encased in quartz or metamorphic rock. Found in Switzerland, Italy, Norway, U.S., Mexico, Brazil, and Australia. Rutile is an ore of titanium.

Sandstone—A compressed sedimentary rock composed of quartz sand, Gypsum, Coral, and heavy minerals. Color is variable, but usually shades of brown. Internationally distributed. Used as building stone.

Sapphire—See Corundum.

Sard—See Quartz, Chalcedony var.

Sardonyx—See Quartz, Chalcedony var.

Scheelite—Translucent to transparent crystals, variable in shape, but often somewhat pyramidal or tabular. Color is yellowish, tawny, green, white, or reddish gray. Semihard, very heavy, fragile, fluorescent. Comes from Australia, Malaysia, Burma, Japan, China, Korea, Italy, U.S. and Bolivia. Important ore of tungsten, used in laser instruments.

Schist—A metamorphic rock, that shows medium banding, various grades of coarseness, but its mineral contents are generally in parallel arrangement. Color depends on the individual content such as mica, Hornblende, chloride, Garnet. Ranges in hardness from paving blocks to talc. International in distribution.

Serpentine—Found in Italy and U.S.; has a greenish color, and a mottled surface with a greasy or waxy luster. Associated with igneous and metamorphic rocks, is light and semihard. Used for building,

ballast, and has a fibrous variety used in insulation.

Shale—A weak, thin-bedded sedimentary rock, formed out of compacted mud deposits. Various colors, most often gray, and has international distribution. Used to make cement or plaster.

"Shamir"—The Hebrew name for Emery.

Slate—Dark gray, shiny metamorphic rock, finely grained, and develops in clay or Shale. Splits readily into sheets, and is used for roofing, flooring, or blackboards. Comes from Finland, France, Scotland, England, U.S. (California).

Soapstone—See Steatite.

Sodalite—Usually compact masses of bright blue stone, or white or gray with greenish tint. Light, hard, fragile, and is found in igneous rocks. Occurs in Burma, USSR, Romania, Italy, Portugal, U.S. (Maine and Arkansas), Bolivia, Brazil, Greenland, and Rhodesia. Used as polished slabs, sculptured ornaments, and in jewelry.

Smaragdus—Ancient and medieval term for Emerald, but could stand for any transparent, green stone.

Spinel—Very hard, octahedral crystals, sometimes masses of rounded granules. Color may be greenish, brown, pink, red, light blue, black, white, or colorless. Transparent to opaque with glassy luster. Used as a gemstone, and comes from Thailand, Sri Lanka, India, Afghanistan, Malagasy Republic, Italy, and U.S. (New York and New Jersey).

Spodumene—Hard, prismatic crystals, heavy, transparent to translucent, may be up to over fifty feet long. Source of lithium and its salts for industry. Gem varieties are pink Kunzite from U.S. (California), and Brazil, also green Hiddenite from U.S. (North Carolina), and Brazil, Malagasy Republic. Other varieties are found in USSR, Sweden, Scotland, Canada, and Mexico.

Staurolite—Commonly called "Fairy Crosses." Very hard, prismatic crystals that may form either a Greek or St. Andrew's cross. Color is reddish brown to black. Found in Italy, Germany, Switzerland, France, Scotland, and U.S. (Georgia and New Mexico). Worn as jewelry. Often associated with Garnet or Kyanite.

Steatite—A soft, talclike metamorphic rock, easily carved. Large deposits in Austria, France, Spain, Italy, U.S., Canada. Used in powdered form as a filler in many industries, and is carved into ornaments.

Sunstone—See Labradorite.

Syenite—A kind of Granite named for its first source, Syene, Egypt. Found also in Norway, Germany, and U.S. (New York). Architectural use as polished slabs.

Tiger's-eye—See Quartz, Crystalline var.

Toadstone—Common name for stones shaped like a toad, or with warty outer texture. Often of volcanic origin and contain trapped gases that explode upon being heated.

Tonalite—A granitic rock, medium gray with dark grains. A building stone found in Italy, Norway, Scotland, western coasts of U.S. and Canada.

Topaz—True Topaz is an aluminum silicate, very hard (8 on Mohs scale), and falls between Corundum (9 on Mohs scale), and Quartz (7 on Mohs scale). It is colorless, yellow, blue, purplish, green, or orange color, forms prismatic crystals, sometimes of enormous size up to a quarter of a ton. Gem-quality stones come from Burma, Sri Lanka, Siberia, Ural Mountains, Czechoslovakia, Germany, Italy, England, Canada (New Brunswick), U.S. (Colorado), and Brazil. "Oriental topaz," which is Corundum, is better than *true* Topaz, while "Brazilian Topaz" is often only Citrine Quartz. Be careful when buying.

Tourmaline—Hexagonal crystals that are very hard, heavy, and give a circular fracture. Transparent to translucent, color may be pink and green in the same crystal. Associated with igneous and metamorphic rock, may be found in marble. Used as a gem and in pressure gauges. Comes from Sri Lanka, USSR, Italy, Brazil, and U.S. (Maine, New York, New Jersey, and California).

Tree Agate—Patterned Chalcedony Quartz, marked with treelike shapes, black, brown, green or blue, depending on the mineral that stained the stone. Used for ornamental display and in jewelry. Most now comes from western U.S.

Tufa—Properly tuff, a porous, stratified rock made from volcanic debris.

Turquoise—Hard, light, fragile, circular fracture, an opaque sky-blue or greenish blue stone with a waxy or porcelain luster. A gemstone from Iran, Turkestan, Egypt, U.S. (Nevada and New Mexico). Stone may be colored artificially by several methods, so beware! It forms in various rocks by a process of alteration, but only in areas that have aluminum-bearing rocks.

Zircon—Prismatic or double pyramidal crystals, colorless, yellow, red, green, gray, or brown in color. Very hard and has irregular granules. Occasionally transparent, but also opaque and dull. Found in Sri Lanka, USSR, Norway, Sweden, Canada (Ontario), U.S. (Maine and Florida), Brazil, and Australia. Occurs in beach sands, and alluvial deposits. Ore of Zirconium, and is used as a gemstone when of good, clear quality. Can be improved by heat treatment.

BIBLIOGRAPHY

General Works

British Museum Guide, London, 1976.

Daumas, M., *History of Technology and Invention*, Vol. 1, New York, 1969.

Doubleday Encyclopedia of Discovery and Exploration: Exploring Africa and Asia, Garden City, N.Y., 1973. *The Glorious Age of Exploration*, Garden City, N.Y., 1973.

Encyclopaedia Britannica, 11th ed., 29 vols., New York, 1910–11.

Fattorusso, J., *Wonders of Italy*, Florence, 1930.

Francis, Sir F., ed., *Treasures of the British Museum*, London, 1975.

Kunsthistorisches Museum Meisterwerke, Wien, 1973.

Kunz, G.F., *The Curious Lore of Precious Stones*, New York, 1971.

Lerman, L., *The Museum*, New York, 1969.

McGraw-Hill Encyclopedia of Science and Technology, 15 vols., New York, 1977.

New York Times Atlas, New York, 1975.

Oxford English Dictionary, Compact Edition, 2 vols., Oxford, 1971.

Pearl, R.M., *Gems, Minerals, Crystals, and Ores*, New York, 1977.

Peck, H.T., ed., *Harper's Dictionary of Classical Literature and Antiquities*, New York, 1963.

Prinz, M., G. Harlow, and J. Peters, eds., *Simon and Schuster Guide to Rocks and Minerals*, New York, 1978.

Rees, A., ed., *The Cyclopedia*, Philadelphia and New York, 1810–24.

Sarton, G., *A History of Science*, 2 vols., New York, 1970.
———. *Introduction to the History of Science*, 3 vols., Baltimore, 1927–48.

Singer, C., ed., *History of Technology*, vol. 1, London, 1954.

Thorndike, L., *History of Magic and Experimental Science*, 8 vols., New York and London, 1923–58.

Webster's Biographical Dictionary, Springfield, Mass., 1957.

Chapter 1

Budge, E.A.W., *Book of the Dead*, New York, 1960.
Clark, G., *World Prehistory*, Cambridge, Eng., 1969.

Delaporte, L., *Mesopotamia*, New York, 1970.

De Rachewiltz, B., *Egyptian Art*, New York, 1960.

Erman, A., *Life in Ancient Egypt*, New York, 1971.

Hawkes, J., *The First Great Civilizations*, New York, 1973.

Huyghe, R., ed., *Larousse Encyclopedia of Prehistoric and Ancient Art*, London, 1962.

Kramer, S.N., *History Begins at Sumer*, Garden City, N.Y., 1959.

Lloyd, S., *Art of the Ancient Near East*, New York, 1961.

Parrot, A., *Arts of Assyria*, New York, 1961.

Chapter 2

Bandinelli, R.B., *Rome, Center of Power*, New York, 1970.

Boardman, J., *Greek Art*, New York, 1964.

Casson, L., *Travel in the Ancient World*, London, 1974.

Charbonneaux, J., R. Martin, F. Villard, *Archaic Greek Art*, New York, 1971.

———. *Hellenistic Art*, New York, 1973.

Demargne, P., *The Birth of Greek Art*, New York, 1964.

Komroff, M., ed., *The History of Herodotus*, trans. G. Rawlinson, New York, 1934.

Pliny, *Natural History*, Loeb Classical Library Ed., Cambridge, Mass.; London, 1950–67.

Suetonius, *The Lives of the Twelve Caesars*, New York, 1931.

Wheeler, M., *Roman Art and Architecture*, New York, 1964.

Chapter 3

Durant, W., *Our Oriental Heritage*, New York, 1954.

DuRy, C., *Art of Islam*, New York, 1970.

Komroff, M., ed., *The Travels of Marco Polo*, Garden City, N.Y., 1930.

Needham, J., *Science and Civilization in China*, Cambridge, 1954–59.

Pratt, K.L., *Visitors to China*, New York and Washington, D.C., 1970.

Rice, T.T., *The Arts of Central Asia*, New York and Washington, D.C., 1965.

Smith, B., and Wan-go Weng, *China, A History in Art*, New York, 1973.

Swann, P., *The Art of China, Korea, and Japan*, New York, 1963.

Chapter 4

Backes, M., and R. Dolling, *Art of the Dark Ages*, New York, 1969.

Evans, J., *Magical Jewels of the Middle Ages and the Renaissance*, New York, 1976.

Hofstatter, H., *Art of the Late Middle Ages*, New York, 1968.

Hubert, J., J. Porcher, W.F. Volbach, *Carolingian Renaissance*, New York, 1970.

————. *Europe of the Invasions*, New York, 1969.

Larousse Encyclopedia of Byzantine and Medieval Art, New York, 1963.

Mâle, E., *The Gothic Image*, New York, Evanston, and London, 1958.

Souchal, F., *The Art of the Early Middle Ages*, New York, 1968.

Vasari, G., *Lives of the Painters, Sculptors, and Architects*, London and New York, 1927.

Wiet, G., V. Elisseeff, P. Wolff, J. Naudou, *The Great Medieval Civilizations*, New York, Evanston, San Francisco, London, 1975.

Chapter 5

Anderson, F. J., *An Illustrated History of the Herbals*, New York, 1977.

Anon., *Hortus Sanitatis*, Strassburg, 1517.

De Givry, G., *Witchcraft, Magic, and Alchemy*, New York, n.d.

Frazer, Sir J. G., *The Golden Bough*, New York, 1952.

Isidore of Seville, *Etymologiarum*, Oxford, 1971.

Linné, C., *Materia Medica*, Leipzig, Erlanger, 1772.

Porta, G. B., *Natural Magick*, New York, 1957.

Quincy, J., *Pharmacopoeia Officinalis*, London, 1720.

Riddle, J. C., ed., *Marbode's De Lapidibus*, Wiesbaden, 1977.

Thompson, C. J. S., *Alchemy*, New York, 1974.

————. *Mysteries and Secrets of Magic*, New York, 1973.

Chapter 6

Cirlot, J. E., *A Dictionary of Symbols*, New York, 1962.

Didron, A. N., *Christian Iconography*, New York, 1965.

Ferguson, Rev. G., *Signs and Symbols in Christian Art*, New York, 1961.

Goodspeed, E. J., trans., *The Apocrypha*, New York, 1959.

Herrad of Landesberg, *Hortus Deliciarum*, New Rochelle, N.Y., 1977.

Holy Bible, Authorized Version, New York, 1959.

Larousse Encyclopedia of Mythology, London, 1959.

Lehner, E., *Symbols, Signs, and Signets*, New York, 1969.

Chapter 7

Descargues, P., *The Hermitage*, New York, 1961.

Durant, W., *Age of Reason Begins*, New York, 1961.

————. *The Reformation*, New York, 1957.

————. *Rousseau and Revolution*, New York, 1967.

Ganz, P., *Holbein Paintings*, New York, 1950.

Her Majesty's Ministry of Works, *The Crown Jewels*, London, 1961.

————. *Hampton Court Palace*, London, 1962.

Menz, H., *The Dresden Gallery*, New York, 1962.

Savage, G., *Dictionary of Antiques*, New York and Washington, D.C., 1970.

Sizov, E. S., *Treasures from the Kremlin*, New York, 1979.

Strong, R., *The National Portrait Gallery*, London, 1969.

Chapter 8

Nassau, K., *Gems Made by Man*, Radnor, Pa., 1980.

Wickersham II, Rev. G.W., *The Cathedral Church of St. John the Divine*, New York, n.d.

INDEX

Personages

214

Places

Topics

ACKNOWLEDGMENTS

Page 11 (left): All rights reserved, The Metropolitan Museum of Art, Rogers Fund, 1910.

Page 18: All rights reserved, The Metropolitan Museum of Art, Rogers Fund, 1918.

Page 19: All rights reserved, The Metropolitan Museum of Art, Gift of J. Pierpont Morgan, 1912.

Page 21: All rights reserved, The Metropolitan Museum of Art, Fletcher Fund, 1926. (Detail)

Page 24 (top): All rights reserved, The Metropolitan Museum of Art, Purchase, Fletcher Fund, 1949.

Page 24 (bottom): All rights reserved, Photography by Egyptian Expedition, The Metropolitan Museum of Art.

Page 27: All rights reserved, The Metropolitan Museum of Art, Fletcher Fund, 1940.

Page 30: All rights reserved, The Metropolitan Museum of Art, Gift of Edward S. Harkness, 1914. (Detail)

Page 31: All rights reserved, The Metropolitan Museum of Art, Purchase, 1966. Inc. Gift.

Page 50 (bottom): The Bettmann Archive

Pages 82–83: All rights reserved, The Metropolitan Museum of Art, The Cloisters Collection, 1947. (Detail)

Page 85: All rights reserved, The Metropolitan Museum of Art, Harris Brisbane Dick Fund, 1958.

Page 86 (left): All rights reserved, The Metropolitan Museum of Art, Gift of J. Pierpont Morgan, 1917.

Page 86 (right): The Bettmann Archive

Page 90 (top): All rights reserved, The Metropolitan Museum of Art, Gift of J. Pierpont Morgan, 1917.

Pages 124–25: The Bettmann Archive

Page 127: The Bettmann Archive

Page 138: The Bettmann Archive

Page 163: All rights reserved, The Metropolitan Museum of Art, The Michael Friedsam Collection, 1931.

Page 174: The Bettmann Archive

Special thanks to the following:

The Collector's Cabinet
153 East 57 Street
New York, New York 10022

Rare Art, Inc.
978 Madison Avenue
New York, New York 10021

Navin Kumar Gallery
967 Madison Avenue
New York, New York 10021

Jamie Androde
17 East 70 Street
New York, New York 10021

The personnel of the Stoneyard
Cathedral Church of St. John the Divine
1047 Amsterdam Avenue
New York, New York 10025